The Rectors of the University of Edinburgh
1859–2000

The University of Edinburgh is supplied
with excellent professors in all the sciences.

Edinburgh is a hotbed of genius – I have had the good fortune to
be made acquainted with many authors of the first distinction.

Tobias Smollett, *The Expedition of Humphry Clinker*

The Rectors of the University of Edinburgh 1859–2000

Donald Wintersgill

Dunedin Academic Press
Edinburgh

Published by
Dunedin Academic Press ltd
Hudson House
8 Albany Street
Edinburgh EH1 3QB
Scotland

ISBN 1 903765 44 7

British Library Cataloguing in Publication data
A catalogue record for this book is available from the British Library

Typeset in Adobe Garamond
by Makar Publishing Production

Printed and bound in Great Britain by Cromwell Press

CONTENTS

Part II 1948 ONWARDS
Actors, Celebrities, and Television Personalities Prevail
– and a dramatic period of student power

How rival groups of students fought each other
The Scots diaspora takes the Rectorship to Canada
The creator of Sherlock Holmes observes an election

ACKNOWLEDGEMENTS

The author records his gratitude to the people who helped in the writing of this book.

Dr Frances Dow, formerly Vice-Principal for Development and before that Provost of the Faculty Group of Arts, Divinity, and Music at Edinburgh University, read the text and suggested many improvements. She helped to bring balance where that was needed.

Dr Jennifer Litster, of the School of History and Classics at Edinburgh University, did devoted work in going through the issues of the *Student* from 1889 to 2000, identifying news and comment about the rectorship. She also helped adeptly in searching the Web.

Melvyn Cornish, University Secretary at Edinburgh, warmly encouraged the project from the start, commented on various sections, and was a great help in furthering the publication.

Sue Paton, formerly of the library at the *Scotsman,* provided a large back-up of cuttings from the *Scotsman*, a wonderful source. Ms Paton gave indispensable help.

The *Student* magazine generously gave permission for the use of many extracts.

Owen Dudley Edwards, Reader in History at the university, has remarkable knowledge of this subject. He pointed the way to sources and gave much advice.

George Foulkes MP, who was a student leader at a crucial time in the history of the rectorship, was a unique source. Bob Cuddihy, who was also active at this time, gave much background material.

Dr A. M. Currie, former Secretary to the university, gave valuable information on the rectorships from 1975 to 1991.

Dr Martin Lowe, former Secretary to the university, gave valuable information on the rectorships from 1988 to 2000.

Arnott Wilson, archivist at the university, and his staff efficiently answered enquiries and responded to requests.

Emeritus Professor Sir John Crofton, who was Vice-Principal with responsibility for relations with students, 1969–1970, and a member of the Court, sent a fascinating memoir he wrote about his times as member of the Court and gave permission to quote from it.

Ivan House gave an assessment of the toxic substances ingested by Sir Robert Christison.

Dan van der Vat, historian and journalist, helped greatly with the entries about Beatty, Hamilton, and Cunningham.

Ahmed Kayssi, Rector of Queen's University, Ontario, sent information about the rectorship there: it is a direct transplant from Edinburgh.

Ian Hawkins of Glasgow University dug up facts about the Self-Governing Schools etc. (Scotland) Act (Commencement) Order 1990.

Reminiscences

I asked former students, through *Edit,* the magazine for alumni, for memories, documents, and photographs. The response was marvellous.

The earliest reminiscences were from Dr Myre Sim in Victoria, British Columbia, and were about Lord Allenby. It was gratifying to receive the letters from Dr Sim and from so many other people. Many memories and anecdotes have been lost.

Dr Ian Lewis sent from Tasmania a section of the "memoir" of his career, produced for his family. It includes material on the election of Pollock in 1942 and a shocking incident: medical students set off dangerous smoke canisters and moved the dean of medicine's car up flights of steps to the war memorial in Old Quad. Marian Shearer recalled her years at the university during the Second World War and sent a copy of the Student's Handbook; she voted for Douglas Young who "seemed a suitably subversive choice" and not for the respectable Sir Donald Pollock.

Dr Philip Myerscough helped with a story about the installation of Admiral Lord Cunningham.

Dr Iain Cowie of Dumfries and His Hon Dr Ralph Lownie kindly provided leaflets about Alastair Sim's election in 1948; Dr Cowie also had some fine reminiscences. Alan Lees recalled stories about Sim's installation and the campaign. Mr Lees also gave help with Sim's installation; and he wrote that he climbed the dome at Old College to inscribe his name on a scroll there.

Hugh J. Kilpatrick sent photographs and a vast store of newspapers cuttings, preserved for almost 40 years, about the events at Sydney Smith's election. He wrote: "About a month ago I finally started excavating the 22 years-worth of boxes and bags in my cellar, hoping to find lots of useless rubbish to throw out. About a week ago I read your letter in *Edit* and, by a strange coincidence, had lying on the table the enclosed newspaper cuttings and snapshots, and I was trying to decide whether to keep them or bin them." Dr Andrew Ramsay had marvellous memorabilia of the same events, including a signed menu from the celebratory dinner.

Dr Eric Morton recalled a facet of James Robertson Justice's character: his delight in seeing a pretty woman. Clyde Reynolds wrote with wonderful stories about Robertson Justice. David Stungo sent photographs and a document from Switzerland of Robertson Justice's installation.

Raymond McCluskey and Bridget Nuttgens (née Badenoch) had detailed memories and charming stories of campaigning for Evelyn Waugh in 1951. The supporters of Waugh provided more help for this book than did any other group.

Bill McDowall of Edinburgh provided documents and facts about Jo Grimond's election. Mrs Eileen Yates of North Carolina sent documents about Grimond's installation, including the strictures about appropriate dress in the audience. She also sent the text of James Robertson Justice's Address and photographs of his installation.

David Simpson was one of Muggeridge's backers in 1957; to Mr Simpson is owed the story of Muggeridge and Compton Mackenzie drinking whisky. May Cruikshank sent amusing photographs and information about Muggeridge.

Dr Jonathan Wills, Dr Donnie Munro, and Dr Malcolm Macleod commented on their tenures. The Rev Iain MacDonald wrote about Dr Munro's tenure.

Douglas Alexander MP recalled his time as Rector's Assessor to Malcolm Macleod.

Dr G. A. Gray wrote about his family's long connections with the university and their tradition of activity in the high jinx.

Charles Guthrie went to much trouble to obtain from a friend in Canada the photographs of a rectorial fight in the Old Quad.

A riot in the Old Quad during the election of Sydney Smith, 1954.

INTRODUCTION

The rectorship

Students at the five oldest Scottish universities have the privilege of electing, every three years, a Rector. This important official ranks second in the formal hierarchy of the university, after the Chancellor and before the Principal. He or she has a seat on the highest governing body, the university Court, and in the four oldest universities has the right to chair it. Rectors may use their high status in the interests of the students, but only if the holder of the office is active and is sympathetic to the students. The office has been held by prime ministers, Nobel prize winners, viceroys of India, and eminent writers, scientists, and academics – a roll call of the great. And it has been held by "colourful" people – celebrities from the worlds of football, broadcasting, film, pop music, and comedy.

The five oldest universities are St Andrews (founded 1411), Glasgow (1451), Aberdeen (1495), Edinburgh (1583), and Dundee (founded as Dundee University College in 1881 and achieving university status in 1967). The four universities founded in the fifteenth and sixteenth centuries are termed the "ancients".

Groups of students nominate candidates for the rectorship. As with any election, leaflets are published, meetings held, and posters put up. Money is sought from the candidate's friends or from political groups. Eminent or famous people are asked to endorse the candidate. Physical violence during the campaign was once a feature: for example, gangs of people from one group commonly smashed up the headquarters of the opposition. Edinburgh had one notable tradition, namely a battle in the quadrangle of the Old College between factions of students, weapons used including rotten vegetables, soot, fish heads, pease meal, which stung the eyes, and dried peas, which stung the skin. The Old College, designed by Robert Adam and William Playfair, is one of Scotland's most noble buildings and damage caused during these battles was distressing to the authorities.

Once elected, the Rector goes through the ceremony of being installed and giving the rectorial Address or speech to the students – an important ritual. A former tradition – now abandoned – was that hardly a word of the Address could be heard over singing, shouting, and playing of musical instruments. Missiles often struck the platform party. Not even great men were immune: David Lloyd George had a very rough time.

A reforming Act of Parliament in 1858 gave rectors the right to sit on the university Court so that the students could have some voice in the way they were governed. Many rectors have, however, been mere figureheads. Rectors appoint an Assessor or co-representative to the university Court who is expected to be active on the students' behalf whether the Rector is an absentee or not.

There are some exceptions to these rules. Edinburgh University's staff, both academic and non-academic, also have a vote in rectorial elections and the Rector represents staff as well as students. Dundee's Rectors do not chair the Court.

Edinburgh's rectors from 1858 to 1948 tended to be Conservative politicians or leading military men. These people were almost always absentee rectors, appearing only to be installed and to give the traditional Address. Glasgow has often chosen Conservative politicians too, but also Whigs, Liberals, and Scottish nationalists. St Andrews has shown a liking for persons of great international fame, especially authors. Aberdeen has been wide in its choices and has often elected people with local links. Dundee has gone for celebrities.

After the Sceond World War a change occurred when at Edinburgh, in 1948, the actor Alastair Sim was elected Rector, defeating Harold Macmillan, a notable Conservative politician and future Prime Minister. Political and military men were out, and later, true "working rectors" were elected: they attended meetings of the Court, promoted the interests of their constituents, held "surgeries", and appeared at events.

Some senior academics and senior administrators have, since the advent of celebrities and working rectors, not been warm towards the rectorship, considering that some of the "showbiz" personalities elected have too often been unsuitable for the dignity and prestige of an ancient university. That is why the constitutions of the newer Scottish universities, such as Strathclyde, Heriot-Watt, Stirling, Robert Gordon, and so on, do not provide for a Rector. Working rectors, active in the university Court on behalf of their constituents, might by some be considered nuisances and intruders. Indeed two Rectors who were also students (they held office in the early 1970s) were seen by some people as too eager to promote certain political ideas.

Nowadays, the Rector and his Assessor are not the only voices for the students on the Court of Edinburgh University: by the year 2000, at the end of the period covered by this book, two members were also appointed by the Students' Representative Council.*

Some academics and university administrators have disliked the rectorship for other reasons. They have been upset by the lively behaviour of students during election campaigns and at installations and Addresses – behaviour bound to be reported in detail by the press and complained about in letters to the editor. That kind of behaviour has now died away.

The colourful candidates and the celebrities

A "colourful" Rector, a celebrity, or a TV personality, might not be comfortable with the university's ways of doing things. Nor might the university authorities be comfortable with a celebrity. A senior figure in one Scottish university (not Edinburgh) has said: "Celebrities are not necessarily accustomed to the ways of modern organisations. Academics and administrators may have mixed feelings about meetings being chaired by people lacking certain skills." Such celebrities can, however, do some excellent work; for example, they can attract the attention of young people and appear at events that need publicity, or go to local schools and

*Edinburgh University Students' Association was formed in 1973 by the voluntary coming together of (not merger) of the SRC, the Union (for men) and the Chambers Street Union (for women); the two unions later united and were joined by the Kings Buildings Union (for science departments).

encourage the pupils to think of studying at university. A person who knows well the way Edinburgh University works has said: "Relationships have improved in recent years. Rectors and university have worked together for the benefit of all."

Edinburgh's first celebrity, Alastair Sim, has been followed by others such as Archie MacPherson, sports journalist, Donnie Munro, leader of the Gaelic band Runrig, and John Colquhoun, professional footballer and sports commentator.

Celebrities are not in the tradition of former rectors such as Gladstone and Churchill, it is true. But a senior academic who is a graduate of Edinburgh has written:

> Just as every American should have the right to stand for the Presidency of the USA, everyone should have a right to stand for the rectorship of a Scottish university. Students nominate the candidates – and the responsibility for the quality of candidates rests with them. If the quality of candidates is poor – and some are encouraged (by being approached by students) to stand for sake of a little more publicity for themselves or a particular cause – then the responsibility or blame lies with the student body.

> The nature of fame, or celebrity status, has changed in recent years. With the rise of mass communications – TV, commercial radio, and the tabloid press – popular culture now accords a large measure of respect to sports personalities, actors, broadcasters and announcers, pop singers, etc. With the change in higher education from providing for an elite to catering for a mass, the composition of the student body has changed, and it reflects this new set of cultural values. The change in the character of candidates is very significant – but its causes lie essentially within the student body.

Love of big names from popular culture has grown in all sections of society. For example, the Beatles in the 1960s were awarded the MBE, while Rolling Stone Mick Jagger, forty years on, was knighted.

The political rectors

Eighteen people held the office of prime minister between 1859 and 1963, the year when the era of political rectors finally ended. Of these, fouteen became rectors or were defeated candidates for the honour. Edinburgh has had five prime ministers as Rector: W. E. Gladstone, Lord Rosebery, David Lloyd George, Stanley Baldwin, and Winston Churchill.

Rectors also reflected the social landscape of the time. In the era of politics at Edinburgh (that is, from 1859 to 1932), a total of twenty-three people held the office. Thirteen of these were graduates of Oxford or Cambridge University; of those who did not go to Oxbridge, one had attended Harrow School and the other Eton College.

The dominance of politicians in Edinburgh lasted from Gladstone's election in 1859 until Churchill's term ended in 1932. The choice was effectively confined not to politicians *per se* but, as a student wrote in 1923, "to politicians of one particular party", the Conservative Party, although a handful of Liberals did win. No Labour figure was elected during the period of political Rectors.

Certain names appear regularly either as rectors or as rectorial candidates at the four oldest universities. Champion rector of all is Lord Rosebery, who was Liberal Prime

Minister in 1894–95. He scored all four of the "ancients", the universities founded in the fifteenth and sixteenth centuries, and in addition was the Chancellor of Glasgow. Of Edinburgh's rectors, nine also held the post elsewhere, including Gladstone, Baldwin, and Churchill.

Many political rectors, however, were not outstandingly distinguished in their own time. Examples at Edinburgh include George Joachim Goschen (elected 1890) and George Wyndham (1908) – who now remembers them?

Rectorships of the Scottish universities were for many decades a part, if a minor one, of the political scene in the country as a whole. A party that won a rectorial election had a feeling of achievement. The university shared some of the great man's prestige. The Rector too had won a trophy.

Another reason for political interest was that public opinion was not tested in the way it is now and the rectorial elections were partly a way of doing so. The General Assembly of the Church of Scotland, in touch with the grass roots, was not able to debate political matters.

All these were good reasons for the parties to get their men elected, and that meant spending a lot of money on the campaigns; on leaflets, posters, meetings, the hire of offices, and day-to-day expenses. We do not know how much money campaigners had because the details were kept secret and have since been lost, but we can guess with some confidence that in an election towards the end of the nineteenth century each of the two sides in the two bigger universities had up to £1000 in the war chest. Money came from the candidates themselves, through appeals to firms and individuals, or from local party organizations.

The great drawback in choosing politicians was that the electors were losing their chance to have a voice in the way the university was run. Their own interests were not going to be properly looked after by an absentee. The average student of those days, however, had little interest in the way the university was organized.

A vigorous condemnation of the political system was made in the 1880s by Sir Robert Christison, who had been a professor at Edinburgh University for fifty years and a member of the university Court for eighteen. The condemnation was written soon after he was defeated for the rectorship by a leading Liberal, Lord Rosebery, in 1880. Christison seems to have taken the defeat rather badly. He wrote in his memoirs of his long experience on the university Court and said that experience had led him to a very different view of the Rector's duty from the view "of every one who has hitherto acted in that capacity". In other words, he thought the Rector should not be a figurehead but should be active for the university and for the students: "The rectorship of the University was intended by the framers of the University Act [of 1858], and the new constitution of the University, not as an ornamental office merely, but as one with important functions, placing its occupant at the head and for the guidance of an important judicial Court."

In 1908, a non-political candidate was put forward, against a Conservative and a Liberal, the first non-political candidate in twenty-five years. He was Professor William Osler, a distinguished medical man. His supporters condemned the monopoly of politicians. Nominations were, Osler's supporters said, in the hands of two small committees representing only a fraction of the electors. "The students deprive themselves of services of those very men who, by their academic training, are best able to serve the interests of our Alma Mater".

By the beginning of the 1930s, feeling among the electorate was turning against the system. People were tired of absentee politicians: a working Rector was wanted by many, or a really distinguished name.

One could also say that interest among young people in politics in general has declined in the last twenty years of the period covered by this book; deference to eminent people has also diminished. Campaigning in the elections has become much quieter: the more recent type of student is intent on getting a good degree, building up a CV, and finding a good job at the end of his or her course.

Few are chosen from science and the arts

Only three people of distinction from Edinburgh's roll have come from the worlds of the arts, literature, and science: Thomas Carlyle (elected in 1865), Sir Alexander Fleming (1951) and Sir Sydney Smith, emeritus professor of forensic medicine (1954). Yet Charles Darwin was a student at Edinburgh and Joseph Lister a professor. Arthur Conan Doyle and Robert Louis Stevenson were both born in the city and studied at the university.

The list of defeated candidates contains many notable names: John Ruskin, art critic and social commentator; Bertrand Russell, mathematician and philosopher; John Maynard Keynes, economist; G. K. Chesterton, journalist, novelist, writer of verse, and satirist; Christopher Murray Grieve (Hugh MacDiarmid), poet; Edwin Muir, poet and critic; Evelyn Waugh, novelist; and Yehudi Menuhin, musician.

A letter to the *Student* magazine at Edinburgh University in 1929, towards the close of the political era, said: "Politics is an absorbing pastime for some; but it will be readily agreed that the fields of literature, art, and adventure, so well employed already at St Andrews University, can present personalities more attractive than the political field."

Edinburgh's fondness for military men

One feature of the roll-call of rectors is the number of military men elected. Edinburgh was far fonder of them than were the other Scottish universities. It began at Edinburgh with Lord Kitchener, the British commander-in-chief, in 1914. The line continued with Admiral of the Fleet Sir David Beatty (later Lord Beatty) in 1917; General Sir Ian Hamilton in 1932; Field Marshal Lord Allenby in 1935; and Admiral Lord Cunningham of Hyndhope in 1945.

How the runners are picked

Candidates do not put themselves forward. How then do their names appear? During the political era, each political club negotiated for a candidate from the political party's local bosses or its central bosses, or a combination of the two. What went on in the negotiations has been lost to history.

When the era of political rectors ended, the field was much more varied. Here is where prominent students in the corporate life came in. They would mull over names and approach a likely person. The running of a campaign – political or non-political – was tremendous fun. There were pranks and stunts and libellous leaflets and kidnappings and raids and speeches.

Sometimes, committed people would choose names close to their interests. Perhaps it might be a medical man or someone with medical connections such as Sir Alexander Fleming; or someone with nationalist appeal such as Hugh McDiarmid; or a campaigner against apartheid such as Albertina Sisulu.

The tradition of campaigning

Arthur Conan Doyle, who studied medicine at Edinburgh from 1876 to 1881, wrote in his novel *The Firm of Girdlestone*:

> A rectorial election is a peculiarly Scotch institution, and, however it may strike the individual observer, it is regarded by the students themselves as a rite of extreme solemnity and importance from which grave issues may depend. To hear the speeches and addresses of rival orators one would suppose that the integrity of the constitution and the very existence of the empire hung upon the return of their special nominee . . .
>
> Great boards appear at the University gates, on which pithy satires against one or other candidate, parodies on songs, quotations from their speeches, and gaudily painted cartoons are posted.

Rowdyism during the election campaigns

One of the traditions that were formerly strong but have now been lost is the fighting that took place between rival factions. Liberals and Conservatives hired committee rooms – not in ordinary buildings but in dilapidated ones. Each side had troops of men, sometimes called "Physical Force Gangs" or PFGs, who raided the other side's committee rooms, the aim being to wreck them. PFGs also might carry out a raid to destroy or capture copies of the opponents' newspaper or leaflets, or do a tricky bit of bill sticking, or remove the opponents' bills (some buildings were smothered in them.) It was a point of honour to fix placards or bills in the most inaccessible places. Another custom was to kidnap a leading member of the other side, partly to remove the brains and the organising force of the other side and partly as a stunt. (See Appendices.)

Here is a defence of the custom by someone who took part in the campaign of 1911. It was written anonymously about 10 years after the events described.

> Great is the satisfaction of being able to smash a window openly and boldly, or to splinter a door with a mighty swing of an axe, free from the horror of war or the terror of a policeman; and the supreme delight of heaving half a pound of ochre bang into the face of another fellow, or tearing a fragment from a rival flag. And then it is a happy memory, a thing which grows more precious as age creeps upon us. In the case of the writer, the memory of the last Rectorial was the means of banishing for a little the terror and misery of the trenches in Flanders on meeting an old student friend and living it all over again.

The convention was that this kind of behaviour, which was most common in the early part of the twentieth century, was tolerated by the university authorities, the police, and the public. Leaders of the contending parties made an agreement at the start of the campaign about how long the fighting would last, how to protect university buildings against permanent damage, and how the fighting would be conducted on the day of the election. No campaigning was allowed on Sundays or between the hours of nine a.m. and five p.m. during the week. The Union building was a place of sanctuary. Everybody knew where he stood.

An example of the rules in action can be seen in an election of the 1920s, when the Liberals captured a Conservative and took him to a distant hotel. As soon as they arrived the victim signed the visitors' book. This act made the hotel his home and, since a student's home was sacrosanct, he was able to go free.

Fighting in the Old Quad: Battle of the Standard

The tradition for more than a century was for a battle – the Battle of the Standard or the Battle of the Steps – to be held on polling day in the Old Quad between factions supporting rival candidates (the historical Battle of the Standard was in 1138, when the English army defeated the Scots at Northallerton; the English were under the banners of their patron saints). Supporters of the outgoing Rector took up positions at the top of the broad flight of steps at the west end of the quadrangle, grouped around their standard bearer. A statue of Sir David Brewster, Principal from 1859 to 1868, stood there, so the site was called the Brewster Steps, but the statue was later moved and replaced by a memorial to the dead of the First World War.

There the supporters of the outgoing Rector were attacked by supporters of candidates in the election about to be held – or that was the theory. In fact, it was a time for a general mêlée. Favourite weapons were dried peas (which stung the skin) and pease meal (which formed a smoke screen and hurt the eyes). Dried peas and pease meal went largely out of use – indeed, they are nowadays hard to find. Ochre, a red or yellow powder used to colour walls, was another favourite, giving a dramatic effect when people were bombarded with it, but that also is now hard to find.

Everything stopped for the election result. The Principal appeared at a window and displayed the figures on a placard, which was seized by supporters of the winner and paraded around town.

A change came in 1929. The Battle of the Standard was not held in that year. Balustrades of the quadrangle were said to be unsafe and it was thought that the combatants might be injured. Graduates all over the world grumbled about the loss of tradition and the turnout of voters was the lowest on record. The low turnout was, however, due not only to the banning of the fight but also to the voters' antipathy to political elections. No more politicians were to stand after that in the traditional way, but the fight was to be revived.

Newspapers loved the event, but not so the university authorities. Exuberance of youth and a disgusting mess in the Old Quad did not suit the dignity of the place.

And in later years, from the 1930s, the campaigning and the fight were less formalized and orderly: no longer were the political clubs in control of what went on.

Here, as an example, is what happened in 1957 when the actor James Robertson Justice was elected.

About 1000 people gathered at ten a.m. in the Old Quad, where the main polling station was; they were dressed in their very oldest clothes. One of the biggest groups was Robertson

Justice's supporters. Another was a crowd of medicals, backing another candidate, Sir Walter Mercer, a well-known Edinburgh surgeon. The factions joined in a furious battle with eggs, fish heads, fireworks, and bags of flour and soot. These bags were the ones used for sweets. Bleeding noses and torn shirts and trousers were abundant. One person had an epileptic fit and was taken away in an ambulance. Another suffered an injury to his ear when a large wooden box was flung among the crowd. He too was taken to hospital.

The Mercer supporters used rockets, launched from milk bottles, against supporters of other candidates who had formed up on the steps of the war memorial. The rockets "caused a certain restlessness" among them (this all happened close to Guy Fawkes day).

The *Evening News* reported: "A large gathering of women students watched from the safety of the Old Quad galleries and cheered on their respective champions . . . It was a bedraggled crowd which dispersed after the fighting at about mid-day [for a lunch break]." Fighting was resumed after lunch and went on for part of the afternoon. While the result of the vote was awaited, students whiled away the time by lighting a bonfire.

One student, after leaving the Old Quad, asked a watchful policeman on the South Bridge: "Can we take you hostage?" Without a smile, the policemen responded: "You can try." When the day was over, a celebratory dance was held in the Union. Nobody was arrested that day.

When the voting was held in 1920, it was reported that 4000 people watched the fight – perhaps an exaggeration. In 1972 four people turned up. An ancient tradition was lost through apathy, changes in attitude, and opposition from the university authorities.

The Installation and Address

One of the traditions is that the Rector gives a speech, 'the Address', to his constituents. During the nineteenth and early twentieth centuries the serious newspapers, both in England and in Scotland, reproduced the texts of addresses in full. That meant a lot of column inches.

Addresses have been notable for noble oratory, as Lord Rosebery's Address in 1882 on Scotland and patriotism certainly was. They have also been trite, banal, commonplace, and dull. Politicians, for example, were faced with the task of speaking for at least an hour to a hall full of young people. Politics was not a suitable subject because many of the listeners were probably from the other side of the political divide. Looking for a suitable theme, speakers often fell into the easy trap of praising the study of Greek and Latin and saying that students should work hard and not waste time. One student at Edinburgh wrote in 1925 about rectorial addresses: "For dull platitudes, for sounding bombast, for the thought of a donkey and the morality of a wolf, they are justly noted. Their emptiness, their tinkling merely echo their authors' thinness of intellect and sparsity of intelligence."

It was a convention that the Rector's speech began with thanks to the students for giving him or her such a great honour. One is reminded of a remark by the Victorian statesman Lord Hartington when he heard a florid speaker say at some event or other that "this was the proudest moment of my life". "The proudest moment of *my* life," said Hartington, "was when my pig won the prize at Skipton Fair."

Traditional installations and addresses have declined in importance. It was usual for the McEwan Hall, the university's great meeting place, to be the venue and for it to be full. Recently, however, very few students have bothered to attend. For the installation of Malcolm Macleod (1994–1997) the McEwan Hall was given up and the smaller Reid Concert Hall, also part of the university, was used instead. Even then, the place had to be filled up by the mustering of staff.

Rowdyism at installations

Installations at the Scottish universities have sometimes been an excuse for rowdy behaviour or even hooliganism. The tradition of rowdiness at Edinburgh seems to have been imported from Glasgow University, as was also the custom of electing politicians.

Often it happened at Edinburgh that not a word of the Address could be heard. The new Rector had to compete against singing, shouting, whistling, the playing of musical instruments, and the throwing of lavatory paper. Dried peas were specially favoured as missiles. One commentator wrote, after the rowdy installation of Sir Robert Finlay in 1904: "Men should realise the cruelty of throwing handfuls of dried peas into the stalls and onto the stage from the gallery. It may be urged that women with bare shoulders should not come . . . but they do, and should be respected. If there were only men below, even bald-headed men, we should say nothing."

Ropes would be slung between the galleries of the hall and bold students would crawl along the ropes. When silence did prevail, the Address was often interrupted by witty comments from the audience.

All in all, rectors often found the delivery of the address an ordeal. That is one reason why the rectors often delayed fixing a date for the ceremony, to the annoyance of the students.

Newspapers loved to report rowdiness at installations; the university authorities hated both the rowdiness itself and the reports about rowdiness. One should remember, when reading newspapers, a rule of journalism: first, simplify; second, exaggerate. That, one feels, repeatedly happened when newspapers in the past reported on rectorial installations.

This ritualized behaviour was partly a release of juvenile high spirits, partly boorishness, and partly a reaction against middle-class conformism and conventions. The Lords of Misrule briefly took over. But customs and attitudes changed in the 1960s. Addresses are nowadays sadly shortened in delivery and are hardly reported in the press – Robin Harper at Edinburgh, elected in 2001, was told: "You have 10 minutes."

Lost traditions

For decades the candidates did not appear while campaigning was underway. That tradition ended in the 1970s. Likely candidates since then have perhaps been put off by the prospect of taking to the hustings.

Torchlight processions were held on the day of the polling. The following account describes a procession in the early 1900s, when about 1000 people took part, each carrying a torch:

> The costumes of many nations, in an exaggerated form, were to be seen; and where nature had failed to supply the complexion suited to the costume, that

defect was remedied by the application of burnt cork and such like devices. Others again, possibly thinking that nature had been too generous to them, sought to hide their good looks under false noses of a comical twist, under artificial beards, and by other disguises.

Although many affected fancy dress, some were attired very much as navvies bound for their work, and a good many burlesqued the ladies' style of dressing. [Cross-dressing was a tradition on students' processions and shows.] The military spirit of the students was exemplified by the presence of two companies of the University Battery [of volunteers] on lorries . . .*

Everywhere there were crowds, either following the procession or witnessing its progress. The greeting which the students got all along the way was hearty . . . this compliment the students acknowledged by waving their torches over their heads and cheering. When not so engaged they sang favourite airs.

Arrived at the Castle Esplanade, the stumps of the torches were piled together, and round the bonfire the students made merry. The National Anthem was played by the band, and a very successful and enthusiastic demonstration was brought to a close by the singing of 'Auld Lang Syne'.

When a Rector was installed, a day's holiday for the whole university used to be announced. This, however, is no longer a tradition.

The working Rector

Political elections, which dominated the scene for nearly a century, had a great disadvantage. Students had representatives on the universities' highest governing bodies: the Rector and his Assessor (his co-representative). Yet the grandees who were elected seldom did more than appear once in the three years of their office, to be installed. They did not attend meetings of the university's supreme governing body, the Court; they left their Assessors to do that. Students thus failed to use their power to put on the Court a person who would actively look after their interests and raise their concerns.

The alternative was a working Rector, an idea that has existed in Edinburgh for as long as the elective rectorship. A working Rector is someone who will be active in the students' interest, attend meetings of the university Court, appear at events important in the students' calendar, hold surgeries, and, if possible, live in the city.

The student Rector – for and against

A refinement of the working rectorship was the idea of a student holding the office, a notion put forward as early as 1957 by an anonymous contributor to the university magazine: "If we want a rectorship of the students, by the students, and for the students, the

---

*"Volunteering" or part-time military training was popular with middle-class young men. The units at the university were infantry, artillery, and medical. This service had patriotic attractions, too; pride in the Empire and, in the early twentieth century, antagonism to Germany, which was seen as a military threat to Britain.

only answer is the student Rector." The contributor also wrote of a real working Rector "who will rule the aristocracy, and, even more important, the bureaucracy, of our university".

It was not until 1968 that a candidate was to stand on that basis. A journalist on the *Scottish Daily Express* commented at the time that this meant the students sought to destroy the office.

> It carries the stamp of naivety which somehow believes that all destruction brings progress. The present day student is howling out for greater representation and few would deny that there is room for greater participation. But whatever can be achieved in that direction can surely be amply supplemented by the workings of an experienced adult in the role of the Lord Rector . . .
>
> It is ludicrous to suggest that any undergraduate could compete. What kind of brashness would it take for an academic fledgling to assert himself in front of a formidable body like the Court?

The headline was, "Why ask a boy to do a man's job?"

The *Express* journalist commented:

> The Edinburgh students could well take their cue from their own Principal, Professor Michael Swann, who says that, while there is nothing to stop them putting up a student for Rector, they would probably find the Court a big disappointment. He suggests that they should seek to use their influence in other quarters. The Court does not deal with teaching, he points out. That is done in the departments and in the Senate.
>
> *That is the kind of wisdom the students should heed.*

A reply came from the Student for Rector group:

> Far from being destructive, this is a positive, non-violent step towards truer democracy, similar to electors in a Highland constituency choosing one of their own number to represent them at Westminster instead of an absentee landlord . . . A student is most qualified because it is he who is living and working in the university, and any non-student candidate, even a supposed 'working Rector', must have his priorities elsewhere.

Any outside Rector could be intimidated by the Court. "From lack of experience he soon abdicates his right to the chair, and often does not turn up . . . But a student Rector would constantly refer back to students for authority and need not be intimidated."

Swann said in the same year: "We ought to remember that students do not pay the bills, that their knowledge, though growing, is limited, and that their experience is slight." He believed in student criticism in academic affairs, but not in claims for a part in major decision-making. Of representation on the Senate, he said: "A few student representatives could not possibly hold their own in these serried ranks of academics." Senior academics and administrators have, however, praised the way students have worked on committees, including the Court.

The idea of a student as rector became real between 1971 and 1975 when Jonathan Wills and Gordon Brown held the office.

Attempts to take away one of the rights of the Rector

Some senior academics and administrators in the ancient Scottish universities have been suspected of trying to take away the rector's right to the chair. Successive governmental inquiries have suggested the same objective. Defenders of the traditional rectorship have protested strongly.

For example, Dr Malcolm Macleod, former rector at Edinburgh, said that to deprive the rector of the right to be chair would rip the heart out of the role. "The Rector is elected by the whole community and not by half a dozen vice-principals and businessmen on the Court." Paul Corrigan, president of the St Andrews University Students' Association, said it was the chairmanship which gave the post its seniority and made people take the job seriously.

Andrew Neil, a leading journalist, editor-in-chief of Scotsman Publications Ltd., former editor of the *Sunday Times,* and former Rector of St Andrews, said: "If students elect somebody sensible, then they have a really powerful figure at the heart of university governance. If they elect somebody stupid they don't, but that's up to them. It works. When a rector has proved not to be up to it, all universities have always managed to get round it. No rector has caused serious damage to a university and a number of them have done great good."

As we shall see, these views were put forward in the late 1990s, at the time of a strong threat to the status quo.

The people who wanted the change were perhaps unhappy about the rectorship as an institution and about some of the people who were elected. But these reformers were also aware that the old way of doing things in universities was under suspicion: reformers were not specifically targeting the rectorship. For example, it was a theme that governing bodies were entrusted with public money and had a duty to keep the highest standards when spending it. Efficient management and correct "governance" were wanted. That theme recurs many times in the reports of Government committees on many aspects of public life.

The office of rector, howver, was an ancient one, and removing the right to chair the Court would have to be approved by the Privy Council, an Act of Parliament would have to be put through, and MPs who had been active in student politics – there was quite a number of them - would block the legislation. So the rectorship could not be abolished.

The Robbins report into higher education (1963) said that old and out-of-date Acts of Parliament governing the Scottish universities ought to be repealed and replaced. Here was an open threat to the rectorship. People who disliked the rector's right to take the chair would have a chance to abolish it. Parliament did follow some of Robbins's proposals in the Universities (Scotland) Act of 1966, but that Act did not affect the rectorship of the ancient universities.

The Jarratt report (1985) was about efficiency in universities. It said that principals and vice-chancellors should be recognized as being the chief executives. That report "set the language of business efficiency against the 'donnish' discourses of senates," said Ann Kettle, a senior academic at St Andrews.

A Bill of 1989, the Self-Governing Schools (Scotland) Bill, mostly concerend with schools and colleges of further education, contained a controversial clause: each university Court would have to right to elect its chair. The Rector was to be downgraded. Muriel

Gray, then Rector at Edinburgh, said: "It is a nasty, shoddy piece of legislation, a piece of nonsense." What was needed, she said, was legislation to make prospective rectors pledge their availability to perform their duties. MPs and past and present rectors came out against that part of the Bill and it was dropped.

Edinburgh's reforms of the early 1990s resulted from a serious financial crisis in 1989–90. As a result, many reforms of the management were put through and some of them affected the Court's membership. For example, the Senate lost two seats and the General Council (which consists of all the graduates) lost one. Representation of students was reduced from three to two. The Rector's Assessor lost the right of full membership – a right that the Assessor had held since 1858. He or she was instead given the right to attend and, when the Rector was absent, had the right to vote. The Revd Iain MacDonald, who was Assessor to Donnie Munro (elected 1991), has said: "I felt it was important to allow full membership. Without that it would be very difficult to stay on top of the issues and to know what was current."

The Cadbury report of 1992 was about corporate governance; its key words were transparency, accountability, fairness, and responsibility. Again, the trend was for modernization and for tidying up anomalies, and the rectorship was seen as one of these. But no concrete changes emerged in this case.

The Nolan Committee into standards in public life, which was set up in 1994, had a hearing in Scotland. One of the recommendations in its second report, of 1996, was: "Appointments to the governing bodies of universities and colleges should be made on the basis of merit, subject to the need to achieve a balance of relevant skills and backgrounds on the board."

On rectors, the principal of Edinburgh, Sir Stewart Sutherland (later Lord Sutherland), told the committee that he did not like the rector having the right to the chair. Sir Stewart said he feared a rector being elected on a "one issue" ticket which obstructed Court business and the running of a £200 million annual turnover.

A spokesman for the university stated that Sir Stewart's remarks did not reflect the university's policy. The principal had "merely expressed his personal view" that the approach in Dundee (where the rector did not chair the Court) placed more emphasis on the rector's "ombudsman" role and that "he felt it had much to commend it". Yet Sir Stewart's comment did reflect the Court's long-standing policy about its chairmanship.

In 1997 the Government commissioned an inquiry into higher education in the United Kingdom, the Dearing Report, and, as part of Dearing, the Garrick Report on higher education in Scotland. Sir Ron Garrick was a Scottish industrialist; the members of his inquiry were eminent people from business, industry, and education.

Rectors, said the Garrick Report, should no longer have the right to chair the Courts of the ancient universities. Rectors were not familiar with the business in hand; Courts shouldelect a chair, and the chair could be the rector. This proposal came near to being made law.

The report said, in stilted, jargonistic, and opaque language:

> The role of the chairman of the university Court is central to the institutional agenda and promoting its strategic aims. The individuals elected to serve in this capacity must be able to do so proficiently and in the best interests of a multiplicity of interested constituencies . . .
>
> We consider the Rector is a valuable asset to Court, and therefore should be retained, to act, as originally envisaged, as a spokesperson for students.

However, we believe that the office of Rector should no longer be linked automatically to the chairmanship of the university Court. We believe that the chairman of Court should more properly be elected by all members . . .

The Rector could, of course, stand for election to this position as chairman.

Sir Ron said: "We felt there is a real need for effective governance. A Rector could have suitable chairing experience and capabilities to effectively lead such a body in the way a modern economy would demand."

Or, as Ms Kettle has said, "Instead of a chairman carefully chosen for his or her business experience or leadership qualities, [the] governing bodies were at the mercy of the whims of a student electorate."

Principal Sutherland of Edinburgh said: "Students are well represented already on university Courts, and the Rector has an important role as the ombudsperson for students. It could be difficult to do that as chairman, who has to be disinterested and independent. The chairmanship of a university Court is a serious burden."

All the rectors, some former rectors, and all the student bodies at the time of the Garrick Report told the Government that getting rid of the Rector as chair would harm the interests of students and would bring no real benefit.

Brian Wilson, the Scottish Education Minister, said in September 1997 that the Government was turning down Garrick's proposal. Rectors, he said, were an important part of the Scottish educational tradition whose power should not be weakened. "The particular role of the Rector as chair of the Court carries great weight. I do not wish to diminish that role by removing the right of Rectors to chair the Court. Rather, I would prefer to see greater democratic representation in all of our universities."

Some people think that Gordon Brown, who was Chancellor of the Exchequer at that time, had a hand in the Government's decision: he may have intervened on this issue at previous times also. Brown was rector of Edinburgh from 1972 to 1975.

The government's rejection of Garrick's proposal annoyed some senior academics and administrators. A spokeswoman for Edinburgh said: "This is yet another recommendation from the Dearing and Garrick committees that has been turned down by Government without consultation."

When the government rejected the Garrick proposal, the whole issue seemed to be shelved. Nevertheless, the tradition of having rectors in the chairs has been regularly threatened.

Edinburgh did make radical changes to the institution during the rectorship (1975–79) of Magnus Magnusson, television personality. His two predecessors, elected when they were students, had angered senior academics and administrators.

A rule was brought in that no student was allowed to stand for the post, nor any member of the staff. At the same time the right to vote was extended from the students to all members of staff, both academic and non-academic. Senior academics and administrators proposed the changes; student leaders endorsed them as a way to integrate the whole community and make it more democratic. These changes diluted the power of the students and gave extra work to the rector.

A remarkable warning was given in 1859 by the Principal of Edinburgh, Sir David Brewster, just before the first rectorial election was held there. He told the students that if they abused their votes, "the legislature would not scruple to withdraw a power which has been abused. High-minded parents would either withdraw their children from a dishonoured institution or find a better reason than they have yet had for sending them to English schools and universities." This was a time when many well-off Scottish people were abandoning traditional education for their youngsters and sending them off to English boarding schools and English universities.

The great reforming Act of 1858

The Scottish universities were in disarray during the first half of the nineteenth century, Edinburgh at least as much as the others. Edinburgh had been founded in 1583 as the "town's college" and for centuries was under the thumb of the town council. The lord provost was for many years the rector, *ex officio*. His job was to keep an eye on what the college was doing.

For almost 30 years from 1829 the town council tried to reduce professors at the university to the status of the teachers in the High School, that is, employees of the council. During that time the town council went bankrupt and the professors' salaries were years in arrears. One commentator wrote of "the present reign of ignorance, favour, passion, and caprice." Another wrote, rather inaccurately, about the occupations of town councillors: "nine law agents, three grocers, one cheesemonger, and one half-pay captain".

In 1834, Henry Cockburn, who was the rector of Glasgow University and Solicitor-General for Scotland, said:

> The voice of the students ought to be very distinctly heard [in the proposed university Court]. It should contain one person, at the very least, directly elected by them . . . I am not, at present, prepared to specify the exact particulars in which I think it [the Court] defective, except that, in general, I think that the students have too little say in it, and the *ex-officio* members rather too much.

Reform was needed and it came in the shape of the Universities (Scotland) Act, 1858. This Act instituted the office of rector, set up the university Court, gave graduates their own body, the General Council, and detached Edinburgh University from the power of the town council. It also reformed the curriculum, but many of the Act's changes are outside the scope of this book.

Another view of the riot in the Old Quad during the election of Sydney Smith, 1954.

PART I

1859–1948

The Era mainly of Politicians and Military Men – and loss of power by the students

THE GREATEST STATESMAN
OF THE VICTORIAN AGE

WILLIAM EWART GLADSTONE, *Liberal statesman (1809–1898).*
Elected 1859 and re-elected, unopposed, 1862.

W.E. Gladstone's election in 1859 was the first after the university was reformed by Parliament, a reform that radically changed the rectorship. No longer was the lord provost of Edinburgh to be rector; from now on the students elected him (Edinburgh was not to have a woman as Rector until 1988).

This election was mostly but not entirely political. The custom of choosing politicians in Edinburgh was adopted in imitation of the customs elsewhere. The students of Glasgow University had seized control of the rectorship in 1820, taking it away from the professors, and the rectors of Glasgow since then had been almost always been politicians.

Gladstone was the Liberal candidate at Edinburgh's first election. The Conservative was Lord Neaves, judge and author. Gladstone was not yet the towering national figure he was to become but he was a master of public speaking and parliamentary debate, had been chancellor of the Exchequer, and was to be prime minister four times, the last time when he was aged eighty-three. His biographer Roy Jenkins, Lord Jenkins of Hillhead, wrote that Gladstone was the quintessential statesman of Queen Victoria's reign and "was the most remarkable specimen of humanity of all the fifty [prime ministers] who, from Walpole to Major . . . held the office." Jenkins, however, later decided that Churchill, not Gladstone, was the greatest.

Charles Neaves was a lawyer of outstanding ability. He had had a brilliant academic career at Edinburgh University before being called to the bar, and had a large practice. He was sheriff of Orkney and Shetland from 1845 to 1852, Solicitor-General for Scotland from 1852 to 1853, and a judge of the Court of Session from 1853. His reputation as an author was also high. He wrote for *Blackwood's Magazine* for more than forty years. Neaves's *Songs and Verses, Social and Scientific* (with music) went through five editions. He wrote about comparative philology and the Greek Anthology, with translations.

During the election, some political arguments went on. This contest was, however, far more than political. Was the holder to be a grandee who was living far away (in this election, Gladstone), or was he to be a distinguished local person who would be active in doing the job (Neaves)? This land of argument was to flourish for the next century.

The debate was carried on in letters to the editor of the Scotsman., with sharp accusations. One writer said that everyone knew about the "lax manner in which [Neaves] administers the law." And it claimed that he was "always the last person who is ever applied to to arbitrate in any difficulty."

Another writer said that Neaves had sent his eldest son to Glasgow University rather man Edinburgh – proof that Neaves thought Edinburgh was inferior. The students, if they elected Neaves, "may depend on his lordship doing everything in his power to raise their university from the low state it has fallen into, until it reaches at least the status of Glasgow."

Religious feelings emerged. One letter to the editor said that Gladstone, if appointed, would be "the more dangerous to the true liberties of Scotland and the best interests of her Colleges and students." Gladstone "declares the establishment of our Presbyterian Church . . . to be a disgraceful blot." Had he not maintained the Church of England, "with her apostolical succession," to be the pure Catholic Church of Christ? And another letter said that if Gladstone was elected, "there may be rejoicing in the Vatican, but the genius, the practical and Presbyterian genius," of Edinburgh University would not want that.

The margin at the election was small: Gladstone took 642 votes and Neaves 527. Neaves had a lot of support among law students; and he had the vote of every divinity student except one. Divinity students were against Gladstone because of his outspoken High Church Anglicanism – he was obsessively interested in Church matters. Gladstone, on the other hand, had a great deal of support among arts and medical students.

At his re-election in 1862, Gladstone was unopposed, something that was to happen very rarely.

Gladstone's oratory was spell-binding and he became addicted to demagoguery. He was able to hold the attention of huge audiences of ordinary people for well over an hour, at a time when loudspeaker systems were unknown. His valedictory address to

Edinburgh University lasted for two hours and fifteen minutes and was printed, at huge length, in *The Times* and other papers. His speech to the House of Commons on his budget of 1853 took four and three-quarter hours.

Gladstone spoke at a public meeting in Glasgow soon after the students of Edinburgh chose him. Someone who was there wrote: "He came on the stage with all the eagerness of an athlete, and from his first sentence of his speech he gripped his audience by his terrific earnestness." Disraeli, however, is quoted as saying that Gladstone was a sophisticated rhetorician, "inebriated with the exuberance of his own verbosity".

Gladstone's ancestors were from the Scottish borders, from the district around Edinburgh, and from Leith, the port of Edinburgh. His father owned slaves and a sugar plantation in the West Indies but became also a great merchant in Liverpool. The young Gladstone went to Eton and Christ Church, Oxford.

William Ewart Gladstone – "the People's William" – was admired and loved in Scotland and his image was in many Scottish homes towards the end of the century. Many Scots saw the Liberals as the champions of progress and the rights of man while the Conservatives were seen as reactionary.

Scottish (and Welsh) votes strengthened the Liberal Party, but Gladstone refused to back a federalist system of government. That would take Scottish Liberal MPs away from Westminster and weaken the remaining Liberal MPs there.

Gladstone cultivated the Scots by talking up his ancestry. At the same time he could point out to the English his roots in Liverpool and to the Welsh his landholdings and his connections there – he had married into the Welsh gentry. It was the Irish that brought disaster. The Liberal Party was to split over his plans for Irish home rule and took a long time to recover.

Other matters that were of great importance to Gladstone were theology, liturgy, and church affairs; the literature of Greece and Rome; and the way that Oxford University was run. A mention of Gladstone's name nowadays will often raise the question of his relations with prostitutes. He liked to talk with them for long periods late at night, trying to "rescue" them and put them back on the path of virtue. This obsession, Roy Jenkins wrote, was semi-innocent and self-indulgent. Gladstone put in his diaries on certain days a special symbol resembling a whip. This meant he had beaten himself for what he regarded as impious or impure thoughts.

Gladstone loved walking – on one day he walked 40 miles. Another of his intersts was chopping down trees. The Conservative politician Lord Randolph Churchill said: "For the purpose of recreation he [Gladstone] has selected the felling of trees, and we may usefully remark that his amusements, like his politics, are essentially destructive . . . The forest laments in order that Mr Gladstone may perspire." It was said of Gladstone as a man that he was always a difficult colleague, "except when he proceeded from the difficult to the impossible."

Gladstone's edited diaries run to fourteen volumes. He wrote many articles for the *Edinburgh Review,* the *Quarterly Review*, the *North American Review,* and others. The titles of some of his books show the range of his interests: *Odes of Horace, The State in its Relations with the Church* (2 vol), and *The Impregnable Rock of Holy Scripture.*

Neaves's writings were very different. The following example of his light verse is one of the judge's better efforts:

OH WHY SHOULD A WOMAN NOT GET A DEGREE?
On female graduation and ladies' lectures
Ye fusty old fogies, Professors by name,
A deed you've been doing of sorrow and shame,
Though placed in your Chairs to spread knowledge abroad,
Against half of mankind you would shut up the road . . . :
Is it fear? Is it envy? Or what can it be?
And why should a woman not get a degree? . . .

But after a few more verses he comes to the conclusion:

A Ministering Angel in Woman we see,
And an Angel should covet no other Degree.

Gladstone said in his Address to his electors that above and beyond professional knowledge and intellectual training the work of a university was to inculcate "a temper and aim" to subordinate all else "to the conscience, and the will of God," with Virtue and the moral law as guidelines.

Of Gladstone's rectorial address his friend and biographer John Morley wrote:

In the midst of the most trying session of his life, he went down from the battle-ground of Westminster, and delivered his rectorial address – not particularly pregnant, original, or pithy, but marked by an incomparable buoyancy; enforcing a conception of the proper functions of a university that can never be enforced too strongly or too often; and impressing in melodious period and glowing image those ever-needed commonplaces about thrift of time and thirst for fame and the glory of knowledge, that kindle sacred fire in young hearts.

The thirst for an enduring fame is near akin to the love of true excellence; but the fame of the moment is a dangerous possession and a bastard motive; and he who does his acts in order that the echo of them may come back as a soft music to his ears, plays false to his noble destiny as a Christian man, places himself in continual danger of dallying with wrong, and taints even his virtuous actions at their source.

Gladstone's address of 1860 especially approved the election of the rector by the students. He said: "The Legislature of our own day has, by a new deliberative Act, invested you, the youngest members of the University, with a definite and not inconsiderable influence on the formation of that Court, which is to exercise, upon appeal, the highest control over its proceedings . . . We think it eminently British to admit the voice of the governed in the choice of governors."

Gladstone the rector visited the university every year and took part in the appointment of professors. He had, however, annoyed some people in Scotland. The great reform of Scottish higher education, the Universities (Scotland) Act of 1858, contained a clause put in through Gladstone's influence, although the Liberals were not in office at the time.

This clause permitted the future unification of the four Scottish universities into one national university, with the individual universities becoming its colleges. The aim was to have an external examining board. A board of that kind would, the theory went, improve teaching and study.

Gladstone argued that it was doubtful in law if the "University of Edinburgh was a university at all" but was "merely a college which had acquired a prescriptive right to grant degrees". His aim, however, was to bring "Scotch degrees generally . . fully up to a par in point of dignity and social effect with the university degrees granted in England." Scotland would gain from having several competing colleges each sending its young men to a central university for examination.

A speaker in the House of Lords during the passage of the Universities (Scotland) Bill said that setting up a central university for Scotland would amount to a "suppression of ancient corporations – the only links almost which connected Scotland of bygone times with Scotland of the present" and that "it was not at all clear that the Scheme would tend to benefit the cause of education in Scotland." But everyone knew that the universities would never co-operate in the change, and so the clause – a permitting clause only - was allowed to go through.

That section of the Act was remembered when Gladstone stood for the chancellorship of Edinburgh University in 1868. It is the graduates who elect the chancellor, and the graduates gave 1780 votes to Lord Inglis, the Lord Justice General, and 1,570 to Gladstone.

Inglis was the person who did most to draw up and put through Parliament the Universities (Scotland) Act of 1858. He was a Conservative and Gladstone was a prominent Liberal, but the contest was not really political. Inglis was esteemed for the services he had given to the Scottish universities.

Gladstone's condescending attitude to the Scottish universities, compared with the English ones, does not quite square with what he said in the rectorial address he delivered at Glasgow, where he was elected in 1877. He told that audience:

> Among your students there is hardly a sprinkling, or at all events there is a very much thinner sprinkling, of youths, who, unhappily for themselves and for others, arrive at an University without any adequate sense of its mission, or of their own . . .

He gave an address at the end of his term. His subject was *The place of Greece in the Providential order of the world*. The speech, which took more than two hours, "was listened to with marked and, indeed, enchained attention, and the distinguished visitor was most enthusiastically cheered when his work was done." Indeed.

A LITERARY FIGURE WINS
– THE GREAT SAGE OF CHELSEA

THOMAS CARLYLE, *historian, philosopher, and essayist (1795–1881).*
Elected 1865.

The newly reformed rectorship was launched in 1859 with Gladstone – a step into having the rectorship dominated by politics and politicians. But his immediate successor, Thomas Carlyle, was a man of letters, a graduate of Edinburgh, and an international figure. He defeated Benjamin Disraeli, the Conservative politician, who was also a novelist of merit. Disraeli had, however, not yet reached the top of the greasy pole, the prime ministership. Carlyle won a decisive victory with 657 votes against Disraeli's 310.

The choice of a literary man was never to be repeated although literary men were to be nominated. Politicians or military men were to rule for almost a century.

Carlyle had a huge reputation during his lifetime and for many decades afterwards and was known as the "Sage of Ecclefechan", the village in Dumfries-shire where he was brought up and where he is buried, or the "Sage of Chelsea", where he lived in London.

Carlyle's family was not very well-off. His father, a stonemason and later a farmer, never travelled further than 40 miles from home. Carlyle, however, walked twice that distance to go to Edinburgh University in 1813. He studied European philosophy and literature especially. In his early years after leaving the university he was a teacher, returning to Edinburgh in 1818 to study law. He wrote articles for the *Edinburgh Encyclopaedia,* took up the life of a scholar and author, and when he moved to London in 1834, started to become really famous. His greatest works included *Frederick II of Prussia; Oliver Cromwell's Letters and Speeches; Sartor Resartus* (The Tailor Re-Patched, a satirical discourse on the philosophy of clothes)*;* and *On Heroes, Hero-Worship, and the Heroic in History.*

Carlyle's thought was much influenced by Calvinism. He became the interpreter of German philosophy, history, and literature to the English-speaking world. His style was, however, eccentric: we shall see (below) an example of that. His marriage, to Jane Welsh, never prospered. Some writers suggest it was never consummated. Carlyle was all his life a martyr to hypochondria.

Backers of Carlyle in the rectorial election talked of Carlyle's literary triumphs and said that his name and fame "would live with that of Macaulay, Tennyson, and Shakespeare".

Isaac D'Israeli, father of Benjamin, Carlyle's opponent, was a writer of Jewish-Italian descent. The young Benjamin was baptized when he was thirteen. Disraeli has been called the most romantic of British statesmen, the most inscrutable, and, according to his great rival, the most courageous. He has also been called a brilliant adventurer, impudent, a poseur, a charlatan, and a gambler of the highest nerve. Carlyle was to call him "a superlative Hebrew Conjurer". Disraeli's manner of speech, appearance, and dress could be flamboyant and he cultivated on his forehead a curl that was the delight of caricaturists.

In the 1840s Disraeli wrote political novels which promoted his ideas of Tory democracy. Their characterisation is lively and they depict well the gulf between rich and poor. When he stood for the rectorship he had been Chancellor of the Exchequer in 1852 and 1858–59. He was to be chancellor again in 1867 and prime minister in 1868 and 1874–80. As leader he imposed on the Conservative Party his beliefs in domestic reform and imperial development.

When the rectorial election was impending Disraeli's backers at the university held a meeting – suitably, in the logic classroom – which passed a resolution saying that the rectorship ought to be filled by a man "eminent in public life and possessing an influence capable of advancing the interests of the Scottish universities". The meeting said: "Mr Carlyle does not possess the qualifications which are essential in the successor of Mr Gladstone." But Mr Disraeli was pre-eminently qualified, they said, "as an author, as an orator, as an independent and original thinker, and as a Member of Parliament of the foremost rank." The backers of Carlyle admitted that Disraeli was a great speaker, but they quoted Carlyle: "Show me a great speaker and I will show you a great ass."

One of Disraeli's supporters told a meeting of students:

> You are asked by one party to choose one of the greatest orators who adorns
> the benches of the House of Commons . . . You are asked by one party to

choose one of the most distinguished novelists of this or any other age while by the other you are asked to elect Mr Carlyle, who, I think, is one of the most one-sided and exaggerating authors in the English language – the perfect Ishmael of politics, his hand being against every man, and every man's hand against him."

A handbill produced by Carlyle's supporters was teasing about Disraeli's Jewishness and said a number of things that would today be looked at askance. These views were, however, not exceptional for the times. The handbill said, in part:

Circumcision must be performed immediately on all Mr Disraeli's Supporters, especially on the Members of his Committee . . .

Every Elector must be prepared to asseverate that he has not had Bacon or Ham for Breakfast . . .

As it is desirable to be able to distinguish the true believers in Rabbi Disraeli from those heathenish men who worship their hero Carlyle, it is particularly requested that the former will appear on the Polling Day with at least Two Hats on, and their Coats turned inside out.

Gentlemen with pug noses are desired to leave them at home, and provide themselves with the real article of proper dimensions.

Each side in the contest claimed that its man was a worthy successor to Gladstone and that politics had nothing to do with it. But politics did have a lot to do with it, under the surface. Carlyle could be called both radical and reactionary. His creed was called "an extraordinary jumble of absolutism and republicanism". But, as a famous person, he attracted Liberal votes.

Carlyle's biographer and friend James Anthony Froude wrote:

The time approached for the installation and the delivery of his speech in Edinburgh. Through the winter Carlyle had dismissed it from his mind as the drop of bitter in his cup; but now it had to be seriously faced. To read would have been handiest to him, but he determined to speak. A speech was not an essay. A speech written and delivered, or even written and learnt by heart was to him an imposture, or, at best, an insincerity. He did not seem to be anxious, but anxious he was, and painfully so. . .

In private talk he had no living equal, words flowed like Niagara. But a private room among friends, and a hall crowded with strangers where he was to stand alone under two thousand pairs of eyes, were things entirely different.

Carlyle told the audience that he thought he should, according to custom, have written a speech to read out. "But on attempting the thing, I found I was not used to write speeches, and that I didn't get on very well. So I flung that aside; and could only resolve to trust, in all superficial respects, to the suggestion of the moment . . . you will then have to accept what is readiest; what comes direct from the heart."

He spoke of his favourite subjects – Cromwell, Frederick the Great, and so forth. His Address was difficult to hear and the audience large. Few people, in fact, were able to follow all he said. He later wrote:

Monday, at Edinburgh, was to me the gloomiest chaotic day, nearly intolerable for confusion, crowding, inanity, and miserable, till I got done. My speech was delivered as in a mood of defiant despair and under the pressure of nightmares. Some feeling that I was not speaking lies sustained me. The applause, etc., I took for empty noise, which it really was not altogether.

Froude wrote:

> He was long puzzled at the effect on the world's estimate of him which this speech produced. There was not a word in it which he had not already said, and said far more forcibly a hundred times. But suddenly and thenceforward, till his death set them off again, hostile tongues ceased to speak against him, and hostile pens to write. The speech was printed in full in half the newspapers in the island. It was received with universal acclamation. A new low price edition of his works became in demand, and they flew into a strange temporary popularity with the public.

One of Carlyle's backers in the rectorial election asked him to give a valedictory address. The great man declined but sent this message to his students:

> Bid them, in my name, if they still love me, Fight the good fight, and quit themselves like men, in the warfare to which *they* are as if conscript and consecrated, and which lies ahead. Tell them to consult the eternal oracles (not yet inaudible, nor ever to become so, when worthily inquired of); and to disregard, nearly altogether, in comparison, the temporary noises, menacings, and deliriums. May they love wisdom, as wisdom, if she is to yield *her* treasures must be loved piously, valiantly, humbly, beyond life itself or the prizes of life, with all one's heart and with all one's soul – in that case (I will say it again) and not in any other case, it shall be well with them.
>
> Adieu, my young friends, a long adieu.

LAWYER AND POLITICIAN BEATS
CRITIC AND MAN OF LETTERS

JAMES MONCRIEFF, *advocate, Liberal politician, and historian,*
later Lord Moncrieff, judge (1811–1895). Elected 1868.

The big issue was what kind of person would the next rector be? The Universities (Scotland) Act had opened up the rectorship of Edinburgh to persons of fame and talent. The first two to hold the office were Gladstone the politician and Carlyle the man of letters. James Moncrieff, politician and lawyer, this time beat John Ruskin, art critic and man of letters, and Robert Lowe, another politician.

Yet Moncrieff was not the type of London-based politician and absentee who was to dominate the office of rector for many generations. He was an Edinburgh man, educated at the High School and university, and he took a lot of interest in student matters.

Moncrieff finished his rectorial address with a promise – a promise that ought perhaps to have been made by many of his successors: "You have placed me in a position of responsibility, and I do not intend that it shall be a sinecure in my hands. Nothing that concerns the interests of the students will fail to have an interest for me."

As a student Moncrieff had been keen on debating and was called "the most precocious bantam ever to teach his grandmother to suck eggs." It was later said of him: "An outstanding writer, speaker, and statesman, he possessed in all categories an admirable mixture of towering knowledge and persuasive deployment of it." At the time of the rectorial election he had been an MP for eighteen years and had been Solicitor-General for Scotland and Dean of the Faculty of Advocates, the premier position at the Scottish Bar. One of his great cases was the trial of Madeleine Smith in 1857 for allegedly poisoning her lover with arsenic: Moncrieff was the prosecuting counsel. The verdict was the Scottish one of "not proven." He was instrumental in preparing the way for the Universities (Scotland) Act of 1858, which gave Edinburgh University students the right to elect the Rector. He was also at the time of the rectorial election the lord advocate, a burdensome post. The lord advocate was in effect the minister for Scotland and Moncrieff guided through the House of Commons more than a hundred Acts of Parliament, especially Acts to reform legal procedure and mercantile law. He failed, however, to reform elementary education in Scotland.

Moncrieff once said of the post of lord advocate that "it does not hold out any golden or glittering temptation" for ambitious lawyers:

> A counsel in large practice is not a gainer by accepting the position I now have the honour to hold; and there is no prospect opening beyond it. There is no promotion, no peerage to look forward to [though he did in fact get a peerage]. There are none of those prizes which are within the reach of the law officers of England and Ireland.
>
> Yet the office has one recommendation, and it is a great one to a generous mind. It has the recommendation that it affords the means of doing much good to the country.

Moncrieff neglected his private legal practice and in that way lost money, but he was more interested in politics than in practising the law. He was to become a judge, as lord justice-clerk, and was made a baron in 1874.

Moncrieff's opponents in the rectorial election were John Ruskin and Robert Lowe.

John Ruskin was the nineteenth century's most celebrated and influential art critic, and a philanthropist, social reformer, artist, and visionary. He can be called one of the fathers of British socialism but was also a great conservative. Ruskin once said: "I am, and my father was before me, a violent Tory of the old school; Sir Walter Scott's school, that is to say, and Homer's."

Ruskin was the defender and promoter of Turner but he also condemned A. W. N. Pugin, the genius of the Gothic Revival style in architecture. Ruskin's published works included *The Seven Lamps of Architecture, The Stones of Venice,* and *Sesame and Lilies.*

Ruskin had connections with Edinburgh. His grandfather John Thomas Ruskin had been an Edinburgh grocer, but became bankrupt; he went insane and took his own life. The family later moved to London where Ruskin's father became a prosperous sherry and wine importer.

Robert Lowe, the third candidate, was a Liberal politician although he had Conservative tendencies. Within a few weeks of the rectorial election he was to become Chancellor of the Exchequer, and was later home secretary for a brief spell. In 1868 he had a bad year apart from his great success in becoming chancellor, for he was defeated for the rectorships of both Edinburgh and Glasgow (the defeat at Glasgow was, however, a narrow one and his opponent was Lord Stanley, a heavyweight politician). Lowe wrote leading articles for *The Times* for no fewer than seventeen years at the astonishing rate of, on average, three a week. He was raised to the peerage as Lord Sherbrooke in 1880.

Moncrieff's candidature was known well ahead of the polling date.

The Tories and other anti-Moncrieff groups looked around for a suitable candidate and lit upon Alfred Lord Tennyson, who had been poet laureate for eighteen years. The anti-Moncrieff groups felt that:

> Wherever the English language is spoken, wherever poetry finds its way to the heart and holds a sway over the mind, wherever part feeling yields to literary merit, Mr Moncrieff will yield to Mr Tennyson.
>
> Party intrigue has been defeated, Politics have been driven from the contest, and the men of the University of Edinburgh have shown that they do not want any one who represents a mere city, a mere Church, or a mere professional section, but a man as renowned as the University which adopts him, a man of world-wide reputation.

Tennyson, however, refused to stand and the anti-Moncrieff elements were flummoxed. A general meeting of the student body was called. The people behind this were "students who are opposed to the return of Mr Moncrieff, or of any other candidate *connected with a political party*." The organizers were in fact pro-Tory and were seeking to promote Ruskin as the anti-Moncrieff figurehead. But the meeting was in the event infiltrated by backers of Moncrieff whose aim was to out-manoeuvre their opponents.

At the meeting several candidates were proposed but almost all of them "met with the most virulent opposition from a mysterious and noisy section of the meeting". Then, "to the horror and amazement of the Chairman, and the promoters of the meeting, just at the last moment, the Right Hon Robert Lowe was proposed and seconded."

A clique of the Moncrieff's backers had managed to get Lowe adopted, but the real contest was to be between Moncrieff and Ruskin while Lowe was a distraction. "At this stage in the proceedings, several gentlemen, known to have strong political leanings, left the meeting with the air of rats leaving a sinking ship." These were the Tories who had failed to have Ruskin adopted. But they could still nominate him.

A "stunt" was carried out by Liberals at the meeting. They took in a bulldog, symbol of Toryism, and offered to give the dog to Ruskin's backers. "This valuable animal is trained so beautifully (on Conservative principles) that it will be able to represent Political Economy in Ruskin's committee, and make up for Ruskin's well-known and pitiable ignorance of that science. It is also said that though the animal cannot *talk* so well about Art as Mr Ruskin, he is generally supposed to *think* a good deal more about it than that *popular* critic."

The Ruskin side wrote that Moncrieff was exclusively a lawyer and politician, "has always been fettered in his opinions and actions by party obligations; and is merely a supreme stump orator of the lawyer kind". To call Moncrieff a genius would not be flattery but "simply uncivil irony". By electing Moncrieff, the Ruskin side said, "you simply hasten that consummation so much dreaded by Mr Carlyle – the 'apotheosis of attorneyism'."

Ruskin's side put out a leaflet backing their candidate:

> STUDENTS! Do not be imposed upon by the flood of printed trash with

which Mr Moncrieff's supporters are deluging the University in the hope of securing a party victory.

Mr Ruskin's qualifications are simply these:

He is the finest living writer of the English language. He will therefore be able to give you a stirring address, more worthy of the literary renown of the University than any heaped up verbiage of legal and theological hair-splitters. He will make a worthy successor to Mr Carlyle, as he belongs to the same open, honest, and independent school of British writers.

No one who has read "The Stones of Venice" can fail to perceive his just claims on an educated constituency.

A leaflet from the Moncrieff side said Ruskin deserved votes:

. . . because, being a *Genius* he is quite above common sense!!!

. . . [because] being an Englishman, and educated entirely in England, he must be thoroughly acquainted with the *Scotch University system*!!!!

. . . [because] he has no Influence, Social or Political, which can be of an service to you!!!!!!

And, because he has expressed a Supreme Contempt for Edinburgh, its Architecture and Inhabitants!!!!!!!!

Ruskin, in lectures given in Edinburgh, praised the streets of the New Town for their "simplicity and manliness of style, or general breadth or brightness of effect". But the New Town, for all its spacious grandeur, was "a wilderness of square-cut stone for ever and for ever; so that your houses look like prisons, and truly are so; for the worst feature of Greek architecture is, indeed, not its costliness but its tyranny." Far preferable was the domestic architecture of medieval Europe.

Students, when they appeared at the polls, declared publicly the name of the person for whom they wished to vote. (The open, public ballot survived at Glasgow University into the 1950s.) A quarter of an hour after polling started, Lowe had received eighty votes out of a possible thousand or so. His committee decided that their man was going to fail rather badly and decided by a majority to withdraw his name. But his committee said: "The votes recorded as a result of the poll must not be taken as showing the number of his supporters." Lowe, said the head of the committee backing him, would have been a useful rector as well as an honour to the university. The final vote was: Moncrieff 607, Ruskin 425.

Moncrieff had not written a line of his rectorial address three days before he was to deliver it. "But he composed with such facility, wrote so fast, and produced such good matter that it sounded as if a long time had been spent preparing it. He also had such fluency, and such a thorough knowledge of his topics, that he could speak from a few scanty notes what seemed to be a carefully written address."

The installation was held in the Music Hall – not a place for populist entertainment but for concerts. A "gay gathering" of ladies, a newspaper said, occupied the galleries. Some students filled in the time between the opening of the doors and the start of the ceremony by making a din, in spite of the disapproval of other students. The noise spoiled an organ recital of works by Bach, Handel, and Mozart.

The rest of the event went on fairly quietly. The rector was warmly applauded during the speech, although a very few students from the defeated factions interrupted a little from time to time. These malcontents "were unable to disturb the harmony and enthusiasm of the meeting".

The chairman of the Moncrieff election committee, George Omond, presented the new rector to the principal with a significant phrase. The students, he said, chose Moncrieff "in consideration of his eminent qualification for the *practical* discharge of the duties of his office" [italics added]. That hints at a "working" rectorship.

Moncrieff's address was better than many others. He began by saying:

> I have no pretensions to rank in a category either along with or second to such names as Gladstone or Carlyle . . . I need not rub up my disused and rusty classics in the vain hope that they may show alongside the genuine metal of Mr Gladstone. I need not affect a shallow philosophy to match the deep and profound meditations of Carlyle . . .
>
> If we are to learn Latin, why not learn to speak it; or rather, why give up learning to speak it? . . . They pronounce Latin there in [in England] such a way that no one but an Englishman can understand it . . . Continental scholars have a perverse habit of pronouncing the language in the same way as that which we ourselves have adopted from them. I have heard it asserted that, after the Reformation, it was used as a test of orthodoxy and a means of detecting Popery, and that students educated at the Continental seminaries betrayed themselves by the breadth of their pronunciation of the vowels of Greek and Latin. Be this as it may, I believe that among English scholars there is a tolerably widespread feeling that it would be better to recur to European practice.

He complimented Robert Lowe, whom he had defeated in the election. The passage reveals the difference between learning and education then and now.

> He is one of the ablest and most finished scholars of his day, and no one exhibits, in his great Parliamentary efforts, more thoroughly the depth and variety of his classical knowledge. Unconsciously perhaps to himself, there is hardly a sentence he speaks, hardly an epigram or a retort which falls from his lips, which does not bespeak familiarity with the great ones of antiquity.

Moncrieff much preferred Scottish education to English, at least at university level. He drew a picture of the Scottish student in a:

> bare garret, up three storeys, scantily furnished with comfort, slenderly lighted and heated . . . Still it is home. It is free of the fetters. The man's mind expands within it, as he feels himself at liberty . . . not condemned to inhabit an artificial atmosphere, and to live surrounded by restraints as arbitrary as they are too often ineffectual . . .
>
> The touch of monasticism, if it cannot be called asceticism, which pervades the discipline of the English colleges, forms the students for the time into a class apart, and has a tendency to give a narrow and distinctive tone of thought, feeling, and even manner, to those who are subjected to it. I prefer what I think the healthier system of day scholars . . . such has been the atmosphere under which the sons of Scotland have risen to greatness.

WOMEN STORM THE MEDICAL SCHOOL

SIR WILLIAM STIRLING MAXWELL, *historian of art, collector of paintings and books, parliamentarian, agriculturalist, and writer of verse (1818–1878). Elected 1871.*

Sir William Stirling Maxwell was elected when a group of women was campaigning for the right to study medicine at the university. He was drawn into the controversy. Students opposed to the women violently disrupted his rectorial installation and address.

Stirling Maxwell intervened in the debate and took a liberal line. The dispute over admitting women is part of the history of feminism; it also gives an extraordinary insight into Edinburgh's academic politics. We know a lot about what went on because the dispute at Edinburgh was followed nation-wide.

Stirling Maxwell was chosen as a landowner, writer, person of wealth and status, Scotsman, and connoisseur. He defeated Sir Roundell Palmer, later Lord Selborne, who was an MP and a brilliant and wealthy lawyer. At the time of the rectorial election Palmer had been attorney-general and was about to become lord chancellor.

Stirling Maxwell was a moderate Conservative and Palmer was ostensibly a Liberal but was in fact independent. Stirling Maxwell received 594 votes, Palmer 502.

Stirling Maxwell was installed in 1872, at a time when the controversy about admitting women was particularly intense.* Some of the people who had voted for him met him at the railway station. They told him they hoped he would not, as chairman of the university Court, favour the women, but he refused to give any promises. What his Address did say was this:

> Few of us will be disposed to deny that the thanks of society are due to the learned persons who have sought to extend to women the higher cultivation which has, till lately, been monopolised by men. For a good many years of his life every man has been under the exclusive care of women, dependent, in all things, no less on their good sense and enlightenment than on their affection and kindness, and probably exposed to more danger by their ignorance than by any other fault which has been detected in woman by the keen sagacity of man.
>
> I can see no surer way of improving the intelligence of boys and girls than by improving the intelligence of their mothers, and other women who are to watch over their most pliant and impressionable years. I am therefore for teaching women everything that they may desire to learn; for opening to them the doors of the highest oral instruction [i.e. lectures and practical work], as wide as the doors of book learning . . .

He also said:

> The chief arguments against the medical instruction of women were these two – that it has not hitherto been the custom to give it; and that for a very large number, perhaps a majority, of women, the medical profession would be an unsuitable calling . . .
>
> The argument arising from custom may, I think, be met by another custom of no less venerable antiquity. From the earliest times woman has been the presiding genius of the sick room, often the sole medical attendant, always the physician's first lieutenant . . .
>
> So long as it is probable that women will continue to minister to their sick children or husbands, and to be charged with the responsibility of fulfilling the doctor's directions, I must hear some argument more convincing than I have yet heard why they are to be debarred from learning the scientific grounds of the art of which they are so often the empirical practitioners, or the docile and intelligent instruments.
>
> But, in truth, the experience of other countries has settled the question. The medical profession is, I am informed, successfully exercised by many women, both in America and on the Continent of Europe.

He said that he wanted the women to have what they asked – a complete medical education crowned by a degree.

---

*It is likely that, many years before these events, the university had admitted a woman to study medicine. Dr James Barry (1795–1865) graduated in medicine at Edinburgh in 1812, joined the Army medical department, served in Malta, the Cape of Good Hope, Jamaica, and elsewhere, and, a skilled surgeon and physician, rose to be inspector-general of the department. Barry was beardless, was considered effeminate, and never married. At his death in London it was openly said that "he" was a woman; the story was a sensation. Barry was never examined medically in a way that would have revealed if he was a woman; nor was a post-mortem examination carried out. No firm proof exists about his sexuality. One of his biographers has concluded that he was probably born female or that he was a hermaphrodite.

Stirling Maxwell's opinions, however, did not actually reach those present, because some people in the audience were so rowdy that nobody heard anything, but the address was widely reported in the newspapers.

According to one report:

> Tambourines, Jews harps, whistles, and many other obscene and undefinable instruments of torture were in great requisition; and as the time wore on, the fury increased and the actors passed from simple noise-making to more decided demonstration . . . the great fire of missiles shortly appeared. Peas were for a time the staple commodity of this trade, but soon enterprising students improved on the traditional projectiles and employed bits of biscuit, slices of orange, and the like.

A thousand people, protesting against Stirling Maxwell's views on women, marched from the venue in George Street to the Old College and from there to the Lord Provost's house in St Andrew Square. The Principal Sir Alexander Grant wrote: "A graceful and charming oration was rendered inaudible by barbarous noises, and was finally broken off amid confusion, as has happened too often on other occasions – when even the poor motive of this disturbance was wanting – in the universities of Scotland."

One student was "rusticated" or thrown out of the university; several others were fined and put on probation for the rest of their time there. It was said that some of the ringleaders of the disturbance were not students at all.

What was called the "woman question" became more and more important in the 1860s. Women wanted education, the vote, and reforms of the laws on divorce and matrimonial property.

Sophia Jex-Blake, from a Norfolk family, is a significant figure in the history of women's rights. She had seen in the United States the efforts of women to become doctors and she decided to seek a medical education. "My thoughts," she wrote, "naturally turned to Scotland, to which so much credit is always given for its enlightened views respecting education, and where the Universities boast of their freedom from ecclesiastical and other trammels." (Oxford and Cambridge admitted only Anglicans. The Scottish universities were more liberal.) Moreover, Edinburgh's medical education was among the best in the country. She applied for admission to Edinburgh in 1869 when she was aged twenty-nine and was joined in her campaign by other women.

Opposition to Jex-Blake was from conservatives and reactionaries in the university, the Royal Infirmary, and the city, who considered that women were suited to become midwives but not doctors. They should not share lecture room and laboratories with men. Women's brains were smaller and therefore less intelligent than men's. Darwin wrote at about this time in *The Descent of Man*: "Man is more courageous, pugnacious and energetic than woman, and has a more inventive genius."

One of the Edinburgh professors said that some women wanting to be doctors could be "basely inclined" – that is, they wanted to learn about carrying out abortions. The medical journal *The Lancet* gave a warning in 1873 to medical men that they should be on their guard when seeing a female patient at her home: "Some women cannot live without an intrigue, if only to procure a new bonnet or a ticket for a ball, and the most platonic and professional attendance of a middle-aged medical man may be warmed up into a romance in the brain of a foolish novel-reading woman with no family cares."

Other forces were active. A fear was that female doctors would attract women patients away from male doctors. That is one reason why some medical students and some young doctors were so strongly against allowing women into medical schools. The profession was overcrowded – for example, some young doctors who were short of medical work became salesmen of soap and scent. The students were easily aroused: they were younger than they are now, many were impoverished, and fewer than half of those who started the medical course became doctors.

Jex-Blake's campaign involved a hubbub of activity in Parliament. There were public meetings and petitions with thousands of signatures, a series of legal actions was raised by her and her group of women against the university. There was an action against Jex-Blake for defamation. Rows took place at the city's Royal College of Physicians and Royal College of Surgeons. Demands were made for the Royal Infirmary to allow women students on the wards. And there was a riot at Surgeons' Hall, where medical teaching was given, during which the women students were abused, pelted with mud, and jostled. Newspapers all over the country reported these events.

Edinburgh University, after great controversy, admitted Jex-Blake and other women as medical students in 1869, the first British university to do so. The reactionary opposition went on, however. The issue went to the Court of Session and the judge ruled in favour of the women. But before they could qualify, the reactionaries managed to squeeze them out. That was achieved through a ruling by the Court of Session, on an appeal in 1872, that the university did not have a right to give women degrees.

It was bizarre. The university had let them in but would not let them graduate. Jex-Blake and the others, worn out with campaigning, controversy, fund-raising, and lobbying, on top of their studies, departed. Jex-Blake graduated in medicine at Berne in 1877 and in Ireland a few years later. She went back to Edinburgh to practise. The first British woman to become a doctor was Elizabeth Garrett (later Elizabeth Garrett Anderson), who qualified in 1865 by taking the examinations at Apothecaries' Hall in London.

The women's campaign for medical education in Britain ended with triumph through an Act of Parliament in 1877. The Universities (Scotland) Act 1889 empowered the universities to provide women with instruction in all subjects (not only in medicine) and to allow them to graduate. Edinburgh University admitted women to its medical examinations in 1894, but excluded them from full membership of the faculty until 1916.

Jex-Blake's great enemy in Edinburgh was Sir Robert Christison, professor of materia medica and therapeutics. He was on the university Senatus, Court, and General Council (the body of graduates) and on the board of Edinburgh Royal Infirmary. He was a representative of the Crown on the General Medical Council, which controlled the registration of all doctors, and he was influential in the Royal College of Physicians and at Oxford University.

Owen Dudley Edwards, reader in history at Edinburgh University and a leading authority on Arthur Conan Doyle, has suggested that Conan Doyle, who studied medicine at Edinburgh University, modelled Professor Moriarty, his arch-villain, on Christison: both controlled a large network of agents.

Christison was made a baronet in the year of Stirling Maxwell's election. His diary says rather unctuously: "The Prime Minister [Gladstone], on his way south from Balmoral, called on me this evening, and informed me in the kindest and most gracious manner, that if it was agreeable to me he would recommend her Majesty to confer on me a baron-etcy, as a compliment to myself, to the medical profession in Scotland, and to the University of Edinburgh." The baronetcy was "a great honour in itself", but he valued it "mainly because it came entirely unsolicited, and was offered in a peculiarly gracious manner by the Prime Minister in person."

A biographer of Jex-Blake has written: "[Christison] was one of the most widely known and respected men in the public life of the city . . . With his tall, lean build and shock of white hair, his appearance was as distinguished as his reputation. He spoke in a rich bass voice and with such an air of authority that he had no difficulty in subduing the rowdiest class of students." Rowdiness in lecture rooms was for many generations a problem for university teachers in Scotland.

Christison believed that "the constitution of the female mind and frame" was "quite unsuited to the exigencies of medical and surgical practice". He denied that "every branch of medical education may be taught to male and female students conjunctly". Christison did not have any sisters, had three sons and no daughters, had been a widower for twenty years, and was aged seventy. "There is no evidence of any adequate demand among females to be edu-cated in medicine . . . There is no evidence of any adequate demand for lady-doctors . . . We have been told that female society is overwhelmingly in favour of having female physicians; but when I appeal to society I receive a very different impression." He thought that women were well suited to help women in labour. But, he said, the public preferred male obstetri-cians, "and now every ploughman's wife expects to be attended by a male obstetrician."

Palmer has been described as follows: "To the practice of the law Palmer brought a mind as keen and subtle as one of the great mediaeval schoolmen, a rare power of easy and persuasive speech, a learning and knowledge of affairs equally wide, profound, and exact, the abstemiousness of an ascetic, a vigorous constitution, untiring energy, and a high and chivalrous sense of the duty of the advocate." He was deeply religious and deeply inter-ested in church affairs. In addition, Palmer's political career was important to him as a certain path towards high judicial office. He married into the aristocracy, bought a landed estate, reformed the English courts system, and wrote a number books on hymnody, liturgy, and the rights of the Church.

William Stirling (not yet Sir William Stirling Maxwell) went to Cambridge Univer-sity. He was twenty-nine when he inherited the Stirling family's fortune and estates. Money had come from estates in Jamaica; they became unprofitable and were sold. But coal, iron, and stone for building had been discovered in the Scottish estates.

He remodelled the family mansion at Keir, near Dunblane, and in particular greatly enlarged the library. He was also able to buy pictures, *objets de vertu*, and buildings. He had a large house in a fashionable part of London, where he entertained Thackeray, Swinburne, and other writers.

He travelled in Spain and the Middle East; the people of Spain and their history cap-tured his interest and imagination. He collected Spanish paintings and published in 1848 *Annals of the Artists of Spain*. A pioneering work, it was also the first book about art to be illustrated with photographs.

The *Art Journal* wrote at this time that few people in Britain admired Spanish paint-ings: "Images of saints and martyrs, attenuated ghastly-looking monks and nuns, innocent of 'damask cheeks' do not constitute the most pleasing pictures, and are certainly not those which our countrymen would choose wherewith to decorate their mansions: living flesh, smiling faces, and joyous sentiment are much more in accordance with their tastes and feelings."

Stirling Maxwell also collected emblem books. Most emblems consist of a motto, verses, and pictures of ordinary objects such as bottles, flowers, or pairs of compasses; the whole grouping is to teach a lesson about life or conduct. Many emblem books were created in the Renaissance period. Stirling Maxwell's emblem books, under the will of his son Sir John, are at Glasgow University.

Stirling Maxwell as a landowner bred shorthorn cattle and Clydesdales, Scotland's great and hardy draught horses which have a good disposition and a graceful, springy step. He was MP for Perthshire from 1852 to 1868 and from 1874 to his death, sitting as a moderate Conservative. His life was changed in 1865 when his maternal uncle Sir John Maxwell died and Stirling inherited his baronetcy. (This baronetcy can descend through the female line.) With the baronetcy came a Georgian mansion, Pollok House, and its estate, in the south of Glasgow. He added Maxwell to his name and became Sir William Stirling Maxwell, sometimes given with a hyphen although hyphens in family names are an English, not a Scottish, custom.

Pollok House houses half of his collection; the house and its treasures are looked after by the National Trust for Scotland, on behalf of Glasgow City Council. The collection includes masterpieces by Murillo, El Greco, Goya, and Blake. The other half of the collection has been scattered.

In the grounds of Pollok House is the magnificent Burrell Collection, formed in the twentieth century by Sir William Burrell, a Scottish shipping magnate, and housed in an exceptionally fine building. The Burrell Collection has paintings, sculpture, furniture, stained glass, carpets, and other treasures from the earliest times to the present.

Stirling Maxwell was married twice. His first wife, whom he married when he was forty-seven, was Anna, daughter of Lord Leven; they had two sons. She died nine years after their marriage. His second wife was Caroline Norton, a woman of spirit and talent who happened also to be an author and a campaigner for the rights of women. She and Stirling Maxwell married when she was sixty-eight and he was fifty-eight. She died a few months after the wedding. He died soon after her.

When she was just nineteen her mother had forced her to marry George Norton; he treated her badly, physically attacking her. The couple ended up in the courts, to huge publicity in the newspapers. Norton claimed that she had committed adultery with Lord Melbourne, the prime minister, but the jury rejected Norton's claims without leaving the court-room.

Norton took their children to Scotland, out of the jurisdiction of the English courts, and Caroline failed to get custody of them. The court ordered him to give her money but he did not do so. He seized all her possessions including her jewellery and he tried to take the money she earned from writing. She was freed only when her husband died.

Caroline Norton wrote polemics, novels, and poetry with the theme of women's rights. The Marriage and Divorce Act was passed in 1857 and later legislation further improved the situation of women.

POLITICIANS TAKE OVER
AND A CONSERVATIVE WINS

Unknown, after William Smellie, Edward Henry Stanley, 15th Earl of Derby. © The Scottish National Portrait Gallery EP VI 79.1

LORD DERBY, *politician (1826–1893). Elected 1874.*

The election of 1874 was a straight contest between representatives from each of the two main political parties. It was the first time that happened at Edinburgh but the pattern was to be repeated many times in the next forty years. Politics had taken over and writers, scientists, and artists had no chance of success.

The Conservative was Lord Derby, a former foreign secretary, and the Liberal was Lyon Playfair, a scientist, busy man of public affairs and MP.

Derby received 770 votes and Playfair 583. Apart from the political split, the English students tended to vote for Derby and the "independent" – or non-political – students for Playfair. More than 400 abstained. Some people may have been discouraged from voting by what happened at polling when students pelted both bystanders and each other with peas, potatoes, small bags of flour, and rotten eggs. Hats were knocked off; shopkeepers in the district put up their shutters.

In the evening a crowd of students marched through the city and some of them invaded the Museum of Science and Art.

The winner had a much greater national reputation than did his opponent. Derby was from a powerful family in the north-west of England. He was the fifteenth Earl and his father had been prime minister for three short spells in the 1850s and 1860s. He entered Parliament when he was twenty-two and was given ministerial jobs by his father.

Derby's name was suggested in the early 1860s as a possible candidate for the throne of Greece. King Otto I, a Bavarian by origin, was unpopular with the people. The politics of the region were unstable, and the great European powers were deeply involved. Who was to take Otto's place on the Greek throne? All sorts of people were mentioned – a Russian prince, Bavarian princes, the second son of Queen Victoria, William Ewart Gladstone, and the future Lord Derby, at that time Lord Stanley.

Stanley was not interested, although perhaps flattered. In the end, on the deposition of Otto in 1863, the throne went to an eighteen-year-old Danish prince, who took the title of George I.

A biographer has written of Derby:

> In his own deep absorption in Home Counties landscape, his youthful love of mountaineering, his inveterate pedestrianism [walking long distances], and his planting of two million trees, he seems to hint at a new range of post-aristocratic, post-religious values . . . His homilies on prisoners' aid, organisation of charity, hospitals, artisans' dwellings, seamen's orphans, technical education, mechanics' institutes, the deaf and dumb, Thrift, and the Conduct of Life, would not have come amiss from Samuel Smiles.

Smiles was a Scot who studied medicine at Edinburgh University and who wrote *Self-help* and other improving books very popular in Victorian times.

Stanley was foreign secretary from 1866 to 1868, succeeded to the earldom in 1869, and was foreign secretary again from 1874 to 1878.

He was, in politics, not a great party man. He was a Conservative at first but inclined to the moderate Whigs later; he joined the Liberals in 1880. When he was elected to the rectorship he had supported reforms to the law, for example on married women's property and civic and legal disabilities of the Jews, but he was keener on foreign affairs than domestic.

Derby's opponent for the rectorship was Lyon Playfair (later Sir Lyon Playfair, and later still Lord Playfair). He was defeated for the rectorship again in 1886. He was described as "below the average height, and . . . strikingly intellectual in appearance. He was gifted with great delicacy and tact, had a strong sense of humour, and was an admirable conversationalist."

Playfair studied at Glasgow, St Andrews, and London universities and had a doctorate from a German university. His main scientific work was in chemistry but he did many other things as well. He helped to organize the Great Exhibition of 1851 and to set up the Royal College of Science and the South Kensington Museum. He was professor of chemistry at Edinburgh from 1858 to 1869. Apart from these posts he was appointed to a number royal commissions on for example the herring fishery, cattle plague, the civil service, and health in towns. He wanted universities to give instruction for the new and evolving professions as well as the law, teaching, and the church.

Playfair was Liberal MP for the universities of Edinburgh and St Andrews from 1868 to 1885 and as an MP was active mainly in social and educational matters.

A former student at Edinburgh University, Norman Fraser, wrote a few years after the election: "The triennial election of a Lord Rector [was] a subject keenly debated on all sides by the young politicians."

Fraser recorded a conversation among his friends, one of whom said: "You will need to take care of yourself on Saturday morning."

"Why so?" asked another friend. "Do you mean to say there is fighting and rioting?"

"Something like it, and if you get an handful of peas thrown sharply in your face, you won't relish it one bit. I have known some fellows have sore inflamed eyes for a month afterwards."

"That shouldn't be allowed at all . . . the Senatus ought to put such things down."

"Not at all. Buying peas helps the grocers, and a little rough fun is enjoyed by nearly all the students . . . I have given you fair warning, so you know what to do . . ."

Fraser's account also includes the following description of the events of election day:

> We entered the University to record our votes. Numbers of students were standing on the stone balustrades of the quadrangle, as well as on the steps; and almost every newcomer was saluted with handfuls of peas, thrown with such dexterity and skill as frequently to strike some part of the face and ears, which stung with a prickling sensation for a long time afterward. Ere we could mount the stairs and get into the Reading Room, where we were to vote, we were also assailed, but having invested in a pound of peas each, in case of necessity, we faced our antagonists, and replied to their attacks.
>
> The opposite party, disinclined to be paid in their own coin, made a simultaneous dash to collar us, but failed to do so. Once inside the Reading Room, I heard the peas rattling louder than hail against the window panes. At the end of the quadrangle where Sir David Brewster's statue is erected, a number of students of opposing parties were endeavouring to put their colours on the head of the statue. Several students, more bold or adventurous than the rest, managed to climb to the top of the pedestal, and were immediately assailed with paper bags containing flour, and others containing yellow ochre, which made a sad mess of their clothes, while all the time a torrent of peas was continually hailing on the advanced sentinel, who was endeavouring to outwit the enemy. . . .
>
> In the evening the students had a torchlight procession . . . there would be some six hundred present. It was a nice sight to see the torches flashing, smoking, and flickering; to hear the students singing various popular songs, and to watch the vast crowds of civilians who crowded on both sides of the streets through which they wended their way.

The Scotsman newspaper said of Derby's rectorial Address:

> Sensible in tone, practical in drift to the verge of commonplace, cautious in counsel, and passionless in pulse – these are the characteristics of the address as they are of the author. There are no flights of eloquence, no gleams of

enthusiasm, to stir the blood of the ingenuous youth who heard it. No one expected these things from Lord Derby, any more than the glow of poetry or the sparkle of wit . . . even the style is homespun and colloquial.

On the evening of the day he was installed Derby spoke to a meeting of 2000 working men. "My speech was well received from first to last," he wrote in his diary. "My argument was all directed to one point . . . that there is no reason why workingmen should not be conservative in regard of politics, since they have . . . nothing more to get or expect from agitation." The next day he was given the freedom of the city. Derby wrote in his diary soon afterwards that he had seen a letter from Charles Darwin, a neighbour in Kent and a friend, about his address at Edinburgh. The letter, Derby wrote, gave him more pleasure than compliments usually did "for three reasons: because it need not to have been written, and therefore is probably sincere: because it comes from one of the very few men who are eminent as thinkers, not only in their own country, but throughout Europe: and because the passages he has selected to praise are those which refer to science."

MEDICAL STUDENTS OPPOSE
ONE OF THE CANDIDATES

Permission of the House of Lords Record Office

LORD HARTINGTON, *Liberal politician and aristocrat (1833–1908).*
Elected 1877.

The contest of 1877 was more complicated than usual. The eventual winner, Lord Hartington, was an eminent political figure and a very grand person indeed: he was the Duke of Devonshire's heir. Hartington was also at this point the leader of the Liberal opposition to Disraeli's Conservative government. The Conservative candidate was Richard Asheton Cross, a remarkably successful home secretary, who was from less grand origins: his father was a lawyer.

Cross had brought in the Cruelty to Animals Act, to limit scientific experiments on live animals. Many doctors and scientists opposed the Act, and the medical students at Edinburgh were generally opposed to Cross's candidature. Hartington gained a decisive victory with 932 votes to Cross's 684.

A newspaper campaign had aroused popular feeling against vivisection. Among the people against vivisection were Browning, Carlyle, Tennyson, Cardinal Manning, and Queen Victoria herself, a great lover of dogs. (Prince Albert, however, had enjoyed killing deer.) She let it be known that she would refuse the royal assent to an anti-vivisection Bill

27

that was weak. A deputation of eminent medical men put their case to Cross, but the legislation went through. Cross did not particularly care one way or the other about vivisection

The future Lord Hartington when he was a boy was taught at home by his father and went on to study at Cambridge University. He was always gruff and uninterested in the minor social graces. One person who knew him well said that his expression was "habitually dreary, and if by chance he said he was glad to see you . . . you would have had some difficulty in believing it had you not reflected that 'no Cavendish tells a lie'." (Cavendish was the family name.) "He once brought down one of the highest partridges ever shot, and was loudly applauded for the feat until his innate honesty forced him to admit that he had been aiming at something else."

Lord Hartington had a confusing number of names. At birth he was baptized Spencer Compton, and given the courtesy title Lord Cavendish. His family did not use his Christian names but called him "Cavendish" or "Cav." The family's name was used in the motto on its coat of arms: *Cavendo tutus* (Caution keeps you safe).

When his father became Duke in 1858 Cavendish became Marquis of Hartington, another courtesy title, and after that was always called Hartington, even after 1891 when he became the eighth Duke of Devonshire. Yet another bunch of titles came with the dukedom: he was Earl of Burlington, Baron Cavendish of Hardwick, and Baron Cavendish of Keighley; but among his friends he was affectionately and endearingly referred to as "Harty-Tarty".

Hartington liked cards better than books. He loved hunting, shooting, fishing, and racing. When he was twenty-eight, and the most eligible bachelor in the country, he began a passionate and romantic affair with a fashionable courtesan, Catherine Walters ("Skittles"), set her up in a house in Mayfair, and gave her an income of £2000 a year for life. She was from the back streets of Liverpool but succeeded brilliantly in her profession. Beautiful, witty, sincere, and charming, she was a daring and skilled horsewoman and understood Hartington's feelings and needs.

Other lovers included Lady Waldegrave, twelve years his senior; but she, Skittles and all others had to yield to the German-born, beautiful, extravagant, and autocratic Louise von Alten, Duchess of Manchester. Hartington's political career would have been ruined if Manchester had decided to sue the his wife for divorce.

Eventually, when the Duke of Manchester and Hartington's father were both dead, Hartington and the Duchess married, in 1892 when they were both fifty-nine. She at once started a strenuous career of dinners and balls at Chatsworth House in Derbyshire and Devonshire House in Piccadilly, London.

Hartington held political office for forty years. He was, among other things, first lord of the Admiralty, secretary for war, chief secretary for Ireland, leader of the Liberal opposition, and secretary of state for India. He declined the prime ministership in 1880, quit the Liberals because he disapproved of Irish home rule, was head of the Liberal Unionists from 1886, and towards the end of his life served in Conservative governments.

Lytton Strachey wrote cruelly about Hartington in *Eminent Victorians*: "People seemed to have got it into their heads that . . . there was some peculiar value in his judgement on a question of right and wrong . . . ." The great mass of the English people, Strachey wrote, felt that here was a man they could trust.

For indeed he was built upon a pattern that was very dear to his countrymen. It was not simply that he was honest: it was that his honesty was an English honesty – an honesty that naturally belonged to one who, so it seemed to them, was the living image of what an Englishman should be. In Lord Hartington they saw, embodied and glorified, the very qualities which were nearest to their hearts – impartiality, solidity, commonsense – the qualities by which they themselves longed to be distinguished, and by which, in their happier moments, they believed they were.

If ever they began to have misgivings, there, at any rate, was the example of Lord Hartington to encourage them and guide them – Lord Hartington who was never self-seeking, who was never excited, and who had no imagination at all . . . As they sat, listening to his speeches, in which considerations of solid plainness succeeded one another with complete flatness, they felt, involved and supported by the colossal tedium, that their confidence was finally assured. They looked up, and took their fill of the sturdy, obvious presence. The inheritor of a splendid dukedom might almost have passed for a farm hand.

The man who was the inheritor of a stately dukedom and was an eminent political figure was not afraid of royalty. Queen Victoria invited him one day to dine at Windsor Castle. The main dish was saddle of four-year-old mutton, a speciality of the royal kitchen. The custom at Court was that as soon as the Queen finished eating a course the footmen removed not only her plate but her guests' plates also. Hartington found his dinner, barely touched, had vanished. "Here," he said sharply, "bring that back." He was so absent-minded that when the Queen gave him her hand to kiss he shook it instead.

His rectorial opponent Cross, a lawyer by profession, went to Eton and Trinity College, Cambridge, where he was president of the Union and was a rower. Cross, as home secretary, tackled slums, drunkenness, bad public sanitation, and harsh conditions in factories. His speeches were "of a type which the House of Commons listens to with respect rather than enjoyment" and he was "very far from being a brilliant man." But he was a person of great good sense. Queen Victoria, in spite of the dispute over the Cruelty to Animals Act, was very friendly with him.

Cross was responsible for a Factory Act and a Licensing Act that earned him the following tribute:

> For he's a jolly good fellow,
> Whatever the Rads* may think,
> For he has shortened the hours of work
> And lengthened the hours of drink.

After the rectorial election Cross brought in more laws to help the poor. He was to be outshone in his party by Lord Randolph Churchill and his career faltered. He did, however, become secretary of state for India. When he was out of office he drew a Government pension of £2000 a year. Cross died a peer and left an estate of £79,299.

* Radicals

FUTURE PRIME MINISTER DEFEATS PROFESSOR

LORD ROSEBERY, *Liberal statesman (1847–1929). Elected 1880.*

Rosebery, according to legend, had three ambitions as a young man: to become prime minister, to win the Derby, and to marry an heiress. He did all three. He also achieved the rectorship of all four Scottish universities – a record. He was exceptionally popular with the students of Edinburgh for decades after his tenure there ended.

Rosebery's ancestors were Scottish and he owned much land near Edinburgh but he was born in London and educated at Eton and Christ Church, Oxford, a very smart college. When he became rector at Edinburgh he was an up-and-coming politician but had not yet achieved great heights.

The Prime Ministership

Rosebery was at this time becoming a dominant figure in Liberalism in the Scottish lowlands. He was to be twice foreign secretary during the 1880s and was to succeed Gladstone as prime minister in 1894.

His Government lost a minor vote the following year. He could have resigned or he could have won a vote of confidence. Instead he dissolved the Government and lost the general election, and his political career after that was in decline. Rosebery said: "There are two supreme pleasures in life. One is ideal, the other real. The ideal is when a man receives the seals of office from his Sovereign. The real pleasure comes when he hands them back."

The turf

Roseberry's love of horse-racing made him unpopular with Nonconformists. His horses won several great classic races, including the Derby three times; two of those wins were in the two years of his premiership. His colours were primrose (after his family name, Primrose) and rose (after Rosebery). But he did not really have a good eye for horseflesh, according to people who knew about those things.

The heiress

Rosebery married in 1878 Hannah Rothschild, the only child of Baron Mayer de Rothschild and a very great heiress. Part of her inheritance was Mentmore Towers, a nineteenth-century mansion in Buckinghamshire that was full of treasures. Hannah Rothschild was an orphan, so Disraeli gave her away at the wedding. This marriage into one of the wealthiest and most influential families in Europe gave Rosebery a higher social and political status. It was a supremely happy and successful marriage, although she sometimes irritated him and he sometimes made fun of her. (He is alleged to have said: "I am leaving tonight. Hannah and the rest of the heavy baggage will follow later.")

Even before he married his heiress, he was rich, with 20,000 acres near Edinburgh worth £18,000 a year in rent. Mines bought in another £2600 a year. He had a mansion near Edinburgh, Dalmeny; a mansion near Epsom, Surrey (handy for the race course); a town house in Berkeley Square, London; and a villa near Naples. The seventh Earl, his grandson, was estimated in 2001 to own land worth between £65 million and £84 million.

Rosebery travelled a lot and loved shooting. He was an accomplished orator, a good classical scholar, and wrote on many subjects, for example, the Turf, Robert Burns, William Wallace, Robert Peel, William Pitt, and Napoleon.

A left-wing view of Rosebery was given in 1909 by Tom Johnston, a rising politician, who wrote in his book *Our Scots Noble Families*: "Lord Rosebery, of course, has done good work on the London County Council – work which it would be foolish and churlish to mitigate or deny. He has however travelled backwards since then; he, the millionaire by marriage, he who spends thousands annually on sport, now lectures the working classes on 'Thrift'."

Rosebery's supporters at the Edinburgh election put him forward because of what they called "his well-known activities and his general fitness for office". His opponent was a venerable and revered figure in the university. Rosebery's candidature was, in some people's eyes, impudent.

His opponent was Sir Robert Christison, who established forensic science as an academic discipline. Of great renown, he appeared as an expert witness in many sensational murder trials. One of the great trials in which he took part was that of William Burke, who with William Hare murdered sixteen people in the 1820's and sold the bodies to

Edinburgh's anatomy schools. Teachers of anatomy always needed a supply of bodies for teaching, but bodies were hard to come by. Hare, the more evil of the pair, turned King's evidence. Burke was hanged.

Christison risked his life several times in the cause of science by taking dangerous substances. He tasted arsenious acid; he ate an ounce of the root of *Oenanthe crocata*; he chewed a large piece of the Calabar bean, not knowing that it was dangerous. Symptoms of poisoning came on, so he swallowed his shaving water to make himself sick. He was saved with the help of two other professors.* Though he often suffered from fever because of his work, Christison lived to be eighty-four.

Christison's supporters for the rectorship pointed mainly to the services he had rendered to the university: he had been a professor for more than fifty years and served on the university Court for eighteen years. He was a power in the university and in the city, able, for example, to delay for years the admission of women to the medical school (see page 21).

Christison was a Tory of Tories, but was put forward as an independent candidate who had served the university well and was someone of great distinction. The aim of the "independent" label was to lure in the voters who were not natural Tory supporters.

Voting in the rectorial election was remarkably narrow: Rosebery won 1024 votes, Christison 985, a majority of thirty-nine or 1.9 per cent of the turnout. Christison wrote frankly, almost bitterly, about his defeat: we are lucky to have this evidence.

Liberals who might have voted for the "non-political" Christison had, he said, violated their promises to his supporters. He spoke of the "gratuitous introduction of the element of irrelevant party politics". Christison said that Rosebery's "student supporters received active encouragement, advice, and assistance from the Parliamentary Liberal Committee of the city, by whom, I was assured by one of their own party, the students were told 'not to spare expense'."

He complained that the Liberals on the election-day were better organized than the Conservatives. This organization, he said, was the work of more experienced people than ordinary students.

He also wrote:

> Throughout the whole contest the [Liberal students] made a point of declaring their regard for me. Nevertheless, they have allowed it to be overborne by the miserable motive of a purely political triumph, in a question in which petty politics had no natural connection whatever. If indeed, as I am informed, they were advised and upheld in their proceedings, by the Parliamentary Liberal Committee of the city, the students may be in some measure excused for having been misled.

*Arsenious acid is the oxide of arsenic. It produces diarrhoea, vomiting and failure of the heart, kidneys, and liver. *Oenanthe crocata* is related to hemlock and cowbane but is not the same plant as the one that killed Socrates. Its effects are a burning feeling in the mouth, severe vomiting, and convulsions. Simply biting the tubers can be fatal; indeed deaths are not rare. Calabar beans can produce a very wide range of symptoms including: paralysis, muscular spasms, diarrhoea, urination, cramps in the stomach and gut, inability to stand, lethargy, mental confusion, and difficulty in focusing. The beans were among substances used in ancient times in trials: the guilty died and the innocent were unharmed. In parts of Africa a person accused of witchcraft was given the beans. Vomiting meant the person was innocent, and diarrhoea meant the person was guilty. (I am indebted to Mr Ivan House for much of this information.)

But how fraught with evil is the lesson which their misnamed Liberal seniors have thus been teaching our ingenuous youth for guidance in future life! – that for offices purely academic, and having no concern with politics or political party, – learning, science, profession, good service, public respect, every generous consideration, in short, must go to the wall of party politics – or rather, to put it plainly, of selfish party interests.

The account goes on: "It is impossible to acquit the students altogether from the charge of ingratitude, when they refused the only honour it was in their power to bestow to the veteran professor who, for more than half a century, had been in a peculiar manner the students' friend."

Most of the electors, however, did not know Christison and were unaware of his services, since he had resigned his chair three years earlier. Moreover, in the same year the Liberal Party, led by Gladstone, was returned to power in a general election.

Christison asked rhetorically of Rosebery's victory: "What as to the interests of the University, of learning, and of the public?" Of Lord Rosebery himself he said: "At the age of thirty-three he was an untried man for such an office as a University Rector. But he had given proof of talent, and I can testify to him being a fluent and clever speaker. The vicinity of his chief residence to Edinburgh put it in his power to . . . discharge the whole duties of the rectorial office."

When the result was announced, a mass of Christison's supporters marched to his house to show their disappointment. He spoke to them from the balcony of his drawing room.

His sons, who edited his memoirs, wrote: "A thousand young faces were turned eagerly towards the erect and vigorous-looking but aged figure that stood alone on the balcony, – his voice, in the perfect stillness that prevailed, commanded the audience as powerfully as of old; there was no hesitation in his manner – no difficulty in finding the words, kind to his friends, generous to his foes . . . it was a great effort nevertheless, and on retiring from the balcony, he was obliged to throw himself down on a sofa in a state of alarming exhaustion." He was aged eighty-three.

Conduct at the installation was, said *The Scotsman,* scandalous and riotous. Students gathered outside the hall, waiting for the doors to be opened. Some were throwing dried peas. Professor Butcher of Greek arrived and went towards the gate: he did not know it was shut. The cry was raised: "Let's give him a squeeze." For several minutes, *The Scotsman* reported, "what with peas and crushing, the Professor had a bad time of it, while attempts were made to knock off his hat with walking sticks. His coat was also torn in the scuffle, but he took this rough reception good-humouredly enough, and shook himself free of the students as quickly as he could."

The galleries of the hall were filled by "the more unruly spirits" who set about pelting their comrades in the area of the hall. *The Scotsman* reported:

> The shower of peas which came from all directions caused the occupants of the floor to seek protection under waterproof coats and umbrellas, of which latter scores were unfurled. Such of the students in the body of the hall as were not possessed of umbrellas retaliated in kind on their assailants; and this mimic warfare was continued until the floor was literally covered with peas . . .

> Crackers were from time to time thrown about the hall, creating no little

commotion among those near whom they exploded; and sawdust now and again showered from one of the galleries on the heads of the students below. The first to take seats on the platform were several of the assistant Professors, who, being vigorously pelted with peas, found it necessary to protect their faces with their academic caps.

The report continued: "Sir Alexander Grant [the Principal] and Professor Wilson having occasion to go upon the platform during the progress of the pea battle, were similarly attacked, and, failing to ward off the missiles by pulling down their hats and turning up their coat collars, the learned Principal and his brother member of the Senatus were fain to beat a hasty retreat."

The professor of church history offered up a prayer but some of the students continued howling, stamping, playing castanets, and making other noises. Some passages in the prayer were greeted with cries of "oh, oh" or "hear, hear".

The hall was left in such a mess that the university had to pay several hundred pounds to its owner, the Free Church of Scotland.

Most rectorial addresses are not of great interest now, nor were some of them very interesting when they were delivered. Rectors often praised the ancient languages, or advised the students to work hard. These themes were not going to be very popular in the audience. Rosebery's rectorial address is a meditation on Scottish nationhood and what that means to Scots and to the world. He expressed with elegance and forcefulness some ideas that Scots have felt for centuries. Rosebery was playing the nationalist card: he was a great sympathizer of the leader of the Irish nationalist movement, Charles Stuart Parnell.

Rosebery's subject was patriotism, which he said was "a motive, or passion if you will, which has animated the noblest efforts, and inspired supreme heroism".

> England's wealth, her power, and her population make her feel herself to be Great Britain, with Scotland and Ireland as lesser gems in her diadem. Therefore, with an Englishman, the love of Great Britain means the love of England . . . He speaks, for example, of the English Government and the English army, without condescending to the terms British and Great Britain – not from heedlessness, but from self-concentration. Where the distinct English feeling shows itself is chiefly in an impatience, if I may so call it, of Scotsmen and Irishmen; perhaps not an unnatural emotion, but not one on which I propose to comment. When an Englishman conducts the government of a country, he at once concludes that it becomes English; the thinnest varnish of English law and English method makes it English in his eye. He is satisfied. Every part of the United Kingdom must be English because it is a part of the United Kingdom . . .
>
> We may hold, without disparagement to the Englishman, that this island is the better for containing Englishmen and Scotsmen; that there is more variety, more depth, more stimulus, and more comparison . . .
>
> There was a shriek of dismay from Scotland when she saw her Parliament disappear, and her delegates proceed southwards to London. But a moment's reflection convinced her that the Parliament had not been so efficient as to demand many tears . . . The Scottish character is well fitted to deal with its institutions, and to perfect them and itself.

Roseberry said that much of the Scottish character had been taken away "by the swift amalgamating power of railways, by the centralisation of the Anglicising empire, by the compassionate sneer of the higher civilisation. The spirit that he wished to see developed was:

> an intelligent pride in this country of ours, and an anxiety to make it in one way or another, by every means in our power, more and more worthy of our pride . . . The dream of him who loved Scotland best would lie not so much in the direction of antiquarian revival as in the hope that his country might be pointed out as one that in spite of rocks, and rigour, and poverty, could yet teach the world by precept and example, could lead the van and point the moral, where greater nations and fairer states had failed.

TORIES ACCUSED OF PLOTS AND POLITICKING

William Brassey Hole, Stafford Henry Northcote, Earl of Iddesleigh. © The Scottish National Portrait Gallery EP VI 73.1

SIR STAFFORD NORTHCOTE, *Conservative politician (1818–1887).*
Elected 1883 and re-elected (as Lord Iddesleigh) 1886.

Hidden forces were at work and some artful manoeuvring by Northcote's backers was going on during the first of his elections. Academics are said to be good at politicking; students can be equally good or better.

Northcote's opponents were Sir George Otto Trevelyan, Liberal MP and John Stuart Blackie, professor of Greek at the university. The result was: Northcote 1035; Trevelyan 983; Blackie 236. Blackie's supporters said he was standing as an independent who would break the monopoly of politicians. But the Liberals believed that Blackie had really been put forward to split the Liberal vote. The plot, if there was a plot, seems to have worked: Northcote's majority over Trevelyan (fifty-two) was surprisingly small.

Blackie had refused pleas from Trevelyan's supporters to stand down. A student politician said afterwards: "I could not characterise the Professor's running for the Lord Rectorship as anything else but a monster advertisement of one thing, and that one thing was Professor Blackie. However, his vanity has suffered."

Northcote's committee had the cheek to send a telegram to Gladstone, the Liberal prime minister, announcing the Conservative victory and beginning: "Thanks for your assistance."

Northcote wrote in his diary: "Elected Lord Rector of Edinburgh University. This seems to excite our friends very much, and I suppose it has a good appearance, which is a good thing for the [Conservative] party." His address was partly about the benefits of knowing Greek literature – a frequent theme for addresses at this time. "It is not easy to convey to you young men the delight with which, when one is wearied with long sittings in the House of Commons, one takes up 'The Knights' or 'The Clouds'." His reference to works by Aristophanes would be understood more fully by students of 1884 than today.

Stafford Northcote, eighth baronet, was educated at Eton College and Oxford University, and studied law. When he was starting his career Gladstone made him his private secretary. He had various jobs in public administration, took lessons in elocution from an actor, and was elected to Parliament in 1855.

Appointed Chancellor of the Exchequer by Disraeli, Northcote cut income tax by a penny, reduced the national debt, and lightened local taxation. Gladstone said: "He seemed to be a man in whom it was the fixed habit of thought to put himself wholly out of view when he had before him the attainment of great public objects."

Northcote had been a candidate for the rectorship of Glasgow University in 1877, but Gladstone defeated him crushingly. Roy Jenkins wrote of this victory in his biography of Gladstone: "To defeat one's former private secretary was not perhaps the most glorious of political big-game hunts."

George Otto Trevelyan, historian, writer, and Liberal politician, backed electoral reform and opposed the purchase of commissions in the army. Trevelyan entered Parliament when he was in his twenties but did not rise in the ranks of the Liberals: he and Gladstone did not get on very well. For twenty-eight years he held the Scottish seat of the Border Burghs, a centre of radicalism.

By the time he stood for the rectorship, Trevelyan's reputation had been much improved by his "courageous discharge of a difficult task" in Ireland. Trevelyan was made Chief Secretary for Ireland in 1881, of which time he wrote to his sister: "The effect of getting used to what is bad in Ireland is that you get more and more disgusted with the whole thing. The perversity of everyone who either writes or speaks is something inconceivable. If these people were left to themselves, we should have a mutual massacre; unless they are not quite as brave as they pretend." During this time his hair started to go grey.

Trevelyan's literary reputation had been made by his *Life and Letters of Lord Macaulay*, who was also a historian, writer, and politician and was Trevelyan's uncle. Another of Trevelyan's notable works was his *Early History of Charles James Fox*, the eighteenth century Whig statesman and orator

After the rectorial election Trevelyan was MP for Bridgeton, Glasgow, and was secretary for Scotland in 1886 and 1892–95. It was in the year of the rectorial election that he introduced the Crofters' Bill with plans for land reform that, when put into law, did much to help the people of the Highlands and Islands. He became the second baronet in 1886; and he was awarded the Order of Merit in 1911.

The third candidate, Blackie, was of picturesque appearance and eccentric habits. He was a translator, poet, and essayist, and lover of walking on mountains. A prominent figure in Edinburgh's political and literary life, he was also a popular lecturer all over Scotland on many subjects.

Blackie was born in Aberdeen and took his first degree at Marischal College there. He studied theology for three years in Aberdeen and spent three years as a wandering student in Germany and Rome. He had planned to enter the Church, but instead took a law degree in Edinburgh and became a member of the Scottish Bar. He obtained hardly any work as an advocate, however, and supported himself by journalism.

In 1839, aged thirty, he became professor of humanity (Latin) at Marischal College and strove for reform there. He wrote later: "The whole style of academical learning seemed so juvenile and pedantic . . . I had to sit down in a sort of intellectual Botany Bay, and teach raw country lads and little boys to blunder through Latin sentences, in the human meaning and purport of which they seemed incapable of taking any interest."

Blackie in 1850 was appointed professor of Greek at Edinburgh, holding the post for thirty years. His teaching was said to be spell-binding but one of his students, Richard Haldane, who was to be a distinguished political figure and also Rector, wrote that Blackie was too erratic in his methods to be an adequate teacher. Another writer said: "He did everything well, except what he was paid to do, viz. teach Greek to his students." One anecdote is that he put up a notice to his students saying that he would not be holding some of his classes. Someone took out the letter "c". Blackie then took out the letter "l".

Blackie espoused the cause of Gaelic and raised £12,000, almost single-handed, to endow a chair of Celtic at the university. He wanted a separate Scottish Parliament and spoke of Westminster's "multitudinous babblement and insolent centralisation".

Blackie died in 1895. A huge crowd turned out for his funeral and the city was almost brought to a halt. The Victorian cult of death and mourning was still powerful. William McGonagall, poet and tragedian, wrote an elegiac work in typical style. Part of it is as follows:

> Alas! The people's hearts are now full of sorrow
> For the deceased Professor Blackie, of Edinboro';
> Because he was a Christian man, affable and kind,
> And his equal in charitable actions would be hard to find.
> Professor Blackie celebrated his golden wedding three years ago,
> When he was made the recipient of respect from high and low.
> He leaves a widow, but, fortunately, no family,
> Which will cause Mrs Blackie to feel less unhappy.
> He was a very kind-hearted man, and in no way vain,
> And I'm afraid we ne'er will look upon his like again;
> And to hear him tell Scotch stories, the time did quickly pass,
> And for singing Scotch songs few could him surpass.

Campaign "songs" were part of rectorial elections, although they were not really meant to be sung. They were usually rather weak parodies. The following example, from this election, is based on *Iolanthe* by Gilbert and Sullivan and is supposed to be sung by Northcote:

I wish I could point to some labours of mine,
    Says I to myself, says I,
In the scholarly, non-Parliamentary line,
    Says I to myself, says I,
My name I am perfectly certain would look
Exceedingly well on the front of a book,
But to such occupations I never quite took,
    Says I to myself, says I

Northcote's installation was boisterous. Nine students afterwards appeared in court: one was found not guilty and two were admonished. One was sentenced to a fine of 10 shillings or three days in jail; another was sentenced to a fine of 20 shillings or seven days. Charges against four were found not proven. Principal Sir Alexander Grant, who appeared for the defence, said his impression was that the police created the riot.

Northcote as rector had much more work than his predecessors, because the university celebrated its 300th birthday during his tenure. The celebrations lasted for four days. A banquet attended by 1000 had seven courses including "haggis á l'écossaise". The town council held a reception for 4000 people. Honorary degrees were awarded to 121 men. Northcote was charmed by the parade of academic haberdashery, writing to his wife: "I wish you could have seen the congregation of all manner of gowns and hoods which assembled in the old Parliament House and formed the procession to the old Cathedral of St Giles."

In 1886, Northcote was re-elected for a second term of office. By that time he had been made Earl of Iddesleigh and had become foreign secretary. His only opponent for the rectorship was Lyon Playfair, a Liberal who had stood against Lord Derby in 1874 and been defeated. Playfair in the meantime had been given a knighthood and in 1892 was to be made a peer.

Voting was rather different this time. Northcote had beaten Trevelyan by only fifty-two votes but this time he (as Iddesleigh) beat Playfair by 1094 votes to 747, a majority of 347. Iddesleigh was expected to win, but not by such a big margin.

The Times reported that after the poll about 400 or 500 students . . .

> . . . marching through the streets in a very excited state, smashed the windows of a tram car. Then, marching to the chief entrance to the International Exhibition in Brougham-street they made a rush for the gates. They were repulsed, but not till some of the officials, including the manager, had received personal injury. The attack on the exhibition was renewed at night, but a small body of mounted police very soon scattered the disorderly youths, though some injury is said to have been done to a case on exhibits in the grand hall.

Iddesleigh died only two months after his re-election.

KEY FIGURE ENSURES STUDENTS' RIGHTS ARE WRITTEN INTO LAW

LORD LOTHIAN, *land owner, diplomat, and Conservative politician (1833–1900). Elected, unopposed, 1887.*

The choice of Lord Lothian as a replacement for the deceased Lord Iddesleigh was a strategic triumph by activists among the students of both political sides. Lothian was the secretary for Scotland for the time he was rector. He was therefore a key figure during the passing of the Universities (Scotland) Act of 1889 which gave students a greater voice in the government of the universities.

Students' Representative Councils had been established as voluntary bodies in the universities but had no legal standing. Lothian, after advice from people interested in Scottish education, ensured that the Act gave statutory authority to the SRCs. Seeds that were sown then have flourished mightily.

The right of students to a voice in the government of universities was to be recognized in the rest of the United Kingdom. The SRCs formed a national body in Scotland to represent students' interests and from that initiative sprang, indirectly, the National Union of Students.

The Universities (Scotland) Act also dealt with other important matters such as entrance qualifications, the curriculum in arts, and the admission of women to degrees.

When the election at Edinburgh was approaching in 1887, the Liberal and Conservative clubs would normally have each put forward a candidate but agreed not to do so. The leaders of the students wanted a Rector who would work in their interests. It was true that Lothian was a leading Conservative, but in the elections the Conservatives very often won anyway. Lord Lothian had certain advantages: he was rich, a great aristocrat, and one of his principal houses was near Edinburgh.

Student leaders produced a leaflet in March 1887, eight months before the election was to be held, saying:

> There has been a growing feeling within the University that the interests and opinions of the Students have not had sufficient weight in its management. The Students' Representative Council has arisen to give tangible expression to these opinions and has done good work in this direction.
>
> The efforts of the Council have been crowned with a success which requires just one thing to render it complete. What now remains to be undertaken is to ensure that the Students have some direct connection with the administration of the University. They have constitutionally two representatives on the University Court [the Rector and the Rector's Assessor].
>
> The present methods of election of a Rector are such that his functions as a member of the Court are treated as a secondary matter, and some undefined benefit arising from political or literary eminence has become the primary consideration.
>
> It is, then, a desirable aim that the election of Rector should be conducted with a view to the importance of these functions, and to the appointment of some one who will attend the meetings of the University Court, and who is in thorough touch with the Students. For thus the students will be using the means expressly provided in the constitution of the University for their taking a real share in its management.

When this was written, in March of the election year, the choice had not yet fallen on Lothian, but the aims of the students' leaders were clear.

The Edinburgh correspondent of *The Times*, within days of the document being produced, wrote that the students contributed more largely than any other body to the finances of the university but were inadequately represented in its government. The students, *The Times* reported, wanted the university courts to have two direct and two indirect representatives of the students and the standing committees to have representatives of the students. These ideas were well ahead of the time and were not to be effected for a century.

The Times also noted one provision of the proposed Act – that the university Courts would have more people on them. Eight people were on the university Court at Edinburgh and that number was to be increased to eighteen. The rector and his assessor, *The Times* reported, would now have only about one eighth of the Court so "the voice of the students is kept in the background and their desires are rendered ineffectual".

One of the MPs who helped the students' cause during the drafting of the law was Richard Haldane, Liberal MP for East Lothian, who was to become rector twenty-seven years later. He said in the House of Commons during the passing of the Act: "I consider that a university should be regarded as a kind of democracy where there is citizenship and where all internal affairs should be under the control of the various classes interested."

Lothian never delivered a rectorial address. He said on one occasion that he was too ill to travel. It may be that he did not want to face the traditional rowdy audience. The *Student* magazine said:

> In our younger days Lord Rectors were supposed to deliver annually *[sic]* an address to their constituents. As yet Lord Lothian has not delivered his rectorial oration, but he has made a public appearance in an academic capacity. Maybe this pleases the body of students rather more than a formal Rectorial Address, which is always more or less inclined to savour of quotations from the classics, which for the most part have become merely memories, or entirely forgotten amid the increasing masses of knowledge of which the youth of Edinburgh are being made the masters.

Schomberg Henry Kerr, future Marquess of Lothian, went to Oxford University but did not take a degree. He entered the diplomatic service and worked in Lisbon, Tehran, Baghdad, Athens, Frankfurt, Madrid, and Vienna.

When he inherited the peerage he took up a political career as a Conservative and was secretary for Scotland from 1886 to 1892. Lothian held a series of other posts, for example president of the Royal Society of Antiquaries of Scotland and captain-general of the Royal Company of Archers (the Queen's bodyguard in Scotland, a kind of exclusive club with fancy uniforms).

The ninth Marquess and chief of the Kerr (pronounced 'Carr') clan, his family had for generations married into the English aristocracy: his mother was the daughter of the second Earl Talbot, and his paternal grandmother was the daughter of the second Earl of Buckinghamshire. Other aristocratic relations were the Marquesses of Londonderry, the Earls of Mount Edgcumbe, amongst others. He himself married the daughter of the Duke of Buccleuch.

As well as being the Marquess of Lothian, he was also Earl of Lothian, Earl of Ancram (twice over), Viscount of Brienne, Lord Jedburgh, Lord Ker of Newbattle, Lord Ker of Nisbet, Langnewton, and Dolphinstoun, Lord Ker of Newbottle *[sic]*, Oxnam, Jedburgh, Dolphinstoun, and Nisbet, and Baron Ker of Kersbeugh.

Among the properties owned by the family was Newbattle Abbey, near Dalkeith, Midlothian, on the site of a Cistercian abbey founded in the twelfth century by King David I. The last abbot, who was a Kerr, converted to Protestantism and retained the abbey's lands for his family. The house in the twentieth century was turned into a residential college for adults.

They also owned properties in England including Blickling Hall, Norfolk, which is everyone's idea of a grand Jacobean country house. It is of red brick and limestone and has gables and turrets, massive yew hedges, a long gallery and great hall, ancestral portraits by Gainsborough and others, tapestries, Chippendale furniture, and ceramics. Blickling is now owned by the National Trust.

Melbourne Hall, Derbyshire, another property, now a Grade I listed building, mainly of the early eighteenth century. It has magnificent gardens which have been described as a mini-Versailles. It was the home of the second Viscount Melbourne, prime minister in the 1830s and 1840s, who gave his name to the Australian city.

A survey in 1872 showed that the family owned 32,361 acres valued at £1,130,075 and worth £45,203 a year in rent. In 2001 the family's land was estimated to be worth £60 million.

ANTI-CATHOLIC PREJUDICE AFFECTS THE VOTE

Permission of the National Portrait Gallery, London

GEORGE JOACHIM GOSCHEN, *later Lord Goschen, Conservative statesman (1831–1907). Elected 1890.*

The election of 1890 had some undercurrents of religious prejudice. George Joachim Goschen was chancellor of the Exchequer when he was elected. He was also a Jew, according to his opponents. In fact he was of German descent; hence his name – but he was not Jewish. Jew-baiting in the campaign was comparatively good-humoured and not unusual for the time.

The Liberal candidate, Sir Charles Russell, was an Irishman. A brilliant lawyer, and devoted to the cause of Irish home rule, he was also a Roman Catholic, and that mattered a great deal. No Roman Catholic was to be elected to the rectorship until 1979.

Russell wrote to his supporters about his nomination: "I thought it a hopeful sign of the times, a remarkable indication of the progress of tolerant opinion, that a Catholic and an Irishman should be, by an important section of the students, asked to assume so high an office in so distinguished a Protestant Scotch university." It was a fine sentiment, but the winner's majority this time was the biggest ever, Goschen receiving 1378 votes, Russell only 805.

Goschen had quit the Liberals for the Conservatives because he disagreed with Gladstone's policy on Irish home rule. Lord Rosebery, the leading Liberal in Scotland, sympathized with Ireland's hopes for home rule and hated religious bigotry. He wrote a message to Russell's supporters in the election. Russell, he said, was the most powerful advocate of the time.

> Outside his profession, his single-minded energy, his wide sympathies, and his general courtesy have made him a man of singular popularity and merit, while within his great calling, to which so many of his electors will devote themselves, he is undoubtedly supreme. It will not be the least notable feature of the contest if you can show that in a University where so vast a preponderance is Protestant, you respect, in choosing a Rector, the conscientious tenure of a faith you cannot share, that in a struggle where religious creed is not even remotely involved you are determined to elect the man you think the best, and that Scottish intolerance, once perhaps necessary and even noble, has been relegated to our national museum of antiquities.

Rosebery, in backing Irish home rule, was showing sympathy with the idea that Scottish people should have more influence in the management of Scottish affairs.

The Russell propaganda sheet, called *The Q.C.* because Russell was a Queen's Counsel, devoted itself almost entirely to maligning the opposing candidate.

> The running of Mr Goschen is the most shameless attempt ever made to foist on a University a man of mediocre ability, of incompetence in public affairs, without an atom of literary or professional recommendation, and without the slightest claim to the suffrages of the students. Mr Goschen is a man of whom many persons are very excusably ignorant . . .

> George Joachim Goschen was the son of a German pawnbroker and moneylender, who emigrated to this country in search of filthy lucre, and the habits of the 'cent per cent' he has found it impossible to get rid of.

> His name was originally spelt 'Goshen', but finding that the seeds of Abraham were not in good repute here, he prudently modified it to a Teutonic form, so that the Goschens, like the Smyths, must be classed among the people who have made a name for themselves. His religion, like his patronymic, was soon thrown to the winds, and from an early period of his career George Joachim has made it his constant endeavour to pass for an Englishman. A nose improver, we have reason to believe, is presently adding the final touch to the transformation . . .

> In a few months he will be the most outcast member of a shattered and discredited party, devoid of influence, principle, or self-respect, a poor ornament to any university. He leaves the Rectorship of Aberdeen without a word of regret from its members, without a solitary voice to bid him remain. He is presented here by those who think that with every principle broken, with every allegiance betrayed, with a reputation soiled and contemptible, he is still good enough for the University of Edinburgh.

Goschen came from a banking family, and was educated partly in Germany and partly at Rugby School and then Oxford University, where he was president of the Union. He made a lot of money as a banker when he was young and became an MP in his early thirties. He was violently against home rule for Ireland, although he never went there and never came up with any other ideas about curing Ireland's woes. Goschen formed with others the splinter Liberal Unionist Party which opposed home rule. Gladstone, the Liberal prime minister, fell; and in 1886 Lord Salisbury, a Conservative, became prime minister. It was then that Goschen rose to be chancellor of the Exchequer.

One of Goschen's biographers says of him that Goschen was "a proud member of the Church of England, and reacted strenuously – though without any sign of bigotry – to taunts by his political opponents that he was the product of Jewish forebears . . . Goschen explored his genealogy and concluded that the oldest verifiable ancestor who he could discover had been a Lutheran minister in the principality of Merseburg in 1609." Roy Jenkins has written that the Lutheran minister "was chiefly useful to establish the non-Jewish credentials of the Goschens on which the future Chancellor seemed excessively keen. These appear to have been impregnable."

His term as chancellor lasted for five and a half years. He was twice in his career given the fairly minor post of first lord of the Admiralty, that is, the political head of the navy. This seems to have gone to his head a little and towards the end of his life he was assumed the airs of an old sea dog and often wore a reefer jacket and a yachting cap. According to one wag, however, "Goschen has no notion of the motion of the ocean."

The Gilbert and Sullivan opera *H.M.S. Pinafore* has a character called Sir Joseph Porter, first lord of the Admiralty, who sings:

When I was a lad I served a term
As office boy in an Attorney's firm
I cleaned the windows and I swept the floor
And I polished up the handle on the big front door.
I polished up the handle so carefulee
That now I am the Ruler of the Queen's Navee! . . .
I grew so rich that I was sent
By a pocket borough into Parliament.
I always voted at my party's call
And I never thought of thinking by myself at all.
I thought so little, they rewarded me
By making me the Ruler of the Queen's Navee!

It should be said here, however, that this lampooning was directed not against Goschen but against another Conservative politician, W. H. Smith, whom Disraeli appointed first lord of the Admiralty. Smith was head of a lucrative company that distributed newspapers. Snobs in the Conservative party and elsewhere thought a mere tradesman should not be given such an office.

One of the few memorable things about Goschen was a mild joke by Lord Randolph Churchill, the Conservative politician. Churchill resigned in a pique as chancellor of the Exchequer in 1886 and found that Goschen had been chosen to take his place. Lord Randolph discovered he was dispensable and said: "All great men make mistakes. Napoleon forgot Blücher, I forgot Goschen."

Sir Charles Russell, Goschen's opponent had a lucrative practice at the Bar: for example, from 1882 to 1892 his yearly income was on average nearly £16,000 and later reached nearly £33,000. He was also an MP.

One of his great cases was when he defended Mrs Florence Maybrick, who in 1889 was accused of poisoning her husband James, a cotton broker, with arsenic. They had married when he was forty-two and she eighteen. He had a mistress and she had an affair. James Maybrick was a hypochondriac and took certain poisonous chemicals as medicines. Five years after they married he died and Florence faced trial for murder. The evidence against her was unsatisfactory but she was found guilty and sentenced to hang. Four days before she was to be executed, her sentence was commuted to life. She served fifteen years in prison then returned to her native America where she died in 1941, in squalor and surrounded by cats.

Another of Russell's famous cases was that of Charles Stuart Parnell, the charismatic Irish politician who was called Ireland's "uncrowned king". Parnell and his friends in Parliament obstructed parliamentary business to draw attention to the cause of home rule. He promoted agitation in Ireland against landlords who mistreated tenant farmers. But he had an affair with a married woman, Kitty O'Shea, and in 1890 was cited by her husband in a divorce case. Russell's speech on Parnell's behalf lasted for six days and was brilliant. But Parnell and Kitty O'Shea lost. The scandal cost Parnell the leadership of the Irish nationalists.

Russell was a great card player and "a familiar figure on race courses . . . he prided himself on identifying the offspring of a famous sire in the paddock." He was successively attorney general, lord of appeal, and lord chief justice and became a peer.

RECTOR WHO WORKED ON STUDENTS' BEHALF

JAMES PATRICK BANNERMAN ROBERTSON, *later Lord Robertson (1845–1909), politician and lawyer. Elected 1893.*

J.P.B. Robertson's term was exceptional. The voters decided that they wanted someone who was not a political figurehead with the single duty of delivering an oration. They wanted someone who was a distinguished figure, lived nearby, and would be a "working" rector. After the result was declared a student wrote: "The many advantages which accrue to us . . . from having a representative on the Court, able to attend its meetings and keep in constant touch with its proceedings, have in the past been almost wholly disregarded. We have been content to have a Lord Rector in London, who might as well, as far as our interests were concerned, have been in Iceland."

But the election was also of a political nature, as was shown by a speech given by the leader of the Conservative students when the result was announced. "The students have let it be known throughout the length and breadth of the country that the wave of Unionist [i.e. Conservative] feeling which is flowing fast has not deserted Edinburgh University but has come here in all its strength." The students, he said, by electing a Conservative had sent a message to Mr Gladstone, the Liberal Prime Minister.

Robertson's victory was predictable. In rectorial elections the Conservative candidate generally beat the Liberal; and Robertson at the time of the election was a former Conservative MP. The Liberal candidate was Lord Reay, a public figure but not an outstanding one. Roberson was educated at the Royal High School, Edinburgh, and at Edinburgh University, where he was a notable speaker at political debates. He became an advocate but he was more interested in politics than in the law. Robertson became an MP and solicitor-general for Scotland in 1885 and Lord Advocate in 1888. But his political career did not flourish and he became Lord President of the Court of Session in 1891. The move was also to secure his income. Robertson went to the House of Lords as a judicial peer in 1899. He remained a politician always.

Voting was 1145 for Robertson, and for Reay 728. This was the first time women had the vote.

The *Student* magazine wrote, when Robertson's term ended: "We are voicing the unanimous opinion of Edinburgh students when we say that never will they have a more real Rector, nor one so universally popular." Lord Robertson, the magazine said, showed his interest in those he represented in many ways. "He presided with an unprecedented regularity at the meetings of the University Court, and has made a record in this respect which his successors will have difficulty in beating . . . He brought all the keenness of his intellect to bear upon the questions under discussion, and he tried as far as possible to act as a representative of undergraduate feeling."

The magazine also said:

> In every possible way Lord Robertson did his best for the students, and his services culminated the magnificent rectorial address which he delivered almost a year ago. It was the masterly production of a masterly mind; it was eloquently rich in thought, and a valuable incitement to strenuous endeav-our. However brilliant the addresses of previous Rectors may have been, that of December 1895 deserves a high place.

Here are some passages from Lord Robertson's address:

> After reading the history of some small country, the controversies of some small sect, or the books of some small writer, one turns away to richer sources for relief and inspiration. Oh for the sonorous voices of many waters! For the words of great men and the fortunes of great nations! Let those who have time explore the barren annals of tyrants and rebels, which begin and end in nothing . . .
>
> Of all subjects, Socialism must be studied to be understood in its practical proposals and ultimate consequences; and once these are realised, it is seen how Collectivism differs from a mere limitation of the old principle of *laissez-faire*. Yet many well-intentioned people, informed only about the excellent motives of the authors of a system which is nothing if not practical, entirely forget Dr Johnson's admonition to Boswell on the important article of Freewill and Necessity.

Lord Reay, Robertson's opponent, was of Scottish and Dutch descent. A branch of the family left Scotland, settled in the Netherlands, and married into the Dutch aristocracy. The eleventh Lord Reay became a member of the Dutch Parliament but came to Britain in 1875. He was governor of Bombay from 1885 to 1890. Reay later held several posts in education: he was chairman of the London School Board and president of the council, University College, London. Other appointments, in diplomacy, followed. Reay had been Rector of St Andrews University from 1884 to 1886.

CONSERVATIVE CLUB SNUBS
UNIVERSITY'S BENEFACTOR

Charles Martin Hardie, Alexander Hugh Bruce, 6th Lord Balfour of Burleigh © The Scottish National Portrait Gallery PG 872

LORD BALFOUR OF BURLEIGH, *Conservative politician (1849–1921).
Elected 1896.*

The Liberals suggested to the Conservatives that for the election of 1896 "political animus" should be abandoned and that the two sides should together nominate William McEwan, an immensely rich local brewer, a benefactor of the university, and a Liberal MP.

He donated most of the money to build the McEwan Hall, the university's principal hall for big meetings and ceremonies.* The hall, in a lavish Italian Renaissance style, cost £115,000 and was being built when the election was held. The Conservative Club, however, refused to back McEwan, the reason being his Liberal politics.

---

*McEwan was a philanthropist and collector. His brewery produced McEwan's Export Ale and India Pale Ale, which were specially made to travel well to the Empire's furthest outposts. Another brewer, Andrew Usher, gave to the city £100,000 in 1896 to build the Usher Hall for concerts.

The Liberal club had to find another candidate and chose Richard Haldane, an MP, lawyer and philosopher who was an Edinburgh graduate. He was to play an important role in preparing the country's armed forces when the First World War was approaching. Haldane won the rectorship in 1905 (for details about him and his life, see page 63).

Balfour of Burleigh was a straightforward Conservative and was Secretary for Scotland. The previous five rectorial elections had been won by the Conservatives and the Conservatives were confident of winning again. The Liberal party was in trouble nationally. It had split in 1886 over home rule for Ireland and the dissidents had formed the Liberal Unionist Party.

During the 1896 election campaign a student politician, Sarat Mullick, who was a Liberal, wrote about the split in the party:

> If broad *principles* of politics be the battle cry, it is the duty of every Liberal Unionist to stand shoulder to shoulder with the Liberals. The Liberal Unionist traditions of a glorious past are the traditions of the Liberals, for the principles which animate the Liberal Unionists and the Liberals alike are the principles of political emancipation, and the extension of civil and religious liberty.

It is hard to estimate accurately the effect of the Liberal Unionist vote, but Haldane's support was creditable. Voting was: Balfour of Burleigh 990, Haldane 771. The Conservative majority was the smallest for ten years.

Balfour repeatedly avoided fixing a date for his installation and address: the Students' Representative Council had to take a firm stance with him. The ceremony eventually took place in the last year of his tenure, with only a few months to go.* He was a busy person, but the delay may also have been because he feared the students would be rowdy. The audience *was* rowdy. The McEwan Hall is suitable for a student audience, having paintings emblematic of Perseverance, Intelligence, Imagination, and Experience. This was the first time it was used for the rector's installation ceremony.

The Scotsman, voice of Edinburgh's respectable middle class, was reproving and gave the students a classic rebuke – a rebuke that could have been repeated scores of times:

> Our Scottish universities are sadly deficient as schools of manners. Lord Balfour's record of public service, ably rendered with untiring devotion to the best interests of his country, should command a respectful hearing from any audience. From an audience which, by its own suffrages, had elected him to the position that he occupied, he had a double claim to an attentive hearing.
>
> Instead of respect, however, he got his share of that discourtesy which is the normal tribute of Scottish students to their Lord Rector, and renders the tenure of that office a burden rather than an honour. To a critical stranger what a strange spectacle it must seem when the appeal to rise to the vast burdens of the Empire, to feel its grandeur, to rise to new enthusiasm for its

---

*Lord Curzon, the Rector of Glasgow University from 1908 to 1911, repeatedly postponed his installation. The students mocked him and rebuked him for that. Curzon, a grandee, thought they were "rather a wild and uncouth lot." He said it was really intolerable that in this fashion they should "lecture and hector" a Rector.

great possibilities, coming from a man in Lord Balfour's position, is greeted with catcalls and noisy ribaldry. The exuberance of youth is no excuse. And there was more in the same manner.

Herbert Asquith, a Liberal MP and future prime minister, told a meeting of Haldane's backers that the Liberals of Scotland and England had a hearty sympathy for the "gallant endeavours which they were making to rescue the honourable office of Lord Rector from becoming part of the spoils of a *particular* political party" (italics added).

The Scotsman said of the result:

> [Haldane's] Liberalism is of a type that is more likely to take the fancy of University undergraduates than of practical men. The Collectivist theories of which he is an advocate represent a sort of milk-and-water Socialism that is calculated to inspire the enthusiasm of callow and unpractical youth. It sounds well and means little. It talks of humanity with a big H, and soars safely in the lofty regions of theory unmindful of the realities of a work-a-day world here below. It is surprising to learn that the vote of the lady undergraduates, now a not unimportant quantity in the Rectorial elections, went in the main to Mr Haldane . . . Edinburgh University has ranged herself with . . . the general political opinion of the country. That is as it should be.

Balfour of Burleigh, the sixth holder of a Scottish barony, was educated at Eton College and Oxford University. He became a representative peer when he was twenty-seven (peers of Scotland were not entitled to sit in the House of Lords but were allowed under the Act of Union to choose sixteen of their number to do so). He was secretary for Scotland during the whole of his rectorship. The *Dictionary of National Biography* wrote that his biography was "largely a record of his work on commissions, the reports of which became authoritative documents". He had, however, "a commanding presence and much charm of manner. Without brilliance, he yet represented the best type of public servant – conscientious, purposeful, and with a gift for mastering complicated details and presenting them lucidly and cogently."

Balfour's kinsman the fifth baron, Robert Balfour, who flourished in the first half of the eighteenth century, led a rather more colourful life. He fell in love when young, but his family thought that the woman was unsuitable because her social status was too low. The family sent him abroad to forget his beloved. Balfour, before he went, told her that if she married when he was away he would kill her husband. She did marry, warning her future husband about the danger. He was Henry Stenhouse, a schoolmaster at Inverkeithing, Fife.

Balfour came back, asked about the woman, found out what had happened, went to Inverkeithing, shot and wounded Stenhouse, and went home. Stenhouse lingered for twelve days and died. Balfour lay low for a while. A local tradition says that he hid in a big hollow tree. But he was arrested, tried, and sentenced to be beheaded, the execution to take place in January 1709. He was confined in the Tolbooth of Edinburgh. A few days before he was to be executed his sister who resembled him, visited him; they exchanged clothes and he escaped.

Balfour was "out" in the '15, and was attainted by Act of Parliament; his estates were forfeited to the Crown. He died in 1757, still unmarried. His descendants knew they were entitled to the peerage but could not prove it to the satisfaction of the House of

Lords. But a discovery was made in 1858 that was worthy of a nineteenth century novel. In an oak chest at the family's main house, Kesnet House, near alloa, Clackmanninshire, an original patent of nobility turned up.

In 1869 the House of Lords decided that Robert Bruce, a descendant of the fifth baron, would have been entitled to the barony but for the attainder. An Act of Parliament was passed to remove the attainder and Bruce became Lord Balfour of Burleigh (the surname had changed as this peerage could descend through the female line).

Among the topics of the royal commissions Balfour worked on were: educational endowments, metropolitan water supply, trade between Canada and the West Indies, commercial and industrial policy after the First World War, and local property tax. When the Conservatives were in opposition and he had less to do, he wrote *An Historical Account of the Rise and Development of Presbyterianism in Scotland*. He worked to bring about the union of the Church of Scotland and the United Free Church.

Balfour died PC, KT, GCMG, GCVO, a DCL of Oxford University, an honorary LLD from each of the four Scottish universities, and chancellor of St Andrews University.

Tom Johnstone, a firebrand Labour politician, wrote of him in *Our Scots Noble Families* in 1909:

> Lord Burleigh [*sic*] draws £100 a month, having as an ex-Cabinet Minister signed a plea that he was too poor to do without some State help. This pension does not, however, seemed to have destroyed his energies or his capacity for thrift, for he 'directs' some 7 public Companies (total capital over £88,000,000), engaged in banking, rails, steamships, and telegraphs. In his spare time he amuses himself with the pleasantries of the Anti-Socialist League, endeavouring to revive antediluvian political theories. He was wildly excited over the introduction of an old-age pension of five shillings per week to working class octogenarians, believing that State pensions destroy self-reliance and individuality. He left us to infer that he spoke from personal experience.

The same sort of criticism was made in parliament and Balfour responded. He said that he had been doing unpaid work for the state for forty years. He had been on nine Royal Commissions and was chairman of seven of them. He said that in some years he had spent more than 180 days in unpaid work. "I took a Commission which involved prolonged absence from the country and a certain sacrifice of emoluments." And so on.

The leader of the House of Commons, Bonar Law, said in a later passage at arms in 1920 that the number of companies which Bonar was connected with was overstated. "Lord Balfour's estate in Scotland, owing to its heavy burdens, yielded little revenue, and is now yielding none."

Balfour left a fortune of nearly £50,000, the equivalent in modern terms of at least £2,500,000.

RECTOR AND STUDENTS HAVE A GREAT QUARREL

LORD DUFFERIN AND AVA, *diplomat and administrator (1826–1902).*
Elected 1899.

Lord Dufferin and Ava, the Conservative candidate, was a very grand person indeed, and a former Viceroy of India. His Liberal opponent Herbert Asquith, was not such an imposing figure at that time as he was to become (he was to be prime minister from 1908 to 1916). Dufferin received 943 votes, Asquith 686.

Dufferin's grandeur did not deter some of the students from having a great quarrel with him. Some student leaders wanted their views to be heard clearly on the university Court but the Rector was going to be an absentee. They wanted Dufferin to appoint as his assessor on the Court a particular person whom they knew and who had helped them. Dufferin favoured someone else and did not talk to the students' representatives about his choice. Dufferin won in the end. Neither side, in this case, showed much tact or diplomacy. Dufferin had, however, the benefit of experience. He had been Rector of St Andrews and had had a similar quarrel with students there – and won.

The quarrel between the Edinburgh students and their Rector centred round a clause in the Universities (Scotland) Act 1889 that gave legal existence to the students' representative councils of the four Scottish universities. This clause said that the Rector "may, before he appoints his Assessor, confer with the students' representative council". Moreover, when this Act of Parliament was being drafted, the Secretary for Scotland, Lord Lothian, had said: "I am most anxious that the students should be represented, and with reference to the Rector's Assessor, I am of the opinion that the students should have a voice in the nomination." Dufferin failed to confer with the Students' Representative Council.

Dufferin, when voted in, told the SRC that he wanted the job of Rector's Assessor to go to David Dundas QC, a Conservative and a friend. (Dundas was to be Solicitor-General for Scotland and a judge of the Court of Session.) The *Student* magazine said of the situation:

> The [Students' Representative] Council rightly refused to have anything to do with such a nomination, and for the excellent reason that Mr Dundas combines in himself every qualification which is unnecessary and useless for the position. We venture to believe that Lord Dufferin may yet agree to accept the one nomination which is acceptable to the students of this University – that of James Walker CA. [Walker had rescued the SRC from a financial crisis and later helped to win for it a grant of £60 a year from the university. He nurtured the Union when it was founded, supervised the building of its premises, and raised almost all the £26,000 needed for an extension to it.]
>
> Every student knows Mr Walker and Mr Walker's work . . . Mr Walker has a record of at least ten years' work given ungrudgingly on our behalf, and for our best interests. But what of Mr Dundas? Who is he? What has he done at any time, rather for us or in our interests, or how long ago is it since he developed this keen interest in our welfare, that without any record behind him, without even the suspicion of work done for us, he is going to prove superior to Mr Walker?

Dufferin wrote to the SRC in strong terms. "I can only regret my inability to reconcile my own view of my duty as Lord Rector with the suggestion of the Students' Representative Council that I should accept their nominee for the Assessorship." He quoted the Act of Parliament that gave the council its status in law. He rejected the Council's attempts to show that the Council was following precedent. He was also aware that the SRC was not unanimous in its choice.

Arguments went back and forward. The Council replied to the Rector in great detail. One of Dufferin's supporters wrote a letter to the *Student,* again in great detail. From the other side, it was said:

> We flatter ourselves that we know a great deal more of what is required of an Assessor than Lord Dufferin. The Assessor may be the Rector's, but we appoint the Rector, and any gentleman who proposes to abrogate the privileges of students, prostitutes the high traditions of his office . . . Lord Dufferin proposes to appoint a man we don't know, and who does not possess our confidence . . . we know as little about Mr Dundas as the Court knows about Lord Dufferin. [He had not attended any meetings.] For all practical purposes we might as well be represented by the Archangel Gabriel or the Lhama of Thibet.

In the end, though, the Rector won and Dundas became the Assessor.

The *Student* magazine said when all was over: "The [Students' Representative] Council has made a good fight . . . It might hope to combat the present oligarchy of intolerant snobbishness which controls these matters . . . Meanwhile it is instructive that Lord Dufferin has now registered his fifth consecutive absence from Court. This is out of five possible."

Dundas was also Assessor to the next Rector, Sir Robert Finlay. Walker became Rector's Assessor in 1907, when Haldane was in office, and took a strong part in the university Court's business. Rector after Rector continued his term in office until he died in 1922. On Walker's death it was said: "The happy relations that subsist in Edinburgh between the 'authorities' and the rest of the academic republic may be credited in no small degree to his wise and sympathetic intervention."

Criticism of Dufferin lessened towards the end of his term. Students may have felt sympathy for him. He was deaf and his health was failing when he gave his rectorial Address, which was "imperfectly heard throughout". It was also an uninspiring Address, although he did say: "Votes are no longer purchased to any great extent with hard cash, but there are only too many candidates ready to buy their seats with promises to give away the property of other people."

Dufferin, when in Edinburgh for his installation and Address, received an honorary degree and the freedom of the city. He wrote to his wife: "Madam, allow me to recall to your mind my various titles to your respect, for I am now a Doctor of Oxford, Cambridge, Trinity [College] Dublin, Edinburgh, Harvard, St Andrews, Laval, Lahore, Toronto . . . and Chancellor of the Royal University of Ireland."

Dufferin's father was an Irish peer and the family was of the Anglo-Irish Ascendancy. He had attended Eton and Oxford University, as had a number of rectors and rectorial candidates, before making a career in diplomacy and politics. He served as Governor-General in Canada and Viceroy of India. He was also ambassador to Russia, Turkey, Italy, and France.

Dufferin was promoted from Baron to Earl and from Earl to Marquess, and was given high decorations: he was a Knight of the Order of St Patrick, and Knight Grand Cross of the Order of St Michael and St George. His title in the British peerage was Lord Dufferin and Ava, 'Ava' chosen because it was an ancient capital of Burma and Dufferin was Viceroy of India when the British Empire annexed Burma. (A photograph of the sixth Marquess's wedding in 1964 was published in a national newspaper. The caption described the couple as "The Marquess of Dufferin and Ava, his bride.")

Dufferin has been described as "remarkable for tact and amiability – and had a florid and rather elaborately literary style of oratory, which also characterised his despatches and reports. For purposes of ceremony his courtliness, dignity, and charm of manner were invaluable, and both in private and in public life he was the 'great gentleman'." He wrote a delightful book about a voyage by yacht to Iceland, called *Letters from High Latitudes*.

Dufferin retired to live in Ireland, on the family's estate. In his later years he was hounded by troubles; his eldest son, a soldier, was killed in the Boer War at the siege of Ladysmith in 1900. Dufferin was chairman of the London and Globe Finance Corporation in 1897, a speculative business which crashed. He spoke in 1901 to a meeting of the shareholders in a "manly and touching address". Along with others, he and his family lost a great deal of money. The promoter of the business, Whitaker Wright, was tried for fraud in 1904; found guilty, he killed himself with potassium cyanide in the precincts of the court.

Dufferin died in office three months after delivering his address. His death gave rise to another dispute when the SRC wanted a day's holiday to mark the loss but the university authorities refused. It was said they feared the day would be spent in skating. The SRC also asked the university to allow the students to hold a service in the university's McEwan Hall, expecting the Senate to join in. But the Senate said that it was going to hold a service in St Giles and refused permission. The SRC persisted and won permission but had to pay £12 rent.

The secretaries of the SRC and the Union were invited to the service at St Giles, which took place on a Saturday. They duly attended in official costume only to find themselves absolutely ignored when the procession was marshalled.

The following day the students held their own service, in the McEwan Hall, to which all professors and lecturers were invited but only seven turned up. A commentator wrote in the *Student* that the conduct of the Senate and Court had been most unworthy. "They have not seen fit to suspend the minutest personal convenience, or throw themselves for a day out of the rut they labour in." In the matter of the holiday they had insulted the students and shown their own petty mindedness. Over the memorial service, "they have once more shown that spirit of aloofness that wrecks their influence with students".

Dufferin's opponent in the election, Herbert Henry Asquith, was a future Liberal Prime Minister. Asquith at the time of the rectorial election was a promising man in the party. When he became Home Secretary in 1890 he acted against sweat-shops and child labour and improved the inspection of factories He advocated one man, one vote and campaigned for free trade.

His candidature for the rectorship was at the start of the Boer War, when the Liberal Party was deeply divided: was the war justified or were the Boers being oppressed? Asquith sided with the imperialists.

Asquith was to be chancellor of the Exchequer from 1905 to 1908 and prime minister from 1908 to 1916. He formed a coalition Government in 1915 but in 1916 some Conservatives and Liberals, led by David Lloyd George, believing Asquith was feeble in prosecuting the war, conspired against him. Lloyd George became prime minister in his place. Asquith led the Liberal Party from 1923 to 1926. He was made Earl of Oxford and Asquith.

Asquith was originally known as Herbert by his family and friends, but his second wife, Emma (Margot) Tennant, wanted him to be known as Henry. His friends therefore used the name Henry after 1894. Historians, however, tend to use Herbert. Margot Tennant was a socialite and hostess who had brilliant gifts, an original mind, and a strong personality.

Some of the people who disliked Asquith called him "Squiff" because of his fondness for strong drink, Churchill writing to his wife in1911: "On Thursday night the P.M. was vy bad: & I squirmed with embarrassment. He could hardly speak: and many people noticed his condition . . . only the persistent freemasonry of the House of Commons prevents a scandal."

Asquith was one of those people who were rectorial candidates comparatively early in careers that were later to flourish. He was Rector of Glasgow University from 1905 to 1908 and Aberdeen University from 1908 to 1911.

ROWDYISM SHAMES THE UNIVERSITY

SIR ROBERT BANNATYNE FINLAY, *lawyer, Conservative politician, and judge; later Lord Finlay (1842–1929). Elected 1902.*

Sir Robert Finlay, when he was elected, was an MP and Attorney-General. He rose to be Lord Chancellor in 1916, serving until 1919. He specialized in international law and at the end of his career was a judge on the Permanent Court of International Justice in The Hague. He was one of those rectors who were elected in mid-career but who went on to greater things in public life.

Finlay's installation and Address were calamitous. The audience was unusually noisy; and the university and city were shocked. The behaviour was deplorable by the standards of the time, but rather similar behaviour was to happen at many future installations.

The Scotsman spoke of unmitigated rowdyism and reprehensible conduct.

> The students, especially the younger section of them, who occupied the first gallery, behaved in so disgraceful and noisy a fashion that scarcely a word of the Address . . . could be heard. The students evidently had not come to hear; they preferred to bawl themselves hoarse, to make noises on whistles and trumpets, and generally to conduct themselves like a lot of . . . 'senseless asses'.

Two students "in female fancy costume" walked up to the platform and presented the Rector with two black dolls. *The Scotsman* said: "The Rector good-naturedly accepted the gifts, but the Chancellor's face contracted, and the incident was evidently regarded by the platform company as one altogether unbecoming to the situation." The Chancellor of the university was no less a figure than the Prime Minister, Arthur Balfour.

Others on the platform were the Secretary for Scotland, MPs, members of the Senate and Court, dignitaries from the other Scottish universities, the presidents of the royal colleges of physicians and surgeons of Edinburgh, the Lord Advocate, and many more persons of rank.

The Scotsman continued: "All this time the Lord Rector took the interruptions in a good-natured manner, and continued to read his Address . . . During the last quarter of an hour the proceedings were a perfect pandemonium, in which the Lord Rector's voice was completely drowned." People knew when he had ended only when he sat down.

The *Student* magazine said, shamefacedly, that it was an overwhelming display of childish disorder. "We must, however, note, in extenuation of this conduct, that, as the *Glasgow Herald* points out, it has become customary for the Rector to address the British public rather than his student audience."

One could call the rowdies foolish, underbred, what you will, said the magazine, "but don't from their conduct draw any such foolish conclusion that it is desirable to abolish the office of Lord Rector."

Other incidents during Finlay's visit were not as bad. During a concert at the Lyceum Theatre attended by the Rector a cab was wrecked, but at an "at home" in the Union the behaviour was better.

According to *The Scotsman*, the police did not put the offenders in the cells because they knew that "incurable bad breeding is the root of the evil, and not *as yet* drunkenness and crime". The two men who presented the dolls at the installation were barred from the university for two years. One of the main offenders was, the *Student* said, an Englishman.

Students held the traditional torchlight procession in Finlay's honour, many of them wearing fancy dress of "conspicuous excellence". The procession went past the North British Hotel where the Rector was attending a university dinner, but he was never told the procession was there, so he missed it.

Finlay's address was about international law and how arbitration can prevent or end war. It was about 8500 words long (this chapter on Finlay's rectorship is about 1500 words). He spoke of ancient Greece and Rome, the Holy Roman Empire, the Papacy, the Declaration of Arbroath, the Congress of Vienna, and other topics. He cited Dante, Grotius, Henri IV, Bentham, John Stewart Mill, Bacon, Carlyle, Andrew Carnegie, and Stair among others.

Finlay attended Edinburgh Academy, graduated in medicine from Edinburgh University, became a lawyer in England, and entered Parliament as a Liberal. When the Liberals split in 1886 over home rule for Ireland he became a Liberal Unionist, that is, he opposed the Liberal proposals for a form of home rule. He later became a member of Conservative governments.

The other candidate, Sir Edward Grey, was a rising man in the Liberal party. His political career was, however, in the doldrums because, except for three years, the Liberals had been out of power since 1886. Good times were to come again when they won the election of 1905 by a landslide. Grey was to be Foreign Secretary for ten years.

Students who picked middle-range figures such as Finlay and Grey might have a future winner or they might have a future also-ran. These candidates turned out to be future winners. Voting was Finlay 916, Grey 621. Turnout was 62.1 per cent.

One of Finlay's most famous trials was *Campbell* v. *Campbell*, a sensational divorce case. The case was also important in the struggle for women's rights. His performance in *Campbell* v. *Campbell* helped to win him the nickname "Hard Head" and it was said: "He has ever (since the long and great Campbell case) been looked upon as the correct counsel to be retained for desperate cases."

Finlay appeared for Lord Colin Campbell, fifth son of the eighth Duke of Argyll, Scotland's most prominent peer. The Duke was a Liberal politician and was nicknamed "the Radical Duke".

Lord Colin married Gertrude Blood, a woman with many intellectual and artistic gifts and a fine sportswoman but not from a wealthy or aristocratic family. The couple became engaged three days after they met. Lord Colin, when they married, suffered from syphilis.

The divorce case lasted no fewer than eighteen days in 1886 and, through the newspapers, kept the nation spell-bound. The law then permitted newspapers to reproduce much fuller details about divorce cases than nowadays. People then, as now, loved to read in the papers about adultery, murder, and domestic violence – especially if the people in the news were rich or titled.

Lord Colin accused his wife of adultery with Lord Blandford (the future Duke of Marlborough), with a general, with the head of the London Fire Service, and with a surgeon. Lady Colin accused her husband of adultery with a pretty housemaid and of cruelty. A husband suing for divorce at this time was able to cite simply adultery; a wife was able to cite adultery but also had to cite cruelty, bigamy, or incest.

One of the leading barristers of the time, Sir Charles Russell, was acting for Lady Colin. Fifty witnesses appeared. The jury found that neither husband nor wife had committed adultery and so the couple remained married. Costs of the case, borne by Lord Colin, came to £20,000, the equivalent of £1 million in today's money.

Finlay's legal career took a more serious course after that sensational trial. He was Solicitor-General and Attorney-General under Conservative governments between 1895 and 1905, but lost his seat in 1905. He went back to practising the law and throve. He got another parliamentary seat in 1910 as member for St Andrews and Edinburgh Universities. Finlay became Lord Chancellor and was made a Baron in 1916, at the age of seventy-four. The Prime Minister, Lloyd George, regarded him as a stop-gap and insisted that on retirement he was not to get the usual pension of £5000 a year. Finlay lost office in 1919 and was promoted Viscount.

He began a new career, at the age of seventy-eight, as a member of the Permanent Court of Arbitration in The Hague and later as one of the first judges of the Permanent Court of International Justice, which was set up by the League of Nations.

Finlay "had the advantage of good stature, striking features, and fine, deep-set eyes . . . he was able to avoid working late at night . . . he never worked on Sundays." He played golf and was captain of the Royal and Ancient in 1903. He was a fine classical scholar and had good French and German and a reading knowledge of Italian and Spanish.

Finlay was a person of many abilities, but his opponent in the rectorial election, Sir Edward Grey, later Lord Grey of Fallodon, was just as exceptional. He went up to Oxford University but the university threw him out for incorrigible idleness (he became Chancellor of the same university in old age). Grey became a Liberal MP in 1885 at the age of twenty-three. While he was Foreign Secretary from 1906 to1916 he had to cope with crises around the world as well as the build-up to the First World War.

Grey was keen on birds and fly-fishing and wrote outstandingly good books both on his public career and on natural history. His later years were marred by blindness. Two brothers were killed in Africa, one by a lion and the other by a buffalo. Fire destroyed both his country house, Fallodon, near Alnwick, Northumberland, and the cottage in Hampshire on the River Itchen where he went fishing and bird-watching.

LIBERAL BREAKS THE CONSERVATIVES' TWENTY-TWO-YEAR HOLD

George Fiddes Watt, Richard Burdon Haldane, 1st Viscount Haldane of Cloan © The Scottish National Portrait Gallery PG 1401

RICHARD BURDON HALDANE, *Liberal politician, lawyer, and philosopher, later Lord Haldane and Lord Chancellor in a Labour government (1856–1928). Elected 1905.*

R. B. Haldane, a Liberal, broke a twenty-two-year run of Conservative rectors,* but with a very small majority, 877 votes to his Conservative opponent, Lord Dunedin's 847.

Haldane and Dunedin were both Edinburgh graduates, MPs, Scots, and prominent lawyers. Dunedin lived in the city and the students were mainly sympathetic to his party,

*Edinburgh returned eight Conservatives in that period; Glasgow returned five Conservatives, four Liberals, and one non-politician.

but at that time the Liberal Party's popularity in the country was soaring. At the general election that same year the number of Liberal MPs went up from 183 to 396 and the number of Conservative MPs went down from 402 to 141. The pattern in Scotland was similar: Liberals up from 34 to 58, Conservatives down from 36 to 10.

The political scene at the university was different in another way. The *Student* magazine said after the election: "In view of the disturbances which took place three years ago [when Sir Robert Finlay won], no attempt was made to obtain a hearing from distinguished politicians in favour of the candidates, and during the last week or two an outlet for party feeling has been found mainly in 'raids' by the one party on the headquarters of the other."

Some songs were produced, as usual. Here is one from Haldane's supporters:

> It needn't be superfine Lager or Bass
> If the quantity's there let the quality pass;
> But purchase the beer and let it flow free,
> Oh it's up with the chances of Haldane MP
> Free trade be the watchword, and bawl with a will,
> The man that bawls loudest shall drink to his fill!
> Free Trade, and Free Will, and Free Beer be the cry,
> The last the most welcome to throats that are dry . . .
> For the man with a sore head is sure to be he
> That's most likely to vote for our Haldane, M.P.

Interest in the election was high with a turnout of just over 65 per cent.

Haldane was always attentive to the Scottish universities. Few things gave him greater pleasure than the vote of thanks he received in 1888 from the Students' Representative Council at Edinburgh for "the able way in which he [as an MP] advocated their claims to direct representation on the University Court, and his careful guardianship of their interests" during the passing of the Universities (Scotland) Act of 1889. It was the Act that gave legal status to the Students' Representative Councils of the four Scottish universities. The Act carried forward the idea that students should have a say in the way universities were run.

Haldane was educated at Edinburgh Academy and his parents at first thought of sending him to Balliol College, Oxford. But his father and his mother were from strongly evangelistic families and felt a violent distrust of the Church of England – and thus of Oxford University also. Haldane went to Edinburgh University when he was sixteen. He also spent a few months at Goettingen University. He graduated from Edinburgh with first class honours in philosophy and won several prizes. He is still remembered there and the class library of the philosophy department is called the Haldane Library.

Haldane went to London and studied for the Bar. He was elected to Parliament in 1885, when he was twenty-nine, as Liberal member for East Lothian and kept the seat for twenty-six years. He became a Queen's Counsel in 1890, again an early age. Haldane was associated with the Fabian socialists Sidney and Beatrice Webb when they founded the London School of Economics in 1890.

Lord Curzon, a Tory grandee, said that Haldane was the greatest master of copious irrelevance the House of Lords had ever known. H. G. Wells said of him: "He carried his words, as it were, on a silver salver, so that they seemed good even when they were not so."

Haldane wrote in his autobiography: "I have avoided being again a candidate for the office of Lord Rector in other Universities, notwithstanding tempting offers. I had said all that I wanted to say in the Edinburgh University Address." He was also the first Rector whose installation was attended by women students.

Soon after his election as rector of Edinburgh University he became Minister for War, one of the greatest that the country has had. Haldane reorganized the Army and set up the Territorial Army, the Officer Training Corps in schools and universities, and the British Expeditionary Force: the BEF was ready for the German onslaught in August 1914. He became a peer in 1911 and was Lord Chancellor from 1912 to 1915 under a Liberal government.

In 1915, Haldane was caught up in a strange political event. Lloyd George persuaded George V, Lord Kitchener, Haldane, and some others to set an example to the nation and take the "King's pledge" – a promise not to drink alcohol until the war was over. Other leading figures in the political and military world did not follow the example. In fact the only person to stick with the pledge was the King himself, much to the regret of the monarch, his guests, and his hosts.

Haldane once said that Germany was his spiritual home and often visited the country for pleasure. He greatly admired the works of German metaphysicians. Before the war broke out he went there on an official mission to improve relations between the two Governments, but it was a failure. Germany's war party was too strong.

When war broke out anti-German hysteria was rife. Lord Northcliffe's newspapers, led by the *Daily Mail,* began a violent, sustained, and spiteful agitation against Haldane, saying he was sympathetic to Germany. He kept his silence and his dignity, but in 1915 the Conservatives insisted he had to leave office. He came back into public life in 1924 as Lord Chancellor in the Labour government. He had drifted away from the Liberals because – as he saw it – they lacked Labour's idealism. He considered Labour the only hope for maintaining social cohesion.

Haldane wrote treatises on philosophy, including: *The Pathway to Reality; The Reign of Relativity; The Philosophy of Humanism; Education and Empire;* and *The Conduct of Life.* He died a Viscount, KT, OM, FRS, and Chancellor of Bristol and St Andrews Universities.

Andrew Graham Murray, Lord Dunedin, was, when he stood for the rectorship, Lord President of the Court of Session, the most senior of the Scottish judges. He went to Harrow School, Cambridge University, and Edinburgh University. He had other advantages, including outstanding talents and influential family connections with the Scottish legal world. He became an advocate and swiftly throve. His career is a catalogue of offices held, but he was more than that.

The *Dictionary of National Biography* said of him:

> The cloistered life of the legal devotee had no attraction for him. He liked to be regarded as a man of the world. His prowess at rackets as a boy at Harrow, and later in life his proficiency at shooting and golf – he was captain of the Honourable Company of Edinburgh Golfers and also of the Royal and Ancient Golf Club at St Andrews – combined with his friendships in his social circles gave to one side of his character as much satisfaction as his pre-eminence in law gave to the other. He was fond of travelling and enjoyed exhibiting his knowledge of French and other languages. Cycling in the early days, photography, and dancing were among his varied hobbies.

Murray became a Conservative MP in 1891, when he was forty-two, although "he had neither inclination nor aptitude for this side of public life". He was immediately made Solicitor-General for Scotland and a QC but lost that job the next year when the Liberals ousted the Conservatives from government. Murray was back as Solicitor-General for Scotland from 1895 to 1896 and he was Lord Advocate in from 1896 to 1903. And in that year he was made Secretary for Scotland.

It was in the year of the rectorial election that he became Lord President of the Court of Session; in 1913 he went to the House of Lords as Lord of Appeal and in 1926 was made a Viscount.

INDEPENDENT CHALLENGES SYSTEM
AND RUNS INTO DIRTY TRICKS

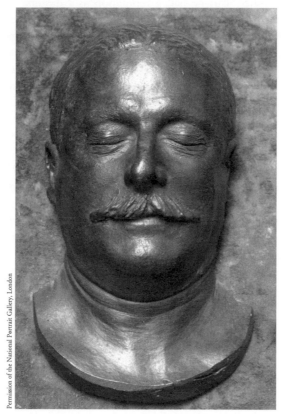

Permission of the National Portrait Gallery, London

GEORGE WYNDHAM, *Conservative politician and man of letters*
(1863–1913). Elected 1908.

The tradition of electing politicians was challenged and the challenge was strong. Nothing like that had happened in the previous twenty-five years and the tradition was not to end for another twenty-four years. The main contenders were the usual politicians from the two main parties. They were a Conservative MP and former minister, George Wyndham; and a Liberal MP and junior minister, Winston Churchill (Churchill was eventually to become Rector in 1929). The challenge came from an independent, Professor William Osler, eminent medical man.

The result was fairly close: Wyndham had 826 votes, Churchill 727, Osler 614. Osler had mass backing from medical students.

Wyndham had attended Eton and Sandhurst and joined the Coldstream Guards, but left the army to marry and went into politics. He became a fairly minor figure in the Conservative Party. Three years before the rectorial election he had held government office and had resigned.

Churchill was at this time Under-Secretary of State for the Colonies in a Liberal government, a minor office. But he had a reputation as a dashing soldier, a daring war correspondent, and author of absorbing books. He was thirty-three years old.

This election was held at a time when the political clubs had large amounts of money for campaigning. The money was raised from local sympathizers and local political organizations. Perhaps each club had as much as £1000, although full details of these funds have been lost. Osler had less money and fewer resources, so his campaign had to be financed by his brother.

The political importance that was attached to rectorial elections was shown again when no less a person than the Chief Whip of the Conservative opposition in the House of Commons, Sir Alexander Acland-Hood, attempted a dark deed – what would now be called a "dirty trick". He wrote to Osler suggesting that Osler should back down in favour the Conservative nominee. Osler informed his backers. The Osler side fired off a telegram to Acland-Hood asking at whose instigation was this attempt made. Acland-Hood replied, rather lamely: "Simply because I regard triple contest as unwise." Again, a telegram from Edinburgh: "At whose suggestion did you approach Professor Osler?" It was a reply-paid telegram but no reply came.

Members of the university Conservative Association said the matter had nothing to do with them – it was a private matter between the Conservative Chief Whip and one of the candidates. Moreover, the Conservative Association said that Osler's party, in revealing what had gone on, was convicted of "a most unscrupulous deed to catch votes, in publishing the matter with the insinuations".

One of Osler's supporters wrote to him when the voting was known: "We could not get motor cabs in Edinburgh to bring men up to the polling, so we had to fall back on the horse cab, a wretched substitute. On the other hand, a host of Conservatives and Liberals in the city put their private motors at the service of the political candidates." And on money: "We are going to try everything we can to cut down the tradesmen's accounts . . . We are proud to have wrought things more economically than our opponents . . . The stone wall of political prejudice we had to face was almost invulnerable." We are lucky enough to have a detailed account of some of the high jinks (see Appendices, page 214).

Wyndham, in addition to his political activities, had edited Shakespeare's poems and a translation of Plutarch's *Lives*. One of his own works was *Essays in Romantic Literature*. He also wrote for journals such as the *New Review* and *Fortnightly Review* and was an admirer of Rodin.

The House of Commons did not appreciate Wyndham's style of speaking. Lucy Tennant, a society beauty and a member of a political family, wrote: "His style was ornate, his phrases smelt of the lamp, and his delivery was marred by certain mannerisms not wholly free from suspicion of practice before the cheval glass." His loquacity sometimes wearied his friends.

But he was much loved and admired by people who knew him. Sarah Bernhardt thought him the handsomest man she had ever met. Lord Curzon, a Tory grandee, said of him: "Poet, statesman, warrior, Adonis." And, Curzon again: "This young and debonair figure, like a Greek hero in his range of attainments and perfections, possessing the physical beauty of a statue and endowed with the chivalry of a knight errant, the fancy of a poet, and the deep tenderness of a woman."

These were generous tributes from Curzon, for he and Wyndham were both suitors in 1887 for the hand of the widowed Lady Grosvenor, and Wyndham won.

Wyndham was an adherent of High Anglicanism, was enthusiastic for the Empire, and believed in government by aristocracy. He held two political posts: Under-Secretary for War and Chief Secretary for Ireland. When Wyndham was at the War Office the Boer War broke out. British forces suffered defeats and humiliation and he had the task of defending the Government's record. When he was Chief Secretary for Ireland he sponsored a law to improve the system of Irish land tenure.

Wyndham resigned from his Irish post in 1905, either from ill health (he was worn out by drink and by six years of overwork) or because both the Conservatives and some Irish nationalists suspected him of favouring an unpopular plan for a kind of Irish home rule. His career was finished. At the end of his life he was voicing anti-Semitic views.

Churchill, at this time, was a romantic figure from a glittering family. His books about his military adventures had brought him fame. Churchill was a twenty-year-old officer in the Fourth Hussars (Queen's Own) when he went to Cuba in 1895 to witness the guerrilla war between rebels and Spanish forces. He spent his twenty-first birthday under fire. His next excitement was in a brutal and dangerous British Army campaign against Pathans near the Afghan border; he was reporting for an Indian paper and for the *Daily Telegraph* but still in the army.

Next was the British campaign in Sudan, a campaign to re-conquer the country and to avenge the death of General Gordon thirteen years earlier. He was attached to another cavalry regiment and took part in the Battle of Omdurman, where he distinguished himself by his bravery. This time he was reporting for the *Morning Post*. Another book came out, and at this time he was also working on his only novel as well as cultivating political ambitions.

During the Boer War he was again a reporter and again showed reckless bravery. He was on an armoured train that broke down; the Boers captured him. Churchill escaped, to the consternation of the Boers because he was famous and came from a famous family. In a thrilling, solitary dash for freedom he reached the Portuguese territory of Mozambique, a journey of 280 miles. He did it by hiding on trains. Churchill had extraordinary luck and had great help from people on the way. He wrote his story for the *Morning Post* and instantly became an international hero at the age of twenty-five. From that adventure came another book. Within a few weeks his political ambitions came true: he was elected Conservative MP. His later switch to the Liberals was because the Conservatives had turned against free trade, and free trade was a fixed principle of huge importance for Churchill.

Churchill's backers in the rectorial election explained why he had switched from the Conservative side.

> His political instinct and that independent judgement, by means of which he
> seeks with the genius of infinite pains to find out for himself the causes of

things, and to bring all problems to the test of a healthy democratic opinion, would not allow him meekly to follow the Tory Party . . .

It was inevitable that he should adopt Liberalism. It was the creed in which he always believed, and by adopting it and by disillusioning himself, at the expense of many friendships, he has found his political salvation.

The social campaigner Beatrice Webb had said of Churchill a few years earlier:

Restless, almost intolerably so, without the capacity for sustained and unexcited labour, egotistical, bumptious, shallow-minded and reactionary, but with a certain personal magnetism, great pluck and some originality, not of intellect but of character . . . Bound to be unpopular, too unpleasant a flavour with his restless self-regarding personality and lack of moral or intellectual refinement . . . No notion of scientific research, philosophy, literature or art."

Webb was, however, to change her tune later, saying: "He is brilliantly able – more than a phrase-monger, I think – and definitely casting his lot with constructive state action." He was to become a Conservative again in the 1920s. Webb and Churchill were both to be among the candidates in the election for the rectorship in 1929 which Churchill won.

William, later Sir William, Osler was from a Cornish family but was born in Canada and educated in North America. He transformed medical education in the United States and Canada and became Professor of Medicine at Oxford University. He was a charismatic teacher, idolized by his students and former students. An outstanding clinician and eloquent speaker, he believed strongly in hands-on learning in the laboratory and at the bedside: "To learn medicine without books is to sail an uncharted sea, but to learn medicine without patients is not to go to sea at all."

Osler's backers said, in their propaganda, that Osler was

a man than whom there are few of greater renown and achievement in the medical profession, a man of letters whose essays have justly acquired for him a world-wide reputation, an academic man in the fullest and richest meaning of this term, who has left the mark of an original and thoughtful mind on every university with which he has been connected. Edinburgh University would honour itself in honouring such a man, and it is not only with hope but with absolute confidence that we submit his name to our fellow-students.

Liberals put out a magazine, called *Alma Mater*, which ran to six issues, each of four or eight glossy pages, and they ran smokers and had blocks of reserved seats at the Empire Palace Theatre; the Edinburgh University Women's Liberal Association had an event with tea, songs, speeches, recitations, and dancing. The Conservatives and Oslerites did the same and had their own glossy magazines.

Wyndham came in for hard words from the Osler camp,

Here, again, what qualifications does he possess? It is true he is an alumnus of Oxford [this was untrue], and is said to have a pretty acquaintance with Classics. But there is one consideration that puts him out of court immediately. He has been Lord Rector of Glasgow University, and by common consent the worst and most inefficient Lord Rector Glasgow ever had. Communications from the SRC [Students' Representative Council], the Union, and other undergraduate bodies were systematically and deliberately ignored; all efforts to get Mr Wyndham to do his duty by his constituents were fruitless.

No evidence was produced for these claims; and he behaved well as Rector at Edinburgh, as we shall see.

Of Winston Churchill, the Osler camp said in their magazine *Ace of Trumps*:

Mr Churchill is a very brilliant politician. We have no grudge against Mr Churchill, we shall watch his development with keen interest. But are the qualities and training which he possesses such as to fit him for the office of Lord Rector of this University? He is a Harrow and Sandhurst man, gained his reputation in the field of battle, the byeways of journalism, the political hustings. . . . What does he [Churchill] know of academic affairs? What experience can he bring to the study of these questions?

Osler's supporters pointed out that Churchill was only in his early thirties. In fact he was the youngest candidate until the elections of the 1960s.

Wyndham wrote to his mother after his election at Edinburgh:

All my congratulators on the Lord Rectorship are more pleased at Winston's defeat than at my victory.

I did not expect to win. But, as I have won, I shall try to say something to them in my Address. Meanwhile new links with real youth have a new joy. The unreal youth of middle age is light-hearted. . . But the real youth of twenty years is portentous in the solemnity of its ignorance. . .

On Monday the Leader of the – Edinburgh undergraduate – opposition and his right hand man sent in their [visiting] cards to me at the House [of Commons]. They were at pains to explain how much they had wished and how hard they had tried to beat me. But – as between gentlemen – that being over, they wished to express their respect for 'The Lord Rector'. So I made them dine without dressing [i.e., without getting into evening wear].

His address was on the *Springs of Romance in the Literature of Europe*. He wrote to a friend after the ceremony:

The youth meant well, but their occasional interruptions, paper darts, and snatches of song would have beat me, if I had not worked so hard at the Address that I knew it by heart. . .The only ones who really made a noise were the Officers' Training Corps. And the jolly, illogical fun of this kind of thing is that immediately after the Address I inspected them in the quadrangle. They stood up like rocks and dared not blink an eyelid . . . Then we had a public luncheon.

The luncheon was for about 250 people and was held in the Union.

Wyndham wrote to his father:

I dined with all the Professors at the Balmoral Hotel. . . .we turned out in the balcony to see the Student's Torch-light procession – a fine sight like the Carnival – with many cars and mounted men. . .I . . . had three of the leading Students to breakfast with me at 9 o'clock. The two leaders of the Conservative and Liberal party and the President of the Union. They were very agreeable and we had a quite a good talk.

Wyndham broke tradition by coming to the help of the students on a special occasion. The *Student* magazine later wrote:

> Mr Wyndham assured his constituents that, should they require his assistance, he would certainly come to Edinburgh, provided his parliamentary duties did not come in the way. Such an occasion arose in the summer of 1911. The governing body was deliberating on a subject of intimate interest to undergraduates, and one where the attendance of the undergraduates' representative was particularly desirable. In spite of the fact that a political crisis was imminent, Mr Wyndham fulfilled his promise by making two journeys to Edinburgh and brought to bear on the discussion a mind unclouded by petty jealousies or narrowness.

Professor Mair of Greek was brought before the university Court on various charges. The professor was popular among the students and they rallied to his help by asking the Rector to take part in the hearings. Wyndham chaired the meeting at which evidence was heard – a meeting that lasted four days – and he chaired the one-day meeting at which the verdicts were passed.

Mair was accused of being drunk at a Faculty meeting; of being in a drunken state after a graduation ceremony; and with being absent from too many meetings. Evidence came from some students that they had found him propped against a shop window: they called a cab for him but he refused to get into it.

There was speculation at the hearings that some of these unseemly moments were a result of opium abuse: various witnesses said they smelt opium on his breath. He said he was taking throat lozenges that may have contained opium.

Most of the charges were found "not proven," a Scottish verdict that does carry a hint that the accused person was at fault. The hearing did, however, conclude that he had been in an "unseemly condition" because of alcohol or drugs on one occasion. The Court concluded that his condition was caused by worry about his wife (she was in a long and complicated labour), by physical fatigue and emotional distress, by his angina pectoris and other medical conditions; and by lack of sleep.

The university Court decided not to dismiss Mair but passed a grave censure on him (and told him to moderate his drinking). He went on to teach for many more years.

The university Court passed a vote of thanks to Wyndham for presiding over the inquiry, "a fact which bore strong testimony to the interest which he had at all times taken in the Welfare of the University."

ARISTOCRAT, ADVENTURER, AND EX-VICEROY

LORD MINTO, *landowner and former Viceroy of India (1845–1914).*
Elected 1911.

Two grandees stood, as was usual at this time. Lord Minto, the Conservative and Scotsman, defeated Lord Crewe, the Liberal and Englishman. Minto was, however, not in the usual kind of public figure. He had been a wanderer and adventurer in his youth and saw fighting in several parts of the world.

The margin in the election was fairly narrow: 1182 votes for Minto and 960 for his opponent. The Liberal candidate may have done better than usual because the Liberal Party was in a long run of government. When this rectorial election was held, the Liberals were passing the Parliament Act, which deprived the House of Lords of power over "money bills" and limited the Lords' power to delay other legislation. That issue and Irish home rule were much debated in the rectorial campaign.

When Minto won, Arthur Balfour, the Conservative former Prime Minister, sent the Conservative students a message of congratulations. Balfour happened also to be the Chancellor of the university, and Liberal students sent him a telegram saying they strongly protested "against your having broken tradition which forbids any official of the university from interfering in the University political [i.e. rectorial] elections."

Minto's impact on university life was small. This was one of the very few Rectors who did not deliver an Address: he several times delayed the fixing of a date and died in office. That kind of delay by rectors who were grandees was a regular irritant to the students. It often took a great deal of prodding before the Rector would consent to turn up. He had got the honour but perhaps did not fancy performing his single duty.

One participant in the election campaign wrote:

> Both parties were supported by real hefty 'physical force brigades,' fairly evenly matched, and the party strongholds, politely called Committee Rooms, soon became storm centres. Much skill (and expense) was employed putting these forts into defensible condition, and many fierce attacks were launched against them, with varying fortune. Windows and doors were removed, and their places barricaded with stout timber, in some cases protected by iron sheeting . . .
>
> On the few occasions when a raid was successful, either by stratagem or battering rams, the destruction defies description. Everything breakable was broken; tables, chairs, windows, doors, gas brackets, grates, pianos, books, papers, and anything were quickly reduced to fragments, many of which were carried off as treasured souvenirs. I heard of a key of the Conservative piano being seen in a study bookcase in India. And great was the delight of the victors if they found the garrison's store of beer.

Minto had been Governor-General of Canada and had only recently ended a term as Viceroy of India. Crewe had been – among other things – Viceroy of Ireland, leader of the House of Lords, Secretary of State for the Colonies, and Secretary of State for India; and was to hold many more offices.

The *Dictionary of National Biography* said, in a passage published in 1927 and remarkable to a later age: "Lord Minto was one of those men who would probably never have risen to the high offices he held except in a country where some deference was still paid to the claims of birth and position; and his whole career shows how much his country would have lost, had such considerations of choice been disregarded." The second edition of the *Dictionary*, published in 2004, said, however: "Lord Minto was a perfect example of the aristocratic pro-consul who was so much the backbone of the British empire. He seemed to be the embodiment of the British belief in the superiority of character, sporting prowess, and integrity over bookish brilliance."

Gilbert John Elliot-Murray-Kynynmound, fourth earl of Minto, lived at a time when a peerage was one of the keys to holding high public office. He was educated at Eton and Trinity College, Cambridge (his father's old school and college). His family bought him a commission on the fashionable Scots Guards in 1867. His regimental duties were small.

He rode five times in the Grand National, rowed, and hunted. As a reporter he witnessed fighting during the Paris Commune in 1871, the civil war in Spain in 1874, and the war between Turkey and Russia which broke out in 1877. He was a volunteer in the second Afghan war.

The next twelve years were spent in looking after his estate in Roxburghshire and in taking part in local and county business. He lived at Minto Castle, near Hawick. Lord Minto possessed 12,595 acres in Scotland bringing in rents of £7748 a year; mines brought in another £2804, but the estate did not prosper.

The life of a country gentleman bored him. Again his career took a different turn: he and his family and friends pulled strings and he was appointed Governor-General of Canada, a job he held for six years. A dispute with the United States about the border with Alaska was settled. Of Minto it was said: "His geniality, directness, and natural shrewdness, his reputation as a soldier and a sportsman, his unaffected manners, all made him very popular, and, in consequence, thoroughly efficient as a moderating and unifying influence." But some people saw him as too much a stickler for protocol.

Minto's next prize was the most glittering in the British Empire: Viceroy of India. Again, he had to deal with political turbulence. Minto got on well with the Indian princes and with the Amir of Afghanistan and carried out some liberalizing reforms. It was however a time of political turmoil: nationalism was growing and Minto was the target of attempts at assassination. A left-wing commentator wrote that he was "suspending the Indian equivalent to the Habeas Corpus Act, and transporting without trial and without indictment peaceable Indian gentlemen, who it is alleged, *might* conceivably one day oppose the continuance of British dominion."

One of Minto's biographers wrote: "The [rectorial] election gave him peculiar pleasure, for if the Borders were the cradle, Edinburgh had been the nursery of his forebears."

Minto's opponent, Lord Crewe, went to Harrow and Trinity College, Cambridge, inherited a peerage at the age of twenty-seven, and was to take part in political life for sixty years. He became Lord Lieutenant of Ireland at a troubled time. The post was later described by one of his colleagues as "the most thankless office that any human being in any imaginable community could undertake". But Crewe "speedily divined the spirit and difficulties of Irish administration".

The Liberals came to power in 1905. Crewe for the next eleven years held important Cabinet posts. When he stood for the rectorship he was secretary of state for India and had recently been promoted Marquess. He lost political office in 1916 but went on serving his country in many ways to as late as 1944. His pastimes were breeding shorthorn cattle and racing.

STUDENTS UNITE IN
A GESTURE OF PATRIOTISM

Permission of the National Portrait Gallery, London

LORD KITCHENER, *Field Marshal (1850–1916).*
Elected unopposed, 1914.

The choice of Kitchener was a demonstration of patriotism. The First World War had started two months before and he was at this time the towering British military figure. In 1916 Kitchener was drowned when he was on a British warship that hit a German mine and sank. He was never installed as Rector and never delivered a rectorial Address. Dozens of his biographies have been written, but his life was so full of great events that none of the books finds space to mention his election to the office.

The political clubs at Edinburgh University had been preparing in 1914 for the election. Conservatives had chosen Sir Edward Carson, an Irish politician, barrister, and future Lord of Appeal, who violently opposed home rule for Ireland. (The saying went: "Sir Edward Carson had a cat; it sat upon the fender. And every time you gave it milk it cried out No Surrender.") Liberals had chosen Sir John Simon, the Attorney-General. (Of Simon, Lloyd George said: "He has sat on the fence so long the iron has entered into his soul.") Simon was a future Foreign Secretary, Home Secretary, Chancellor of the Exchequer, Lord Chancellor, and Viscount.

When war broke out, the political clubs agreed that the usual kind of election would not be right. Both prospective candidates agreed to withdraw, Kitchener's name was agreed upon, and a mass meeting was held. The president of the Conservatives said that Kitchener "was the one on whose skill, courage, and sanity the whole future of the Empire depended." The president of the Liberals concurred and Kitchener was adopted unanimously "amid scenes of great enthusiasm".

The other three Scottish universities elected similar figures during the war. Glasgow chose as Rector the President of France, Raymond Poincaré, as a mark of solidarity between the two countries with a common enemy. Aberdeen chose Winston Churchill, who had become First Lord of the Admiralty in 1911 and since then had been giving warnings that a war with Germany was likely; he pushed up the naval estimates from £39 million a year to more than £50 million. St Andrews chose Field Marshal Sir Douglas Haig, commander-in-chief of the British forces on the Western Front; Haig was to becomean Earl and Chancellor of St Andrews as well. All these men were returned to the rectorships unopposed.

Horatio Herbert Kitchener's story spans a remarkable period. When he was a high-ranking officer at the end of the nineteenth century the British Empire was at its very peak. By the time Kitchener died in 1916, Britain and the world had drastically changed.

Kitchener commanded the force that defeated the Dervishes at the Battle of Omdurman (1898). That was revenge for the death of General Gordon, who was besieged at Khartoum for ten months by the forces of the Mahdi, the Sudanese political and religious leader. Gordon was killed two days before a relief force arrived. Victory at Omdurman gained back the Sudan for Egypt and confirmed British power there. Kitchener, a national hero, was made a baron.

In the Boer War (1900–1902) he was at first chief of staff and later commander in chief of British forces. Kitchener fought the Boers ruthlessly, even brutally. The British burned farms and removed Boer women and children to concentration camps, where many of the captives died of disease or starvation, especially the children. These methods helped to weaken the Boers' resistance.

The Boer War was the longest, costliest, bloodiest, and most humiliating war that Britain fought between 1815 and 1914. It divided British public opinion, split the Liberal Party, and broke the old Imperialist spirit.

When the war ended Kitchener was promoted Viscount, awarded the Order of Merit, and given a Government grant of £50,000.

Kitchener was moved to India in 1902 as commander in chief, where he had a power struggle with the Viceroy, Lord Curzon, over control of the army, and was victorious. From India he went to Egypt in 1911 as pro-consul, ruling Egypt and the Sudan. When the First World War broke out he was appointed Field Marshal and Secretary for War and was made Earl.

Kitchener organized manpower and the armaments industry on a vast scale. More than 3 million men volunteered in the first two years. Recruitment posters showed him with splendid moustaches and pointing at the viewer, saying: "Your country needs YOU." He became a symbol of the national will to win the war. * Margot Asquith, wife of the Prime Minister Herbert Asquith, said: "Kitchener is a great poster."

The Allies' defeat in the Gallipoli campaign of 1915 damaged Kitchener's reputation. Allied losses of men were heavy. A historian has written: "Kitchener was handicapped by bureaucracy and his own dislike for teamwork and delegation. His cabinet associates did not share the public's worship of Kitchener and gradually relieved him of his responsibilities for industrial mobilisation and then strategy."

The Government decided in 1916 that Kitchener would go to St Petersburg to rally the Russian allies in fighting the war against Germany. He and his staff set sail on a cruiser, *HMS Hampshire,* from Scapa Flow, a great natural harbour in the Orkneys.

Hampshire was in the Pentland Firth, in a severe gale, with huge waves, and torrents of rain, when she struck a German mine, laid by a U-boat. On the shore a boy aged sixteen named Fraser saw what happened: "We saw a small cloud of black smoke at water-line under the bridge. Then came a sheet of flame and yellow smoke from under the forward gun turret and all round it. But we heard nothing – the storm was too loud."

On board the *Hampshire* all lights went out, water gushed in, and the captain gave the order to abandon ship. Boats were lowered but great waves smashed them against the side. A few rafts were launched and they floated. Ten or fifteen minutes after the explosion the *Hampshire* went down, a mile and a half from shore. More than 600 men were killed by the explosion, or were drowned, or died of exposure. Only twelve survived. Kitchener's body was never found and some patriots refused to believe he was dead.

*The design reappeared many times. The United States had one of the great icons of the twentieth century: Uncle Sam pointing at the viewer and saying: "I want YOU for the U.S. Army." A poster produced by the Bosheviks during the Russian civil war of 1918 to 1921 shows a dramatic military figure and the slogan in Russian: "You – are you a volunteer yet?" Britain during the Second World War had a poster with a sailor saying: "You can help to build me a ship," a soldier saying: "You can help to buy me a gun," and so on. The original poster did not show the cast in Kitchener's eye and shows his moustache as fuller and darker than in life.

ANOTHER MILITARY LEADER IS CHOSEN
– THIS TIME AN ADMIRAL

ADMIRAL SIR DAVID BEATTY, *later Lord Beatty (1871–1936).*
Elected 1917.

The choice of Beatty, like that of Kitchener, his predecessor, was patriotic: he was a national military hero. Both were unopposed.

Beatty had been a commander of the British fleet at the Battle of Jutland against the German fleet in 1916. Jutland, as a battle, was indecisive. But the German fleet never again ventured into the North Sea, which was a triumph for British arms.

The *Student* magazine wrote: "To our new Lord Rector, Hail! Never in all the annals of the University has she made a better choice. Never was Edinburgh more to be congratulated than she is today in securing the services of our splendid and universally popular Naval Commander-in-Chief, Sir David Beatty."

Nevertheless, he was to be criticized for going on holiday instead of delivering his rectorial Address on the day proposed. And he delivered his Address only two days before the end of his term of office. That meant that many people who voted for him never heard his Address because they had graduated or gone away or been killed in action.

Beatty was a knight when elected but by the time he gave his rectorial Address was an Earl. All through his adult life he was promoted very quickly, often to the dismay of his fellow officers. For example, he was made Rear-Admiral when he was thirty-seven years old, the youngest flag-officer for more than 100 years. Churchill and Sir John Fisher, naval commander-in-chief, hailed him as a new Nelson.

Beatty entered a naval training school at thirteen, seeing his first active service in the Sudan with Kitchener's campaigns: the Royal Navy had a small fleet of gunboats on the Nile. He served in China during the Boxer Rebellion and on his return to Britain worked closely with Churchill, who was First Lord of the Admiralty.

Beatty's rise was not impeded by a series of blunders by him in the early stages of the First World War, when he commanded a force of battle cruisers. At the Battle of the Heligoland Bight in August 1914, a raid by British naval forces, he intervened with his capital ships without telling his colleagues. Confusion followed – confusion that might have been lethal to his own side. At the Battle of the Dogger Bank in January 1915, appallingly bad signalling led his battle cruisers to concentrate their fire on one already doomed enemy ship while the others were able to get away.

Beatty's great day came at Jutland, in the North Sea, in June 1916. The British Grand Fleet, under Sir John Jellicoe, and the German High Seas Fleet clashed in confused order. No fewer than 250 ships took part.

Three of Beatty's battle cruisers, *HMS Indomitable, HMS Indefatigable,* and *HMS Queen Mary* blew up. Beatty's comment to his flag captain was: "There seems to be something wrong with our bloody ships today."

Visibility was bad, information was muddled and inaccurate, signalling between ships was yet again poor, and the war could possibly have been lost in an afternoon. Debate about the battle went on for a long time: did the British do as well as they should? Nevertheless, Jutland ended the threat from the German fleet

Beatty was one of the first people to press for convoys as the way to protect merchant shipping from U-boats in the Atlantic: at that time the German blockade threatened to defeat Britain. He took the surrender of the German fleet after the Armistice.

Beatty's rectorial Address was also a political speech. He spoke about the nation's glorious naval history but also gave a solemn warning about its naval destiny. He feared the Royal Navy would soon be cut to the bone unless he spoke out. That is why, at around this time, he made many public appeals to keep the Navy strong. He had plenty of chances to speak out, for example at ceremonies when he was awarded the freedom of cities and towns and of livery companies in London.

One of Beatty's biographers has written: "He was gifted with an unusual power of oratory. The short, clipped, forceful delivery was always lightened by touches of humour. His distinguished bearing, immaculate appearance, and flashing eye all contributed to a magnetic personality which held his audience in rapt attention from first to last."

His Address said, in part:

I cannot deliver an address which will rank with those of my predecessors. I have been brought up in a Service in which silence is a tradition, and I have read that Thomas Carlyle, the great Lord Rector of a former day, said: 'Silence withal is the eternal duty of man: he won't get to any real understanding of what is complex, and what is more than aught else, pertinent to his interests, without keeping silence, too'.

Nevertheless, Beatty spoke out, quoting Sir Walter Raleigh: "Whosoever commands the sea commands the trade; whosoever commands the trade commands the riches of the world and, consequently, the world itself." And again from Raleigh: "Peace is a blessing from God, and blessed are the peacemakers; therefore, doubtless, blessed are the means by which peace is gained and maintained: the which means of our defence and safety, being shipping and sea forces, are to be esteemed as His gifts."

He spoke of Empire:

To a great world-wide Empire like our own, which must get food from over-seas, and can get it by sea routes only, sea power is not a desirable luxury; it is the essential condition of existence. Without such power the British Empire would not possess liberty. Its every act, its very existence would depend upon the goodwill of other nations. . . .

The exploits of the great sea captains of the Elizabethan era form some of the greatest and brightest pages in the history of our islands: exploits which brought about the decline of Spain, and laid the foundations of what has been, and still remains, the greatest sea power of all time; the means whereby the British Empire came into being.

Sea power, he said, was essentially a power for peace:

Unaggressive in itself, it is a shield against aggression. If wisely employed, it will not excite the odium of others, nor the suspicious jealousy that is the lot of those who pin their faith in armies. Hence there is no greater fallacy than to speak of 'navalism' as the sea counterpart of 'militarism' or to refer to the British Navy as a baneful influence.

Wellington, speaking of the Peninsular War, said: 'It is our Maritime superiority gives me the power of maintaining my army while the enemy are unable to do so'.

Beatty also gave a swift survey of power, empire, and naval strength from the earliest times to the present day.

Beatty has been described as impetuous, self-willed, arrogant, and vain enough to design his own uniform (against naval regulations). He was buried in St Paul's Cathedral; his tomb is marked with the single word: Beatty.

I am indebted to Mr Dan van der Vat for much advice about Beatty.

ROWDY AUDIENCE DEFEATS GREAT ORATOR

Edinburgh University

DAVID LLOYD GEORGE *(1863–1945), Liberal statesman, later Lord Lloyd George. He was Prime Minister when elected in 1920.*

Lloyd George was Prime Minister of a coalition government from 1916 to 1922. His dynamism made him "the man who won the war". Winston Churchill said of him: "When the English history of the first quarter of the twentieth century is written, it will be seen that the greater part of our fortunes in peace and war were shaped by this one man."

Only very rarely were incumbent prime ministers elected as rectors of the Scottish universities. Prime ministers were reluctant to risk the humiliation of defeat at the hands of students. But Lloyd George had a thumping victory.

Lloyd George was, of all British prime ministers, perhaps the greatest orator. His skill as an orator was challenged when he delivered his rectorial Address. And he did indeed suffer humiliation on that occasion from his audience, some of whom surpassed themselves in noisiness, rowdiness, and rudeness.

Something very unusual happened when Lloyd George gave his Address. His text was distributed before he spoke. When he did speak, elements in the audience, with the text in front of them, yelled out the punctuation marks: FULL STOP and COMMA and so on. When he asked a rhetorical question, people in the audience shouted the answer.

The Times reported:

Even Mr Lloyd George has probably never experienced anything quite so trying to a speaker as the 'ragging' which he received . . . Once he appealed for a courteous hearing. It was explained to him that the boisterous conduct was in reality a species of hero worship, and it is a fact that the students of Edinburgh University let themselves go on these occasions without meaning any disrespect towards their Lord Rector. Yet there were moments when the proceedings caused some alarm . . . The shooting of peas and paper darts was comparatively harmless, but there were also fireworks and even a live hen came fluttering down from a gallery.

The Scotsman wrote that a gigantic leek appeared on a wire above the speaker.

This symbolic vegetable was agitated by students at either end of the wire in the course of the Lord Rector's speech, at appropriate points, and had the effect of a grotesque and new form of applause . . . Over the lower gallery was projected an effigy of a bearded man, the head equipped with prominent ears, and the expression being one of remarkable fatuity. This figure was arranged in front of the balcony, and some of the students manipulated arms and head during the delivery of the Address in such a way as to suggest that the figure was listening with interest and appreciation to the remarks being made.

The *Student* magazine was contrite and angry about the behaviour:

The treatment of the Lord Rector was a disgrace . . . The minority mistook hooliganism for humour. Interruptions can only be tolerated because they are clever. There is nothing clever about turning a rectorial address into a bear garden. There is nothing clever about shouting like prehistoric savages on the warpath . . . The unpleasant incident of the hen was simply torture, which displayed callous brutality.

A student wrote:

Even granted that Mr Lloyd George did about everything which lay in his power to increase instead of allaying the disturbance, this is no excuse. What if he did show that he was annoyed? Any other man in his position would most probably have done the same. What if he did make the fatal error of asking rather too many rhetorical questions? . . . The unpleasantness came from an undisciplined minority.

One passage in Lloyd George's Address reads as if he had known what was to happen in the hall:

I put courage, enduring courage, in the forefront of the qualifications for the real politician's life. What else do you need? You ought to have the gift of speech . . . The personality of the speaker also counts and makes an impression that is absent from the merely written word. In the conflict between the written and the spoken word the latter has hitherto been the most powerful.

His Address was delivered when he was no longer Prime Minister, for by then a Conservative government had replaced the coalition. Lloyd George was then at the beginning of a long sad twilight in his powers and status.

Lloyd George was first elected to Parliament in 1890 and was to hold the same seat for 55 years. He was inspired by radical politics, Welsh patriotism, and Nonconformist religion. One of his obsessions was the disestablishment of the Church in Wales, an obsession that became wearying to even his strongest supporters. One meeting has been recorded: "And now," said the chairman, "I haff to present to you the Member for Caernarvon boroughs. He hass come here to reply to what the Bishop of St Asaph said the other night about Welsh Disestablishment. In my opinion, ladies and gentlemen, the Bishop of St Asaph iss one of the biggest liars in Creeashion! But, thank God, yess, we haff in Mr Lloyd George a match for him tonight."

Lloyd George became a leader of the radical wing of the Liberal Party and opposed the Boer War. He was appointed Chancellor of the Exchequer in 1908 and squeezed the rich. This brought the House of Commons, which the Liberals dominated, into conflict with the House of Lords, which the Conservatives dominated. That conflict resulted in the Parliament Act of 1911, limiting the powers of the House of Lords. He went on to bring in health insurance and Old Age pensions, the first steps towards the welfare state.

During the early part of the First World War Lloyd George vigorously backed efforts to increase the output of munitions. But munition workers were thought to be drinking so much that production from their factories was lessened. Drink, it was said, was hampering the war effort in general. Lloyd George said: "We are fighting Germany, Austria, and the drink, and, as far as I can see, the greatest of these deadly foes is the drink." Laws were brought in to limit the hours when pubs could open, laws that were not to be fully liberalized for nearly a century. The legal strength of beer was brought down. Tax on drink was put up; a bottle of whisky cost five shillings in 1914 and by 1918 was £1, a four-fold increase. Buying a round – "treating" – was forbidden. Just before the war, about 36 million barrels of beer a year were being drunk; by the end of the war it was 13 million barrels a year.

Britain's conduct of the war had lost its vigour by 1916, under the leadership of Herbert Asquith, the Liberal Prime Minister. No end was in sight to the slaughter on the Western Front. A group of Conservative MPs combined with many Liberal MPs and forced Asquith to resign. Lloyd George took his place. Removing Asquith in 1916 was as necessary as removing Neville Chamberlain in 1940, but the Liberals split, some following Lloyd George and some Asquith, and the party was never to recover. As a result, the Conservatives became the "party of Government" for decades.

Lloyd George, with astonishing drive, versatility, and energy, drastically altered the way the war was being waged. He set up a War Cabinet of five people and a special secretariat to serve it. He and the War Cabinet mobilized men and resources. He recruited the help of businessmen. Conscription was brought in for men up to fifty. He clashed with the heads of the army over strategy, but dared not remove the Commander-in-Chief, Sir Douglas Haig, because Haig was a national hero.

German U-boats were sinking large numbers of merchant vessels bringing food and other supplies to British ports. Men and horses had left the farms and gone to the Front, so home-produced food was dwindling. Indeed some people were starving. Admiral Lord Jellicoe refused to have merchant shipping protected in convoys. When Lloyd George ousted Jellicoe and convoys were brought in, the loss of shipping was much reduced. The historian Lord Blake has written that Lloyd George's achievement as a wartime Prime Minister is rivalled, but not surpassed, by Churchill's.

Lloyd George was a womanizer, had several illegitimate children, and was nicknamed the "Welsh goat". His great extra-marital affair was with his secretary, Frances Stevenson, an affair that was never revealed in his lifetime. Exposure when he was alive would have ruined his political career. The economist John Maynard Keynes called him: "This goat-footed bard, this half-human visitor to our age from the hag-ridden magic and enchanted woods of Celtic antiquity," and asked, "Who shall paint the chameleon, who can tether a broomstick?"

Lloyd George's opponent at the rectorial election was Gilbert Murray, a distinguished Greek scholar, radical critic of society, and campaigner for liberal causes. Voting was: Lloyd George 1764, Murray 509. The winner's vote was about 3.5 times bigger than the loser's – the biggest victory in the period covered by this book.

Murray from the end of the First World War was devoted to preserving peace; he was chairman of the League of Nations Union from 1922 to 1938. He was a Liberal, a follower of Asquith rather than Lloyd George, and a campaigner for women's rights and similar causes.

Murray was born in Sydney, New South Wales, came to Britain at the age of eleven, and became Professor of Greek at Glasgow University when he was twenty-three. He was an outstanding teacher there for 10 years. He became Professor of Greek at Oxford University in 1908 and was to hold the post until 1936. Murray was awarded the Order of Merit in 1941. He was six times a candidate for parliament, but was in any case not much suited to parliamentary politics. He was twice a candidate for the rectorship of Glasgow University.

THE PRIME MINISTER WINS,
BUT POLITICIANS ARE ON THE WAY OUT

Permission of the National Portrait Gallery, London

STANLEY BALDWIN, *later Lord Baldwin, Conservative statesman (1867–1947). Elected 1923.*

Stanley Baldwin became Prime Minister shortly before this election. The days of the political nominations were, however, coming to an end. The tradition was being seen as harmful to the interests of the students: more worthwhile candidates, it was said, should be chosen. A student wrote at this time of "the contumely" in which politicians were held: "Why should an honourable position be deprived of its dignity by thrusting into it a political carpet-bagger?"

Another tradition was temporarily abandoned for Stanley Baldwin – the tradition of rowdiness during the installation. That was a reaction to the embarrassment brought on the university by extraordinary behaviour at the installation of Lloyd George, the predecessor of Baldwin.

Precautions were strict for Baldwin's installation. Large numbers of policemen were stationed outside the McEwan Hall, where the ceremony took place. Stewards lined the stairways and galleries. "There was a determination, in view of Mr Baldwin's position, to keep down the usual unordered and quite juvenile hooliganism. It resulted in the Rector's address being perfectly heard."

Baldwin's opponents were a Socialist, Bertrand Russell, and a Liberal, Lord Buckmaster (Stanley Owen Buckmaster), a lawyer, politician, and judge. This was a straight line-up of candidates linked with the three national political parties. It was the only time that Edinburgh University had a line-up of that precise kind. Voting: Baldwin 1236; Buckmaster 488; Russell 261.*

At the start of the election campaign the political clubs set up their usual committee rooms and made the usual raids on their opponents' rooms. But that kind of activity was costly and, because of the cost, was on the way out. So also was lavish spending on propaganda "newspapers".

The *Student* magazine reported: "The Liberals struck the first blow . . . by ransacking the Tory committee rooms in the Potterrow, destroying most of the furniture. A counter-offensive was delivered that afternoon, and the Liberal rooms in West Richmond Street reduced to a state of desolation."

Liberals carried off a piano and other items from the Conservatives; it figured in Liberal battle songs. Conservatives raided the Liberals headquarters and after an hour's struggle forced the Liberals to retreat. The Conservatives threw the piano out of a window, not realizing that it was their own.

Baldwin's family was very wealthy. He was educated at Harrow School, which was at that time more famous than it is today. Harrow "was much nearer to being on a level with Eton as a ruling-class school," wrote Roy Jenkins. Baldwin went on to Trinity College, Oxford and from there to work in the family's iron and steel business. He did not enter Parliament until he was forty and for many years spoke rarely in the House.

Nevertheless, he became President of the Board of Trade in 1921, Chancellor of the Exchequer in 1922, and Prime Minister in 1923. His competitor for the job of Prime Minister was a much more glamorous figure, Lord Curzon, who said when Baldwin won the prize: "Not even a public figure. A man of no experience. And of the utmost insignificance." No wonder Curzon was vexed, for Curzon had held high office for decades, including being Viceroy of India.

Baldwin was to be leader of the Conservative Party for fourteen years and was Prime Minister for about half that time – from 1923 to 1929 and from 1935 to 1937.

Baldwin's premierships were marked by the General Strike (1926) and the Abdication Crisis (1936). He helped to end the General Strike peacefully and got rid of Edward VIII without getting rid of the monarchy. He was, as a politician, a conciliator.

He was, however, accused of betraying the principles of the League of Nations by his policy towards the Italian war against Ethiopia and towards the Spanish civil war. He was opposed to Britain rearming during the 1930s and was regarded by many as one of the guiltiest of the "guilty men" who failed to recognize the Nazi threat. When the Second

---

*Baldwin's big majority is very different from his majority when he was chosen Rector at Glasgow University five years later. Baldwin then received 1044 votes and the Scottish Nationalist candidate, R. B. Cunninghame Graham, 978. Baldwin had appeared certain to win with a big majority, but unemployment was severe and Scottish nationalist feeling was strong. Scots had come to think more and more that the Government at Westminster was neglecting Scotland.

Women students at Glasgow, however, in general preferred Baldwin, perhaps because the Conservative government in the same year passed an Act giving votes in parliamentary elections to women over twenty-one. The age limit had been thirty. Baldwin, after this backing, was nicknamed Glasgow's first Lady Rector.

World War broke out he was vilified. Churchill said of him in 1947, the year Baldwin died: "It would have been better if he had never lived."

Baldwin was, as a public figure, a man who was known to love his pipe, his pigs, cricket, and farming, but a leader of the Labour Party said that these images were deliberately cultivated, like Disraeli's ringlet.

An anecdote is told of Baldwin at the height of his fame. He was supposedly in a railway compartment with one other man.

"Excuse me, sir," said the other man. "Is your name Baldwin?"

"Yes, it is."

"Not S. Baldwin?"

"Yes, my first name is Stanley."

"S. Baldwin, who was at Harrow in 1884?"

"Yes, I was there then."

"My dear fellow, what have you been doing since?"

Bertrand Russell, Baldwin's opponent, was a philosopher, mathematician, and controversialist, and was to win a Nobel prize for literature. He was a campaigner for nuclear disarmament. His greatest work is *Principia Mathematica*. This was written from 1910 to 1913 with Alfred North Whitehead; their contribution to logic has been described as the greatest since Aristotle's.

Russell during the First World War had been active in the No-Conscription Fellowship, which encouraged men to refuse war service. For this, Trinity College, Cambridge, took away from him in 1916 his fellowship there. His pacifist activities also brought him six months' imprisonment in 1918. Russell became the third Earl Russell in 1931. The first Earl, a Liberal and reformer, was twice Prime Minister.

Russell was backed at the rectorial election by a Socialist group but at that time socialists and Labour supporters at the university, while keen and enthusiastic, were very few. They took little part in the elections.

Lord Buckmaster, the third candidate, was the son of farm labourer who became a public speaker in favour of free trade and rose to be a professor of chemistry. Buckmaster went to Cambridge University and became a barrister and MP. Like his father, he was a strong free trader and social reformer. He tried to liberalize the laws on divorce, for example, and was partially successful.

Buckmaster was appointed Solicitor-General in 1913 and Lord Chancellor in 1915, but his patron, Herbert Asquith, was ousted as Prime Minister the following year and so Buckmaster held the office for only eighteen months. He spent almost all the rest of his career as a judge in the House of Lords and on the Judicial Committee of the Privy Council.

Lord Dunedin, another distinguished judge (see page 65), was once asked: "Whom do you regard as the greatest colleague you have had?" and answered: "You will be surprised when I tell you – Buckmaster. I have not and never have had any sympathy with Buckmaster's political ideas and performances and I think him to be a sentimentalist – unless he is sitting on his arse on the bench; there he is one of the most learned, one of the most acute, and the fairest judge I ever sat with."

POLITICAL FIGURE DEFEATS
TWO LEADING INTELLECTUALS

Unknown, Sir John Gilmour of Montrave, 1845–1920, Admiral © The Scottish National Portrait Gallery SP VII 40.1

SIR JOHN GILMOUR, *Conservative politician (1876–1940). Elected 1926.*

Sir John Gilmour was Secretary of State for Scotland when the election was held. His four immediate predecessors in the rectorship and his successor were far more eminent than he, but he did the job well. "Sir John Gilmour's name," said the *Student* magazine, "will be remembered as a most honourable one in the long line of distinguished holders of the office. Very few Lord Rectors have been so assiduous in their duties, and very few Lord Rectors have displayed such enthusiasm and interest in Edinburgh University student activities."

His opponents were remarkable in intellectual life. They were John Maynard Keynes, economist, put forward by the Liberal Club, and Richard Henry Tawney, economic historian, put forward by the Socialist group. Other intellectual or radical figures had recently been defeated at Edinburgh: for example, Gilbert Murray in 1920 and Bertrand Russell in 1923. Voting was: Gilmour 1027; Keynes 568; Tawney 268.

A tradition, long lost, was for supporters of one candidate to kidnap leading supporters of another candidate. We have a good account of one of these kidnappings, written by Albert Mackie many years later: "I was shanghaied away to sea."

He and two others were pounced on by a gang in George Square as they were leaving a dance in the Women's Union. "We were carried off by car to Roslin [in Midlothian], kept in a hotel there overnight, and motored to the Forth Bridge next morning and taken over the ferry to Inverkeithing, where we were thrown aboard a tramp steamer carrying stones to England." One of the victims pleaded a business engagement and was let off on parole. The two others stayed aboard until the ship arrived at Great Yarmouth in the midst of the herring fishing:

> We were tossed about on a wild North Sea for a day and a night and were pretty seedy by the time we hopped ashore at Yarmouth. I had enough money to wire home for my fare back to Edinburgh. A kindly railway guard at one stage in my journey insisted on me eating his lunch of bread and cheese. He had been reading about my kidnapping in his morning paper.

> Well, I was back in Edinburgh only a couple of days when I was seized again, this time in Bristo Place by a gang who chased me from the men's union in Park Place. [He was carried off to a cottage in the Pentland Hills.] My clothes were removed to keep me from escaping and so I had to spend the five days in bed . . . We [Mackie and two fellow-captives] were kept alive on sausages, the only things our captors could cook, and beer . . .

> There were several people victimised in that election. One was left naked in the middle of the Meadows [a green space near the centre of Edinburgh], another was left chained high up on the Old Quad gates . . . A certain amount of craziness is inevitable. The Lords of Misrule take over.

Gilmour was a worthy figure from an establishment background. He was the only Scottish minister in *Who's Who* to give his hobbies as hunting, shooting, fishing, and golf. He became Captain of the Royal and Ancient, a very great eminence. The Captain went through a ceremony at the start of his tenure. He "played himself in" – that is, drove a ball from the first tee. An ancient cannon was fired off. Caddies waited to get hold of the ball – the caddie who did so gave it back to the Captain in exchange for a sovereign (a gold £1 coin.) Gilmour did all that in plus fours and a tweed cap, the golfers' uniform of the day. Among the waiting caddies were some unemployed miners hoping for a sovereign. This was in the year after the General Strike and a disastrous stoppage by miners.

Gilmour was a baronet, owned a large estate, and was educated at Trinity College, Glenalmond, a public school near Perth (it is an Episcopal foundation on the English model), and at Edinburgh and Cambridge universities. He had a great interest in agriculture and was master of the Fife foxhounds. He was a member of the Orange Order and was the highest-ranking member of a British Government to be an Orangeman.

Gilmour was a High Commissioner to the General Assembly of the Church of Scotland and Brigadier of the Royal Company of Archers (the sovereign's bodyguard for Scotland.) He served in the Second Boer War and, during the First World War, at the Gallipoli landings and in Egypt and Palestine, being awarded the DSO and bar.

Gilmour was a Conservative MP for Scottish constituencies from 1910 until his death. He was appointed Secretary for Scotland in 1924, but the post was raised in 1926 to Secretary of State for Scotland. He was the first person to have that title since 1746. The post was difficult because it spanned many departments – health, education, transport, and others – but Gilmour was hard-working and successful. During this time he sought to transfer authority from London to Edinburgh, so that decisions could be reached faster and be more to the wishes of Scottish people. He was Minister of Agriculture (1931–32), Home Secretary (1932–35), and Minister for Shipping (a vital job) from 1939 until he died, in 1940.

Gilmour's speeches were described as feeble and his company as dull. An authority on Scottish government, George Pottinger, has written of Gilmour: "He was not flamboyant. He proceeded by way of disarming reasonableness . . . His officials respected him and admired the manner in which he defused potentially explosive situations . . . He was a skilled Parliamentarian."

John Maynard Keynes has been called the most influential economist of the twentieth century. His principles allowed governments to intervene, for the benefit of the people, in the running of the economy. Unemployment was not inevitable, he said. Keynes opposed the harsh terms imposed on Germany by the Allies at the end of the First World War and he opposed Winston Churchill's restoration of the gold standard in 1925. At the time of the rectorial election his most influential writings were still to come, in 1930 and 1936.

Politicians and economists were mostly unable to cope with the calamity of the Depression – traditional policies did not work. One of the traditional ideas was that the unemployed could always find work if they accepted lower wages. Keynes denied this and said it was wicked to blame the unemployed for their plight. He said that in a Depression the best policy was to increase private investment. If that did not happen the State ought to spend money to fill the gap.

Keynes said in 1936: "I believe that there is a social and psychological justification for significant inequalities of income and wealth, but not for such large disparities as exist today."

When he did poorly in examinations for the civil service, he said: "I evidently knew more about economics than my examiners."

R. H. Tawney, the third candidate, was an ardent socialist and one of the most influential reformers and social critics of his time. Among his reforms he advocated were the fixing of minimum wages and raising the school leaving age. His publications influenced the thinking of the Labour Party in the 1920s and 1930s. He is remembered for *The Acquisitive Society* (1926), *Religion and the Rise of Capitalism* (1926) and other writings. *Religion and the Rise of Capitalism* argued that Calvinist Protestantism was a source of strength for the northern European economies. He was a leading figure in the Workers' Educational Association at the time of the rectorial election. When he was offered a peerage, he asked: "What harm have I ever done to the Labour Party?"

THE LAST OF THE POLITICAL ABSENTEES

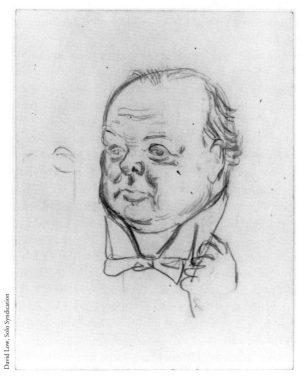

David Low, Solo Syndication

WINSTON CHURCHILL *(1874–1965). Elected 1929.*

Winston Churchill was to be the last of the old-style politicians to be chosen. Opinion was turning against electing distant figures who took hardly any interest in their constituents. The voters paid little attention to the campaigning; and turnout at the polls was the lowest to date. But if the character of the rectorship was changing, who was to receive the honour in the future? The honour was to be won by military men, academics, celebrities, scientists, and student activists, but not by any mainstream politician and not by any literary or artistic figure.

Commentators in the *Student* magazine sometimes looked with envy at St Andrews, which had many people of real eminence: for example, Rudyard Kipling, Guglielmo Marconi, Andrew Carnegie, Fridtjof Nansen, Sir James Barrie, and Jan Christiaan Smuts.

Also significant, at this election, was the abandoning of violence. The university Court put strong pressure on the Students' Representative Council for reform, and students fell into line. During the summer before the election, leaders of the political clubs held meet-ings and decided not to have "physical force gangs," as they were called. The gangs' activities were called "indiscriminate kidnappings and senseless horseplay".

The Edinburgh *Evening Dispatch* reported:

> There is to be no physical force employed in the University Rectorial Election this year. Why? Because there was too much damage done three years ago. Broken windows and other destruction to property cost, it is said, £600 to repair. Because five professors were thoroughly drenched in a hose attack by one party. Because the rectorial fight was developing into a very serious rivalry in which personalities were becoming too prominent.

One student argued that the gangs favoured the rich:

> A Physical Force Gang is an expensive luxury, and is no longer a necessary adjunct to any election. The Rectorial Campaign should be a battle of wits, not of bank balances. Its result should be determined by brains, not by beer. Hired mercenaries – which is what the P.F.G.s had become – merely distract the attention of the electorate from the real issues, and bring the good name of the university into disrepute . . . [members of the Physical Force Gangs were parasitic and] accruing to the wealthier parties.

For the first time in memory, "the real issue at a Rectorial Election has not been obscured by a haze of rotten eggs, decaying cabbages, putrefying fish-heads, stale person-alities, political catch-words . . . for the first time, at any rate since the [First World] War the student body have really known what they were voting about and whom they were voting for . . . it has been an Election, not a Dog-fight."

This outbreak of peace did not last, and fighting was revived the next time around.

Churchill was defeated for the rectorship in 1908, when he was a junior minister. When he stood this time around, he had been in the thick of politics for more than a quarter of a century: he had been involved in five wars, contested thirteen general elec-tions, fathered five children, written fourteen books, and been Chancellor of the Exchequer. He was playing polo until 1927, when he was fifty-three years old.

His political career had recently been erratic, and his backers stressed his achievements as a literary figure as well.

Early in his career Churchill was a Conservative MP but switched to the Liberals. In 1921 he lost his Liberal parliamentary seat at Dundee, in a crushing defeat. In 1923 and 1924 he stood again as a Liberal for other constituencies and lost. He drifted from the Liberals back towards the Conservatives, and he was such a great man that the Conserva-tives at last allowed him a safe seat, in 1924. He said at this time: "Anyone can rat, but it takes a certain amount of ingenuity to re-rat."

Churchill's absence from the Commons had lasted twenty-three months, but he was to achieve a total of sixty-three years and ten months there. Almost as soon as he returned to Parliament, the Conservative Prime Minister, Stanley Baldwin, made him Chancellor of the Exchequer.

Churchill played a big – and bellicose – part in the Government during the General Strike of 1926. But the Conservatives were out of office in 1929, the year of the rectorial election. Churchill was not to appear on the Government front bench for another ten and a half years

The Liberal candidate in the rectorial election was Gilbert Keith (G. K.) Chesterton, novelist, poet, journalist, literary critic, essayist, ardent Roman Catholic, and a co-founder of Distributism, a political movement. Distributism appealed to the young and to idealists but almost entirely died out in the late 1930s. Some of his most popular works of fiction were the Father Brown stories, about a priest who was also a detective. Other notable works were the novels *The Man Who Was Thursday* and *The Napoleon of Notting Hill*. Chesterton wrote biographies of St Francis of Assisi and Thomas Aquinas.

Chesterton is always linked with Hilaire Belloc, another Roman Catholic writer of that time. Both hated Protestantism, progressive opinions, Jews, materialism, and the modern state.

Beatrice Webb (née Potter), later Lady Passfield, was the first woman to contest any rectorial election. The Labour Club put her forward but the club had few members. She was a social reformer, social historian, and economist. Though from a conventional, wealthy bourgeois family, her interest in politics and social matters began when she was young and single and infatuated with a charismatic radical politician, Joseph Chamberlain, who was in the Cabinet at that time and a widower twice over.

Potter, however, found Chamberlain's attitude to women unacceptable: despotic, he thought a wife should hold the same opinion as her husband. She instead married Sidney Webb, social researcher. The Webbs were among the founders of the London School of Economics and Political Science, the Fabian Society, and the *New Statesman*, and were dedicated to improving the conditions of working-class people. They had a strong influence on radical thought and public institutions through books and reports.

Webb kept a diary for seventy years; in it she wrote of her award of an honorary degree from Edinburgh University in 1924, when she was one of seventeen honorary graduands. She mentions a grand dinner with speeches, the whole lasting four hours; walking through the city in cap and gown to the High Church of St Giles, a lunch given by the students' Union, at which she spoke; a reception given by the Principal, another evening function she refused to attend (she "struck work," she said), and a talk she gave to local Fabians. Her diary, however, does not mention her defeat in the rectorial election.

Voting was: Churchill 864, Chesterton 593, Webb 332.

Churchill had stood for the rectorship of Edinburgh in 1908, as Liberal candidate and as was usual in that era the Liberal candidate lost and the Conservative won. He had been chosen unopposed as Rector of Aberdeen in 1914 and nearly stood there again in 1924. He was to stand once again for a rectorship, at Glasgow in 1939. The Glasgow result was remarkably different from the Edinburgh one. The clear winner at Glasgow was a pacifist campaigner and the founder of the Peace Pledge Union, the Revd Dick Sheppard; the runner-up was a former professor of English at the university, W. Macneile Dixon; in third place was Churchill, with only 20 per cent of the vote; last came J. B. S. Haldane a Communist and biologist. This election was, however, held before Neville Chamberlain resigned as Prime Minister and Churchill took his place.

Churchill's rectorial Address at Edinburgh was a very fine one, especially when compared with some others. A lot of his points are of interest nowadays. He said that the House of Commons had steadily declined in public repute and was showing itself to be increasingly inadequate to deal with the real topics of public interest.

Democracy seems to mock and disdain the institutions to which its rights and liberties are due.

Not only is the assembly declining, but the foundation on which it stands has degenerated. When the vote was given to a few, all coveted it; when it was given to many, some coveted it; now that it is given to all, you can hardly get them to go to the poll. The sustained discussion of great public questions of vital concern to our national fame and security does not proceed as it used to do. A sort of universal mush and sloppiness has descended upon us, and issues are not brought to the clear-cut cleavages of former times. In fact we are drifting and in a sense dissolving as we drift. The time has come when we should endeavour to put more bone and structure into our political organism and to make it more truly responsive to the national need.

The vacuum formed by the shrinkage of our parliamentary institutions has been imperfectly filled by a Press, unquestionably superior in every standard of strength, quality, probity, and decency to the Press in any other country in the world. But these British newspapers for all their growing strength are increasingly abandoning the political theme. I have been told that nothing will kill a newspaper so quickly as too much politics. The readers of newspapers are not worrying much about politics. They take it for granted that they will be very unsatisfactory, but will not do any serious harm. The Press, except at election times, is no longer, as it used to be, the forum of continuous public discussion. It has not filled in any effective manner the gap caused by the shrinkage in the repute of the Parliamentary machinery . . .

Can any sincere and thoughtful man believe that the House of Commons, elected as it is, composed as it is, burdened as it is, biased as it is, changing its colour with every General Election and always living in trepidation of the next, is capable of affording our vast Empire a sure centre? Can this unstable body form the sole pivot upon which the interests and the hopes of so many peoples and States may rely? . . . The House of Lords, in its present unreformed and restricted condition, lacks the authority which is needed at the centre and at the summit.

Churchill then gave a glance at the Scottish Nationalist movement. He spoke of larger organs of local government than county and municipal institutions. "Supposing that other bodies – deeply rooted in history and tradition, harmoniously adapted to local requirements, larger and more powerful than county councils or any of the existing local institutions – were to come into being naturally throughout the United Kingdom, might that not be an immense advantage both for progress and for security?"

THE TRADITION OF POLITICAL RECTORS
IS ENDED

GENERAL SIR IAN HAMILTON, *soldier (1853–1947). Elected 1932.*

This election was non-political, breaking a long tradition. Candidates were far more varied than ever before: they included an artist, the Lord Provost of Edinburgh, and a former professor at the university who was on a "working Rector" ticket. The voters still went for a nationally-known name: a commander of British forces in the Middle East during the First World War.

General Sir Ian Hamilton was unique at that time, combining as he did the prestige of a famous person and the diligence of a "working" Rector.

Hamilton had been a most distinguished soldier, although his career had ended in disgrace. His downfall came during the Gallipoli campaign, when the Turks inflicted severe losses on the allied powers and repulsed them. Hamilton was the commander of the allied forces there and was removed.

The rectorial contest in 1932 was more lively than previous contests because the political basis had been given up and because five people stood – the usual number was two or three. And they were more interesting people than the usual Conservative and Liberal politicians. The turnout was 2426, an increase of about 39 per cent compared with the previous election.

The year before this election, the president of the university Labour Club wrote to his fellow political presidents: "On the whole, the University is profoundly uninterested in politics: a fact evinced – if (to be quite frank) our small and struggling political parties did not prove it even more conclusively – by the ridiculously few matriculated students who have voted at the past few Rectorials." He gave figures. In 1923 the vote was 1985 out of a possible 3736 (53 per cent); in 1926 it was 1833 out of 3635 (50.4 per cent); and in 1929 it was 1749 out of 3904 (44.8 per cent).

"It is to be doubted," the president continued, "if, in the welter of political animosities artificially created for the occasion, the man with the most qualifications as rector is ever nominated, let alone elected." The most suitable Rector would be one whose interests and profession were alike removed from the political sphere. "And, finally, politicians are busy folk, less able to devote the necessary time to rectorial duties than many another." The political Rector, he said, was an anachronism.

The *Student* magazine commented that abolition of politics from the contest would ensure that "no longer would the duties of the Rector be attended to at long intervals by party leaders in their spare time, in the 'limited leisure' they are able to snatch from bricklaying [a dig at Churchill's hobby] and pig breeding [a dig at Baldwin's]." A commentator wrote about the Rector who was coming to the end of his term: "Mr Churchill has devoted to his duties, for the period of three years, a proportion of his scanty, scarcely snatched leisure, amounting to thirteen hours ten minutes."

And: "We must cease wasting energy and money on a farce . . . and set about electing a local man, preferably a graduate of Edinburgh, who will attend to his duties, protect the rights, privileges, and general welfare of the student body, and put an end to the bad old tradition."

A student wrote after Baldwin's election in 1923:

The field of choice in reality is narrowed to politicians of one particular party, and the speeches delivered as Rectorial Addresses to the Scottish Universities should be sufficient warning that this system must come to an end. For dull platitudes, for sounding bombast, for the thought of a donkey and the morality of a wolf, their tinkling merely echoes their authors' thinness of intellect and sparsity of intelligence.

Why, then, should not the election be conducted on non-political lines? Why should our candidates not be chosen from those outstanding in the ranks of explorers, or scientists, or poets, or physicians, men who are not parasites preying on the human organism, but choice specimens of humanity. Able to give a lead to youth? Statesmen would still be eligible, but they would be chosen not because of their adherence to a political creed, but because of their service to the cause of man.

Representatives of the political clubs signed a declaration that they would not put forward candidates: the declaration was to be renewed before each election. Any twenty students were able to put forward a candidate.

When the result was announced, *The Scotsman* commented that an advantage claimed for a non-political contest was that the Rector would not be a distant Londoner coming to pay a single visit to Edinburgh, but might be expected to take a more active part in the business of the university.

> As it turns out, the only candidate with academic qualifications and a knowledge of conditions at Edinburgh University was Professor Schlapp who proved to be runner-up . . .
>
> In adopting the non-political system the students seem to have fallen between two stools. They have sacrificed certain advantages of the old system without securing all the theoretical advantages of the new.

Nevertheless, Hamilton turned out to be one of the hardest-working Rectors and was genuinely interested in student life and in the university. For example, a serious fire damaged the offices of the *Student* magazine. Hamilton sent a telegram: "If you have lost any money please let me help you make it good." – and that happened more than ten years after his term ended. His archives in King's College, London, have many documents about his activities as Rector and show his concern for the welfare of his constituents.

At the end of Hamilton's three years, a student wrote: "After many years we at last have the good fortune to have a Rector who realises that both duties and privileges attach to the office, and who is prepared to perform the duties while enjoying the privileges." Another wrote:

> He has honoured with his presence almost every important function which has taken place in the University in the last three years. His interest in the social side of University life has been far above that of any previous Lord Rector for many years back. His genial and attractive personality has made him known and liked by quite an exceptional number of Edinburgh undergraduates, and he is one of the few Lord Rectors who were recognised immediately in whichever part of the University they might choose to appear.

It is fairly certain that Winston Churchill, the outgoing Rector, "fixed" the nomination of Hamilton. The men were old comrades in arms and had known each other for thirty-five years. Both served in the army in India during fighting on the North-West Frontier. Hamilton was a senior officer during the Boer War, and Churchill reported the war for newspapers. Churchill was a member of the Cabinet during the Gallipoli campaign and supported it strongly.

Hamilton in his turn, when his term as Rector came to an end, was to encourage another old soldier and friend, Lord Allenby, to stand for the rectorship as Hamilton's successor – and Allenby won.

Hamilton's main opponent was Dr Otto Schlapp, the emeritus professor of German. One of his supporters said: "Today he possesses the freshness and vigour of mind that is associated with youth and with youth only. He is absolutely free from the crystallised prejudices that so often form a barrier between the generations. He is young now and always will be." To the rectorship he would bring "his wide culture, his profound knowledge of the University, his immense sympathy, his plastic and inquiring intellect."

Dr Schlapp was educated at German universities and Edinburgh University, was for a while a schoolteacher in Edinburgh, and became a lecturer and professor at the university. He wrote school textbooks and *Kante Lehre von Genie und die Entstehung der "Kritik der Urteilskraft"* ('Kant's teaching on genius and the genesis of "Critique of Judgement"'). He was an artist in clay, oils, watercolour, and wood.

James Pittendrigh MacGillivray was a sculptor, painter, architect, orator, poet, and philosopher. He was born in Aberdeenshire, the son of a sculptor, and trained in Edinburgh and Glasgow. MacGillivray was linked with the group of artists known as the Glasgow Boys and was a co-founder of the *Scottish Art Review*. He also produced a report for the Scottish Education Department which led to the setting up of the Edinburgh College of Art. He became King's Sculptor for Scotland in 1923. And he was an authority on clans and tartans.

MacGillivray had several important public commissions, many with a Scottish flavour: statues of Robert Burns in Irvine, Ayrshire; the third Marquess of Bute in Cardiff; John Knox in the High Kirk of St Giles; and Lord Byron in Aberdeen. He also did a great deal of sculpture for the great memorial to Gladstone in Coates Crescent, Edinburgh: the main figure, 9 feet 6 inches high, and eight life-size figures.

An example of MacGillivray's poetry is an elegy for his dog Flinc – could we call this *doggerel*?

> My ain wee doggie – dainty Flinc:
> I miss ye mair than folk would think,
> For aye ye were a heartsome link
> Wi' happy hours
> In woodlands spent, whar rabbits jink
> Mang bushy bowers. . .
> Your faithfu' een were hazel brown –
> Your coat o' black hung wavy down –
> A splash o' white, like eider-down,
> Your breast did mark;
> But o' your gifts I'd ca' the crown,
> Your welcome bark!

His backers said he was the greatest sculptor Scotland had produced. This opinion, they said, was endorsed by his fellow-artists and by art critics in Britain and on the Continent;

> While other Scottish writers and artists anglicised themselves and caricatured Scotsmen for the benefit of foreigners in the Lauderesque* style, Pittendrigh MacGillivray patiently strove to create a definitely Scottish art, drawing its inspiration from Continental models.
>
> His own creations and the literary, artistic, and cultural revival in Scotland illustrate his success. It is due to Pittendrigh MacGillivray's efforts in sculpture and poetry that Scotsmen are now gathering up their national traditions and creating a national literature and art.

---

* Sir Harry Lauder, a singer of comic or sentimental Scots songs. He had great success in Scotland, England, and especially in the United States and Commonwealth.

MacGillivray was outspoken: he sharply criticised the state of Scottish art colleges and some of the Royal Scottish Academy's rules. It has been said that his outspokenness cost him a knighthood and the rectorship of Edinburgh.

Sir Iain Colquhoun of Colquhoun and Luss, another candidate, was seventh baronet and thirty-first chief of Clan Colquhoun, KT, DSO and bar, and laird and baron of Luss. Of the Colquhouns it has been said: "Since the very earliest records that have come down to us, the deer-haunted hills and wooded glens and loch-side lands of Luss have belonged to the ancestors of the present Chief." That description is by Sir Iain Moncreiffe of That Ilk, a great authority on genealogy and heraldry, who was to become Albany Herald at the court of Lord Lyon King of Arms, the supreme authority in heraldry in Scotland.

Moncreiffe also wrote of Sir Iain Colquhoun's achievements:

> A true Highland chief, he was lightweight boxing champion of the British Army, killed a Prussian officer with his revolver and five Bavarians with an improvised club [both weapons were, Moncreiffe wrote, preserved at Rossdhu, the family's Georgian mansion on the banks of Loch Lomond], kept a fairly tame lion in the trenches, and won the DSO and bar, though wounded more than once in the First World War: on the first occasion by a German bullet striking the hilt of his drawn sword at the First Battle of Ypres. [This story about war service is in several versions.]

He had also been a member of an Arctic expedition and had fought in the Egyptian Camel Corps.

Colquhoun's other achievements were worthy but not quite as colourful. His backers listed them: "Lord High Commissioner of the General Assembly of the Church of Scotland, Vice-Chairman of the Scottish Committee of the National Playing Fields Association, Chairman of the Society for the Preservation of Rural Scotland, Lord Lieutenant and JP for Dumbartonshire, and Chief Scout's Commissioner for the West of Scotland." One can add that he was Grand Master of the Scottish freemasons and was to be elected Rector of Glasgow University in 1934 as a non-political candidate.

The last contender was Sir Thomas Barnaby Whitson, Lord Provost of Edinburgh, an accountant, and worker for many causes. He was educated at George Watson's College, Edinburgh, Loretto School, and Edinburgh University.

In the election Hamilton beat Schlapp by 1448 to 978, with the others trailing far behind. Hamilton's cause had received messages of support from Lord Baden-Powell, Earl Jellicoe, the Chancellor of the Exchequer Neville Chamberlain, and Winston Churchill's wife Clementine.

Physical Force Gangs (PFGs) had been abandoned during the previous contest but violent behaviour was revived this time. Very early on polling day:

> ... an encounter between a party of Sir Iain Colquhoun's supporters and the students supporting Sir Ian Hamilton took place early in the morning, when an attempt was made to imprison a number of Hamiltonians in the dome of the University.
>
> As a result of the ensuing fight, it is understood, several students were injured. One who was taken to the Infirmary had received minor concussion, and another required seven stitches put in his arm. The majority of the students received minor cuts and bruises, and many blackened eyes were in

evidence. Evidence of the intensity of the scrap was to be found at the University yesterday forenoon. Windows were broken, the stairway was strewn with litter, [and] a door wrenched off its hinges . . .

Later in the day another encounter took place at the Old Quadrangle ... A party of about fifty Hamiltonians loaded with ammunition in the form of soot, ochre, and decayed fruit, issued a challenge to all the other parties. Though a large number of students were present at the time, no opposition was forthcoming. The belligerent Hamiltonians, resentful of inactivity, thereupon attacked a party of students supporting Dr MacGillivray, who were later joined by a number of Colquhounites. Against superior numbers, however, their efforts were of little avail.

Intruders broke into the Fine Art Department and vandalized plaster casts and models, using the plaster to replenish the supplies of ammunition. *The Scotsman* commented: "The late Professor Baldwin Brown in the course of his long tenure of the Fine Art Chair had made a collection of plaster casts and other teaching material. His old students will remember the care which he bestowed on this collection, and will regret the statues and other plaster casts have been smashed up . . ."

The Scotsman said that such vandalism was unlikely under the old system of political elections.

If the political contests of the past were better conducted, that may be due to the fact that the heads of the political societies in the University could be held to some extent responsible for the behaviour of a candidate's supporters. At all events they had some sense of responsibility. On the present occasion a sense of responsibility has been entirely lacking.

Hamilton joined the army in 1875 and was mainly with the 92nd Highland Regiment of Foot, the Gordon Highlanders; his father for some time commanded the regiment. He served in Ireland, India, Afghanistan, South Africa, the Sudan, Malta, and elsewhere. In India he achieved an ambition: he "bagged" the biggest-ever head of a markhor, a member of the goat family with unusual spiralling horns.

The Gallipoli campaign was part of Europe-wide strategy. The allied powers wanted to strengthen Russia against Germany by sending Russia munitions. The allied powers also needed to import Russian grain. Men and horses in the allied countries had left the farms for the front and output of food had collapsed. The route for this planned exchange was to be through the Dardanelles, the straits between the Black Sea and the Mediterranean.

The straits, however, were defended by Germany and Turkey, who, at the start of the war, had made an alliance, and they prevented ships from passing through. The Royal Navy was ordered to force the straits, defended by the Turks who were helped by German military and naval commanders and by German artillery. The defenders were down to their last eight armour-piercing shells when the allied fleet, on the brink of victory, withdrew.

The task was turned over to a British-led army, which Hamilton commanded. The landings, on the area called Gallipoli, were chaotic. The terrain of the beaches was appalling for the attackers – steep rocks and ridges, deep ravines. Turkish troops on the high ground poured fire on the allied troops.

Britain lost more than 21,000 men in the action, France 10,000, Australia 8700, and New Zealand 2700. Hamilton was sacked. The consequences of this defeat were extraordinary. The Germans led the Turkish fleet into the Black Sea and it shelled the Russian coast. Russia was forced to declare war against Turkey.

Russia received almost no help from its allies; its plight precipitated the Communist revolution. The Turkish empire, already moribund, collapsed, and that destabilized the Balkans and the Middle East.

The allies were deprived of Russian grain and had to import supplies from North America, which meant that allied merchant vessels in the Atlantic were exposed to attack by U-boats.

It has been said that Hamilton had the enthusiasm, self-confidence, and personal courage demanded of the military commander-in-chief: "But he lacked the iron will and dominating personality of a truly great commander." He never again held any significant post in the army. Nevertheless, his obituary in *The Times* said: "To many laymen it appeared that the criticism to which he was sometimes subjected by the Army sprang from the Army's short-sightedness and narrow-mindedness . . . If he had not been starved of resources he would have achieved an outstanding victory."

I am indebted to Dan van der Vat for advice about the Dardanelles and Gallipoli.

ONCE AGAIN, VICTORY GOES TO AN OUTSTANDING MILITARY FIGURE

Permission of the National Portrait Gallery, London

FIELD MARSHAL LORD ALLENBY *(1861–1936). Elected 1935.*

Allenby was an outstanding commander in the Middle East during the First World War. His public record outshone those of the other three candidates in the election. Nevertheless, the runner-up, an eminent medical man and local figure, did well, which implied – again – that the "ornamental" Rector was falling out of favour.* Moreover, Allenby's military achievements, although great, were fading in the public memory and were not as important to young people as they were to older people. Far more important was the universal dread at this time of another war in Europe.

A group of students approached General Sir Ian Hamilton when Hamilton's term as Rector was coming to an end. They asked him for advice about who should follow him. He suggested Allenby, his old comrade-in-arms, and he got Allenby to agree.

*Glasgow University never had a military man, but in 1937, two years after Allenby's election, chose Canon Dick Sheppard, a pacifist campaigner. Sheppard founded the Peace Pledge Union in 1935.

Allenby commanded the Egyptian Expeditionary Force in 1917 and his forces won decisive victories over the Turks, Germany's allies. His part in the destruction of the Ottoman empire made him a hero to the Zionist cause. He commanded the last of the great cavalry campaigns – his successes were partly due to his skilful use of cavalry. Allenby had served in Bechuanaland, Zululand, and South Africa. He also served in France during the First World War but his biggest successes were in the Middle East:

Allenby's supporters among the students said his qualities as a soldier and statesman made him pre-eminently suitable for the rectorship:

> That strange admixture of human kindness, that love of children and animals, show us the human side of a character at the same time able and tenacious in purpose, merciful yet absolutely just. It is written of him that 'in days to come, when the history of our times is written with that calm deliberation . . . which only the passage of years can bring into due perspective, the name of Allenby will be considered among the greatest who have devoted their lives to the British Empire.

Allenby's nickname in his early years as an officer was "Apple Pie", because of his exaggerated concern for neatness and order. He was obsessed by minor breaches of regulations, particularly regulations about the wearing of chin-straps. He had a tantrum about chin-straps even during the retreat from Mons in August 1914. He became more and more quick-tempered and bullying as he rose in rank and took on bigger responsibilities. It was after one of his outbursts over a minor matter that he was given his later nickname, "Bull".

Allenby had three opponents.

Douglas Douglas-Hamilton, the Marquess of Douglas and Clydesdale, was heir to the Duke of Hamilton. He was educated at Eton, represented Oxford University at boxing and was nicknamed the "fighting marquess". He was chief pilot of an expedition that flew an aircraft over Mount Everest in 1933. The Marquess came from two great Scottish families and was "the scion of an illustrious house". The head of his family was the Premier Peer of Scotland and Hereditary Keeper of the Palace of Holyrood House.

Lord Douglas was an MP and was ADC to the Duke of Kent. Douglas-Hamilton's supporters in the election said: "Everyone who has known him has remarked not only his quiet modesty but also the streak of determination which lies just behind it . . . He would make not only a decorative but an active Lord Rector."

He was to hold senior positions in the RAF during the Second World War and was mentioned in despatches. He succeeded to the dukedom in 1940. The Duke was at the centre of one of the most bizarre events of the war. Rudolph Hess, Hitler's deputy, baled out of an aircraft in 1941 over Eaglesham, near Glasgow, close to the Hamilton estate, and surrendered to the Home Guard and the police. Hess said he was on a solo mission to end the war. He said he wanted to meet the Duke, whom he erroneously believed to be a leader of a "peace party". Churchill was unimpressed. Hess was taken prisoner and remained captive until he died in 1987.

Douglas Chalmers Watson, an eminent Edinburgh doctor, went to school at George Watson's College in Edinburgh and to the university. He was a former chief physician at Edinburgh Royal Infirmary and was an expert on nutrition. This background meant that he had the automatic backing of most medical students.

His supporters said: "His advanced outlook and his courage in investigation and treatment of disease have largely revolutionised modern medicine . . . During the [First World] War Dr Watson's outstanding knowledge of food was recognised by the Government, and he founded the Patriotic Food League during the time when Britain's existence was in such deadly peril from the submarine blockade." (U-boats had interrupted imports of food and farms in Britain were producing less.)

Christopher Murray Grieve is better known as Hugh MacDiarmid, who has been called the greatest figure in twentieth century Scottish poetry. He was the leader of the Scottish literary renaissance. His greatest work is probably *A Drunk Man Looks at the Thistle*, "full of political, metaphysical, and nationalistic reflections on the Scottish predicament . . . He dedicated his life to the regeneration of the Scottish literary language . . . He succeeded brilliantly by employing a vocabulary drawn from all regions and periods, intellectualising a previously parochial tradition." He was a pioneer in the Scottish National Party and a Communist.

MacDiarmid's supporters in the rectorial election said of him:

He uses peasant, and, in *Hymns to Lenin,* gutter Scots with sureness and greatness. His supreme medium is synthetic Scots – a revitalisation of the tongue's potentialities for treating large ideas by the resurrection of apt words peasants devise. Seeking to express *all* Scotland's qualities he has recourse now in his fine versions of Gaelic masterpieces to a real Scots English, distinct in manner and word range . . . Heir of our radicalism, he is always a left-wing man, possessed with the idea of Freedom. In thought as in his attitude to language it is for the masses of us that he is working. Our inner longings, our 'benmaist resolves,' so long inarticulate and half-conscious, find in Grieve the voice they have lacked since Burns and the great Highland poets.

A leading critic of the twentieth century, Ian Hamilton, has, however, written:

Scotland may well be grateful to MacDiarmid for his early efforts to achieve a Scots Renaissance, but to the unkilted reader there still seems something quaint, and rather bogus, in the dredged-up archaisms of literary Lallans . . . If poetry cannot be wrung from the language Scotsmen speak, no amount of nostalgic pedantry is likely to bring about the cultural reflowering for which MacDiarmid said he yearned.

This was the first election at which the single transferable vote was used. When the votes were counted, Grieve was the first to be eliminated: he had 88 votes. The next to go was Douglas Douglas-Hamilton, with 300. At the last run-off, Allenby had 1047 votes and Chalmers Watson 916, a majority of 131.

Leon Trotsky, in exile in Paris, was asked to stand but declined, saying:

The freedom from all nationalist considerations which this [invitation] demonstrates does the greatest honour to the spirits of the students of Edinburgh . . . I do not believe that I can properly accept your invitation. You write that the rectorial elections are held on a *non-political* basis and indeed your letter is signed by representatives of every tendency of political thought. But I myself occupy a political position which is only too clearly defined. All my activity has been and is dedicated to the revolutionary liberation of the proletariat, bowed beneath the yoke of capital. That alone entitles me to occupy any position of responsibility. I should therefore regard it as a felony towards the working class and as an act of disloyalty to yourselves if I were to appear in any public arena otherwise than under the flag of Bolshevism . . ."

Allenby appointed as his Assessor to the university Court a well-known person: Donald Pollock (see pages 112-17). The Rector did not consult the Students' Representative Council about his decision and the *Student* magazine spoke of "the flagrantly unconstitutional method adopted . . . in the appointment of Dr Pollock, whose nomination certain prominently placed persons were suspiciously anxious to procure." (Pollock was wealthy. One of the "prominently placed persons was the Principal, Sir Thomas Martin, who was anxious to please a potential benefactor.) The writer in the *Student* implied that Allenby was obliged by law to consult the SRC over the appointment, but in fact this was not true. Consulting the SRC was optional.

The rectorial installation was a disaster. A small section of the audience made the Address inaudible. The *Student* magazine said they were hooligans and cads and their behaviour was shameless blackguardism. Allenby died within a month of the installation. Rumours immediately said that the rowdiness and the stress had hastened his death. Allenby was, however, aged seventy-five.

Allenby said in his Address, tongue in cheek: "We soldiers are sometimes looked down on as below the average educational standard; especially so, perhaps, cavalrymen – of whom I am one. However, I assure you that your armed forces take their profession seriously; are as earnest, industrious and competent as any equal number of civilians."

He urged the need for an international police and the creation of a wide comity of nations independent yet interdependent – a world federation or fellowship . . .

> Lust for expansion is not yet quite dead, but the glory of conquest is departing; its gains are Dead Sea fruit, its legacy bitter memories alone. We earth-dwellers are prisoners on the planet; there is no way out. So, as we cannot escape from the proximity of our neighbours, it is surely better to live with them as friends than as enemies . . .
>
> There is a danger in delay, for its seems likely that unless an effort in the right direction – a successful effort – is made soon the present social system will crumble in ruin, and many now alive may witness the hideous wreck. Then will loom the dreadful menace of the dark ages returning, darker, black, universal in scope, long lasting . . .
>
> At the present moment, many years after the close of the war that was to bring enduring peace to all, we find the cleverest brains everywhere busily experimenting with new inventions for facilitating slaughter, building more horrible engines of destruction, brewing more atrocious poisons, designing more monstrous methods of murdering their fellow men and women . . .
>
> Is it too much to believe that the human intellect is equal to the problem of designing a world state wherein neighbours can love without molestation, in collective security? It does not matter what the state is called; give it any name you please – League of Nations, Federated Nations, United States of the World. Why should there not be a world police just as each nation has a national police force?

The *Student* magazine said:

Probably no past Rector has delivered an oration more inspiring, more worthy of prolonged and serious consideration, than that of Viscount Allenby. Our Rector's plea for internationalism and his condemnation of war – both of which appear the more important when we remember that no one is better qualified to speak of war than the Conqueror of Jerusalem and the former High Commissioner for Egypt – come at an opportune time . . . the countries which are supposed to hold the moral and intellectual hegemony of the world are daily preparing for another and a bloodier war.

Dr Myre Sim was one of those who promoted Allenby's cause in the rectorial election. He has written:

Allenby established a reputation as a distinguished Christian gentleman, for, before entering Jerusalem he dismounted, removed his hat, and said that Jerusalem was so sacred to the world's religions that no one should enter it on horseback like a conqueror. Because of his very distinguished military career the university's OTC [Officers' Training Corps] was asked to support his candidature with canvassing and what little I did indicated that he was a very popular candidate even though he was not a Scotsman . . .

On his departure, the OTC pipe band was recruited for his send-off at Waverley Station [the main station in Edinburgh] and we all marched behind. It was a rather feeble band because of the numbers but when we entered the station the glass roof magnified the sound greatly. and I looked round to see whether other bands were involved. I recall that one of the tunes was *The Flowers of Edinburgh*, which was one of the band's favourites. When we arrived at the platform, Viscount Allenby was already seated in his carriage and we sang, to the accompaniment of the band, 'Will ye no' come back again.' When we had finished, the new Rector lowered his carriage window further and and popped his head out and shouted the appropriate response 'Will I no'.

This impressed us all, coming from an Englishman but as an old soldier he must have had considerable experience of Scottish regiments and was frequently exposed to this farewell. Yet there were quite a few wet eyes, including my own, I thought he brought considerable nobility to the office.

Allenby's ashes were buried in Westminster Abbey. One of his biographers wrote: "His death and burial made little impression in the newspapers, which were filled with ominous news of an Arab uprising in Palestine, Mussolini's invasion of Ethiopia, and Japanese incursions into Manchuria." Only *The Times* gave a full obituary, saying he had been "a man of powerful physique and determined will, a bold sportsman and a fearless rider," who possessed extensive powers of physical and moral courage coupled with straightforwardness of speech.

EMINENT EX-PROFESSOR IS CHOSEN AS A WORKING RECTOR

SIR HERBERT GRIERSON, *critic and scholar (1866–1960). Elected 1936.*

Grierson had been professor at the university for twenty years and had retired a year before. His full and elegant title was Professor of Rhetoric and English Literature. His supporters rightly spoke of his "his prowess as a scholar, the range and force of his intellectual powers, and, last but hardly least, the unforgettable voice in which . . . he delivered facts, opinions, and judgements in his capacity as Professor."

Grierson promised: "Should I be elected, I would take my duties seriously and would endeavour to discover what are the grievances of the students and what are their wants, and would keep in as close touch as I could with their representatives."

His backers said that he was familiar with university affairs and especially with the needs and wishes of the students. "His skill and tact, his reputation and the high esteem in which he is held by the authorities as well as by the students, will always carry great weight and command respectful attention." He was "not the figure-head of a party, not the tool of our University Olympus."

He had four rivals.

The poet Christopher Murray Grieve (who wrote as Hugh MacDiarmid) had been soundly beaten in the previous election but his defeat was not quite as decisive this time. His supporters said:

> C. M. Grieve now occupies in Scottish letters and affairs the commanding position enjoyed by no one since Thomas Carlyle. The University has the distinction of being Alma Mater to both. As the old-time students paid tribute to Carlyle by electing him Rector, a like honour is due from us to Grieve.
>
> Grieve has greater claims on our support than had Carlyle. Carlyle initiated the ruinous tradition of Scottish brains for export to England and Empire [by going to live in London], but Grieve himself is the first to reaffirm the principle that the work of Scottish brains lies among the Scottish people. Carlyle was a *figure-head Rector;* it is characteristic of Grieve's whole career that he comes before us willing and able to be the first *Working Rector,* ready to put at our disposal his profound grasp of our University problems.
>
> . . . Let the students unite under Grieve, the only man in Scotland competent to carry through a national protest. The first necessity is to rally the students of Edinburgh, and all Scotland, since we are all affected similarly, in a general agitation for increased grants.

Donald Pollock was to be a notable name in the university for more than ten years and Rector for six of them (see pp. 112-17). His name lives on also through his benefactions. Among them was money for the building of hostels – what would later be called halls of residence (Pollok Halls). That made some students suspicious. The backers of Grieve said: "Hostelisation is not even meant as a solution for the University's disunity . . . its increase means the growth of an Anglified ascendancy bloc, under the authorities' thumb, dominating their fellow-students, and out of sympathy with the Edinburgh populace."

The Grieve camp also said that students should have the right to determine "how money is to be outlaid that is meant to improve our amenities. What is wanted as a remedy for disunity is the exact opposite policy to that pursued – a demand for a new, free Union as a centre for University life. Where hostels grow, the Union always weakens."

This was the first election in which Pollock was a candidate. He was to be comfortably elected Rector in 1939, re-elected in 1942, and quite heavily defeated in 1945.

Lord Salvesen, former judge of the Court of Session, was from the well-known Edinburgh shipowning family. He was aged seventy-nine and had been Rector's Assessor on the university Court from 1929 to 1933. He was active in several causes: for example, he worked for an extension to Edinburgh Zoo and helped to foster the youth hostels movement. He was chairman of the Scottish Public House Reform League, which sought to improve pubs so that they were like clubs for the working man.

An anonymous student wrote:

> Nothing did Lord Salveson's candidature more harm than the remark that he had done such excellent work for the Royal Scottish Zoological Society and for public house reform. The electors were not interested in these admirable attainments. They wanted, not necessarily a man with a distinguished and dignified past, but someone who they felt would fight for their freedom and their traditions.

Douglas Chalmers Watson was an eminent retired doctor who also stood in 1933 (see page 104). His advocates mentioned the achievements put forward in his favour during the previous election. They also pointed out that he had studied the rare disease of acute gout in fowls and "laid the foundation, now accepted as correct, that acute gout is an acute infective disorder."

On the first count, Pollock came top with 795. At that point, according to the rules of the "single transferable vote" under which the poll was held, Grieve with 266 votes and Salvesen with 134 were eliminated. When their votes were redistributed, the count gave Grierson 864, Pollock 838, and Chalmers Watson 696. When Chalmers Watson was eliminated and his votes were redistributed, the final result was: Grierson 1329, Pollock 960.

Grierson taught lovers of literature the delights of metaphysical poetry, especially the works of Donne, and he edited the letters of Walter Scott in twelve volumes and wrote on Scott and Carlyle. He was an inspirational lecturer but away from the rostrum was shy, nervous, and impractical: he was not happy in tutorials. These characteristics and his great eminence (he had twelve honorary degrees) isolated him from all but his family and a few colleagues. Perhaps his nature was unsuited to the post of Rector.

Grierson was one of those university teachers who think that some students do not approach their studies properly. They want to learn the facts off by heart. Here is a description of a class being taught by Grierson: "Three-quarters of the students sat crouched over their notebooks, feverishly striving to get every word down on paper, without the slightest comprehension of what he was driving at. Later they would read over their confused notes and wonder what it was all about." Grierson sought to counter this. "He spoke discursively, almost conversationally, to bring home to them the beauty of a certain passage."

It is unfair to blame the students alone for the eagerness to take down every word of lectures. Until recently, lecturers and professors were hardly ever taught how to lecture effectively. Many generations of students have been disappointed with their instruction and have found by the end of their courses that their enthusiasm has been dampened, their initial love for their subjects much diminished. At that time lectures were the main method of instruction; later generations of students have tutorials and seminars.

A view of lecturing has been given by Sir John Crofton, who was professor of respiratory diseases from 1972 to 1977, Dean of the Faculty of Medicine from 1963 to 1966 and Vice-Principal from 1969 to 1970. He has recorded: "I once passed the door of a law lecture theatre and heard the lecturer reading out his lecture at dictation speed. I believe a senior lecturer in surgery at that time read out his lectures from his own book." Sir John and associates held a series of residential seminars on teaching, examinations, continuous assessments, and so on.

Grierson's remarks about students were paralleled by another in his rectorial Address: he said he found "something melancholy in the plight of the professional man who has no resources outside his profession or subject beyond golf, bridge, and perhaps the novels of P. G. Wodehouse.".* Specialisation, he said, was to blame: it had taken over the university curriculum and it prevented students from gaining a liberal education.

*For all Grierson's disdain, the numerous admirers of Wodehouse have included T. S. Eliot, W. H. Auden, Evelyn Waugh, Cardinal Basil Hume, and Ludwig Wittgenstein.

Grierson believed that the Universities (Scotland) Act of 1889 Anglicized the Scottish curriculum. The Scottish universities until then had their own traditions – democratic, not elitist. These traditions included a broadly-based curriculum and unrestricted entry for all who were in their mid-teens – all males, that is.

But the Act brought in a matriculation or entrance examination that was fairly difficult. This meant that one or two years had to be added to the school curriculum. And it gave an advantage to pupils from good, fee-paying schools. Another anglicizing factor was the introduction at universities of Oxbridge-style honours courses, so that students were encouraged to specialize.

Grierson wrote that the arts class at a Scottish university before the Act of 1889 was unparalleled. It:

> was a heterogeneous but united body, from first to last . . . the atmosphere was one of work and competition. The best students scorned delights and lived laborious days . . . Our intercourse had not the charm and grace, the freedom of mind and wide range of cultural interests, the critical spirit that one found in intellectual circles at Oxford. But no one who remembers it in tranquillity but must feel he owes a deep debt to the spirit of arduous and generous emulation which breathed from these lads carving out their own careers on the rudely cut and hacked benches.

Grierson himself was educated at Aberdeen University and Oxford University; and knew what he was writing about.

WEALTHY BENEFACTOR IS TWICE ELECTED

Edinburgh University

SIR DONALD POLLOCK, *industrialist, philanthropist, and doctor*
(1868–1962). Elected 1939 and re-elected 1942.
(He was defeated in 1936 and 1945.)

Pollock, of all the rectors, was the one who left the greatest permanent impression on the university. He did this by giving it land, buildings, and large amounts of money. Among his benefactions to the university were a gymnasium, playing fields, and a building for the students' union. Pollock was awarded a baronetcy in 1939 for his charitable gifts; the university and Oxford University gave him honorary degrees.

He was especially generous towards halls of residence. He had a vision of making Edinburgh University residential, as Oxbridge was. That, as we shall see, aroused opposition. Some people in the student body believed that a residential system would anglicize the university. He also was the first Rector for generations, apart from Sir Ian Hamilton (1932–1935), to do more than appear at a few official functions.

He never married but he was devoted to the interests of young people – the Boys' Brigade, the Sea Scouts, and students. He also, as a son of the manse, gave money to a trust for the benefit of missionaries.

Pollock wanted George Square, near the heart of the city, to become a centre for halls of residence. Pollock's halls of residence were in the end built not at George Square but on a nearby site that he gave to the university.

The story of George Square is one of vandalism and folly by the city and the university. A beautiful group of buildings was erected there in the second half of the eighteenth century. On two sides of the square are now blocks of buildings in the twentieth-century brutalist manner: concrete hulks. One side has survived complete but the university has taken over the buildings for administration and teaching – even the house where Sir Walter Scott lived. The fourth side is of old buildings, but not interesting.

Pollock studied science at Glasgow University and medicine at Edinburgh University; he was lonely during that time and the loneliness affected him deeply. He wanted, later, to foster a better way of life for students.

Pollock held hospital posts in Edinburgh and after that went to work in London as a general practitioner. A long-standing friend wrote: "The Scottish colony in South Kensington, including several Members of Parliament from Scotland, soon discovered the young Edinburgh doctor, whose skill was as notable as his personality was pleasing." He served as a doctor in the armed forces during the First World War.

The same friend also wrote, about the benefactions:

> Dr Pollock might have chosen to live a life of leisured ease. But to him money as a personal possession has no meaning, and such a life for him has no attractions. He lives modestly in his bachelor home, with three dogs to keep him company; he digs in his garden; he oils and greases and drives his own unpretentious car. He is quite unspoiled by wealth and success. These are heady wines; but he maintains a balance of judgement and a sanity of outlook which are quite undisturbed by these dizzy happenings. His great joy is to give to others that which he has acquired.

The writer was Lord Alness, a former Liberal MP and former Secretary of State for Scotland.

Of Pollock, the *Scottish Biographical Dictionary* says:

> After a time in medical practice in London (1895–1908) he obtained one of the most lucrative medical charges of those times, private attendant on a wealthy lunatic, in this instance the sixth Duke of Leinster, in which service he moved to Edinburgh while maintaining the duke at Morningside (Royal Edinburgh) Asylum and attending him as 'Personal Physician and General Adviser'.

Pollock was the Duke's companion in travel – yachting off Norway, relaxing in the tropics, playing tennis at Cannes. The Duke died unmarried, aged thirty-four, in 1922 and Pollock looked for something else to do. He and business associates profited from "war surplus". During the 1920s they had a contract with the Government to break up obsolete British warships for the metal. Pollock moved on to bigger prizes.

At the end of the First World War, the German High Seas Fleet sailed to Scapa Flow, the great natural harbour in the Orkneys, to await the outcome of the Paris peace talks. The future of the fleet was causing serious friction between the victorious allies. What vessels would go to the French, the Italians, the British?

The commander of the German fleet ordered his men in June 1919 to start scuttling the ships. To the bottom of the sea went ten battleships, five battle cruisers, four light cruisers, and thirty-two destroyers – by far the greater proportion of the ships. British reaction was at first a mixture of exasperation and anger, but that changed to a feeling of relief: the French and the Italians would not be able to acquire most of the fleet.

Pollock and his associates in the mid-1920s won contracts to raise the warships and recover the metal. Pollock was on the way to make a fortune.

One of his companies produced liquid oxygen, needed for the cutting up of ships for scrap; he later had a stake in the British Oxygen Co. He was also part owner of Metal Industries Ltd; a dairy business; and an engineering company. He held several public appointments, serving on the Scottish Milk Marketing Board and the Carnegie Trust for the Universities of Scotland.

Pollock gave money to Oxford University for a readership in engineering and to the Cavendish Laboratory at Oxford University for research into low temperatures. Oxford gave him an honorary doctorate in science and Edinburgh an honorary doctorate in law.

Pollock was associated with the rectorship for a long time. He was Rector's Assessor to Lord Allenby (elected 1935) and was one of the defeated candidates in the election of 1936 which Sir Herbert Grierson won. Pollock continued as Assessor under Grierson.

The Students' Representative Council considered whom to recommend as Grierson's Assessor. A member of the Council suggested: "Why not elect a young man, a recent graduate, who would work in close touch with the S.R.C?" That idea was not carried out but foreshadowed the election of a student as Rector, which was to happen in 1971.

The Second World War had started two months before Pollock's first victory. Campaigning was muted. The *Student* magazine said: "Since we are not suffering from war hysteria or misguided patriotism there is no danger that we shall vote with blind enthusiasm for a war hero. [This was a reference to the elections, unopposed, of Field Marshal Lord Kitchener in 1914 and Admiral Sir David Beatty in 1917.] The military virtues of courage and cool-headedness are excellent things, but we are looking for other qualifications also when we come to choose a Rector." (A war hero, Admiral Lord Cunningham, was, however, to be elected in 1945.)

Most of the principal student office-bearers backed Pollock's nomination in 1939. A student wrote at that time:

> Sir Donald is a man whose capacity for work is well known and whose interest in the students of this university has been shown time and time again. Sir Donald, as he himself would admit, is not an orator. He is neither picturesque nor flamboyant. He has, on the other hand, the more commendable qualities of modesty, energy, and genuine sympathy with the students. His election at this time would only be a just recognition of the good he has gone about doing quietly for some years.

That favourable view would be challenged the next time Pollock stood.

His opponent at the election of 1939 was Edwin Muir, poet, novelist, critic, journalist, and academic. Both he and Pollock were candidates on a working Rector ticket. Muir's father was a crofter in Orkney but the family moved to Glasgow when he was fifteen. Muir worked in Sussex, St Andrews, Edinburgh, Prague, Rome, and elsewhere and held a post at Harvard University for a year. He believed that Scotland could create a national literature only through English, not the Lallans of MacDiarmid and others.

Of Muir one of his backers wrote:

> It is only reasonable that Scottish students at a Scottish university should be anxious to have a Scotsman like Mr Muir as Rector . . . Mr Muir, however, is put forward not merely as a poet and critic of recognised merit, but by reason of the personal qualities of the man himself. His life has not been that of a sheltered scholar. He worked as a young man in various offices and as a free-lance journalist. He has made himself at home in Czechoslovakia and in the other countries of Europe. He has made a name for himself with his translations. We would welcome Mr Muir's presence in the university. He would bring to the Court a freshness of outlook, an imagination, and an intelligence that would not be wasted.

But the Principal, Sir Thomas Martin, backed Pollock, who was giving the university lots of money.

George Bernard Shaw was asked to stand but declined, saying: "Any candidate with a suspicion of intellectual or academic qualifications will be ignominiously defeated by Sir Donald Pollock. A totally illiterate one would have a much better chance. Universities are like that." The Revd George MacLeod, leader of the Iona Community, which was a strong force in the ecumenical wing of the Church of Scotland, was suggested as a peace candidate, but he too declined the honour. Anthony Eden, Secretary of State for the Dominions, former Foreign Secretary, and future Prime Minister, also declined.

Voting was Pollock 1010 votes and Muir 367. Turnout was 50 per cent

The election of 1942 was different. The *Student* magazine was far less respectful towards the candidates than before. Its editorial line did not, however, necessarily represent the general opinion of its readers.

Pollock had two opponents at this election.

C.E.M. (Cyril) Joad, philosopher, wit, and controversialist was originally a civil servant and then became head of the philosophy department at Birkbeck College, London University. He was famous from his appearances on a weekly radio programme called "The Brains Trust", which started in 1941 and in which eminent people discussed topical questions. Joad had a catch-phrase: "It all depends on what you mean by . . ." He would pick out a crucial word in the question and analyse the question from there. He became a household name. His obituary in *The Times* said he was "a star performer as a popular educator . . . he had zest, gaiety, wit, agility, combativeness, and an unfailing lucidity and an equally unfailing glibness."

Joad was convicted in 1948 of "unlawfully travelling on the railway without having previously paid his fare and with intent to avoid payment." He was fined £2. The nation was amused that this should happen to a person who was so famous as a pundit and philosopher and was the author of such works as *Philosophy and Ethics*, *Decadence*, *The Future of Morals*, and *Guide to Modern Wickedness*. Joad was sacked from "The Brains Trust".

When he stood at Edinburgh Joad made a recording of an election speech and sent it to his supporters, who were mostly arts students. They held public meetings to play it. One of the Pollock team, Jimmie Payne, a medical student, went to the Old Quad, where the arts people were, and grabbed the record. The Arts students were in hot pursuit, but Payne threw the record to a medical friend, Ian Lewis, saying what it was. Lewis headed towards the medical quad and shook off the pursuers. He has recalled: "Jimmie Payne sold the record in a second-hand shop for sixpence. I believe the arts students traced it and brought it back." Other accounts say it was found in a pawnshop.

The other defeated candidate was Douglas Young, a classical scholar, polymath, poet, and dramatist. He was born in Tayport, Fife, and went to St Andrews and Oxford universities. When he was at St Andrews his fellow students nicknamed him "God" because of his height, black beard, and omniscience. His friend Ian Hamilton wrote: "Douglas Young was a big long streak of joy."

Young was for thirty years a passionate writer and speaker for the Scottish Nationalist movement. Young was aged twenty-six when the Second World War broke out and he was called up for military service. He held that the Treaty of Union between Scotland and England of 1707 did not allow a government in London to conscript Scots.

He said: "The Scottish people through a democratic Scottish government should have control over whatever war effort the Scottish people wish to make." For his refusal to serve in the armed forces he was jailed for a year. He took Greek texts with him when he went to jail. Some of his supporters went to Barlinnie Prison in Glasgow and played the bagpipes there, to encourage him and hoping he would hear them. People wondered what would happen if he was elected as Rector when in prison. Would he be brought in a "Black Maria" (a police van) to deliver his Address?

Young was chairman of the Scottish National Party from 1942 to 1945. His chairmanship split the party. He later left the Scottish Nationalists for Labour, believing that independence for Scotland could come only through the main parties. He was chairman when the rectorial election was held.

Young's best poetry was in Lallans and among his finest works were translations into Lallans of *The Frogs* and *The Birds* by Aristophanes, as *The Puddocks* and *The Burdies*. Young was a distinguished scholar and taught at Aberdeen and St Andrews universities but was never given a professorship at a Scottish university – something his friends regretted. He became professor of classics at McMaster University, Ontario, and of Greek at the University of North Carolina.

His supporters at the election said: "Douglas Young will defend our democratic educational tradition against all attacks now directed against it from powerful quarters . . . He has travelled widely throughout Europe, has a command of eight foreign languages . . . In his 29 years he has done more than most able men do in a lifetime . . ." He was in jail "because he keeps faith with all Scots at home and abroad by fighting to preserve something of freedom and justice in our laws . . . he turned down the soft job for this task and the prison stool. He gives his talents and dedicates his life in the service of his own people."

One student wrote during this election that Sir Donald wanted the residential system for the university because it had benefited the English universities.

> A plausible argument, but quite false. There is a certain type of Scotsman who can see no greater good for his fellow-countrymen than that they should adopt the customs and manners of England.
>
> These gentlemen send their sons to English Public Schools to acquire a refained [*sic*] accent, thence to Oxford or Cambridge to give it polish, and

finally to the outposts of Empire or a job in the BBC. What they quite forget is that we have in Scotland a tradition for learning tempered by education which is incomparably greater than that in England. If the slavish aping of English institutions, because they are English, is allowed to proceed, it can lead only to the destruction of the Scottish nation.

And, again from 1942: "A steady influx of Englishmen will come from the second-rate Public Schools because they just have not enough to support living at Oxford and Cambridge. The poor Scots student will slowly, through economic reasons, be unable to come here unless his home is in Edinburgh itself . . . The building of residences means the Anglicising of Edinburgh University."

And: "In the matter of residences and a mixed Union he is completely wrong . . . We do not think he will change his mind. However, mark our words, in twenty years' time we shall triumphantly say: 'I told you so'." Such ideas were not necessarily shared by the majority of students.

Voting was Pollock 1077 votes, Joad 375, and Young 142.

Some students were angry that Pollock broke tradition by never giving an Address, but perhaps an Address would not have been appropriate when the country was at war. He did, however, send messages in the Student's Handbook. One reads as follows: "I would lay great stress upon bringing your health and physical fitness to the acme of proficiency. This is of vital importance, not only as an insurance against the rough and tumble of life, but for the more immediate assistance it will give in securing appointments."

One is reminded of advice from Dr Thomas Gaisford, Dean of Christ Church, Oxford, to undergraduates there in the 1850s: let young men concentrate on "the study of Greek literature, which not only elevates above the vulgar herd, but leads not infrequently to positions of considerable emolument."

Pollock chaired the university Court and took a lot of care in overseeing the way his benefactions were used. It is said that the university authorities found him obstructive, but it was his money that was being spent. For all his generosity, on his death he left a fortune of £874,582.

THE LAST OF THE MILITARY LEADERS

Photograph by Yousef Karsh, Camera Press London

LORD CUNNINGHAM OF HYNDHOPE, *Admiral of the Fleet (1883–1963).*
Elected 1945.

Cunningham was the last of the military men to be elected. He was the outstanding British naval leader of the Second World War, Britain's best fighting admiral of the twentieth century, and has been described as the greatest British naval commander since Nelson.

The other candidates in this election were Sir William Beveridge, architect of the Welfare State, and Sir Donald Pollock, standing for the fourth time and seeking his third term. Voting was: Cunningham 904, Beveridge 567, Pollock 451.

Beveridge (later Lord Beveridge) was of Scottish descent and was an economist, social reformer, and outstanding authority on unemployment and similar issues. He was director of the London School of Economics from 1919 to 1937 and Master of University College, Oxford, from 1937 to 1945.

Beveridge's great work, the *Report on Social Insurance and Allied Services,* called the Beveridge Report, was published in 1942. It sought to banish "want, disease, ignorance, squalor, and idleness." That was to be done by a National Health Service and a comprehensive system of social security. The Beveridge Report was a great testimony of hope at the height of the Second World War and was the gospel of the Labour governments from 1945 to 1951.

Pollock had by this time lost his appeal for the electorate. He had never given the traditional Address and his benefactions had been criticized by some students. He received 23.5 per cent of the votes cast.

Dr Ian Cunningham has remembered an incident from this time. "We found we had access to tear gas and smoke canisters in the University Corps armoury. We helped ourselves, raiding the Old Quad. A smoke canister followed by a tear gas canister in a lecture theatre produced dramatic effects."

Admiral Cunningham's rectorial Address was received rowdily by a group of about fifty of the people in the hall. One student said: "I felt so embarrassed and hot under the collar that I could look only at my feet." The *Student* magazine has often in its long history had to deplore such behaviour, and so again this time. It noticed with pleasure what had happened to one of the hooligans. He was thrown head first down the steps of the Union building and was heard to say – as he lay on the ground: "You will be fined for this." The phrase quickly became a catchword. But the magazine added that the Address was unsuitable and that much of it was trite.

Dr Philip Myerscough was at the rectorial Address and installation. He has written:

> Cunningham, because of his war-hero status, was welcomed to the ceremony with almost God-like respect, and perhaps no one had dared to brief him about what was expected of him and, in particular, that he was expected to announce to the student body the boon of a rectorial holiday from classes. [He failed, at the beginning of his Address, to follow tradition and ask the Principal to grant the students a day's holiday.]
>
> His Rectorial Address was delivered rather like an address to his midshipmen – much too serious, and much too long.
>
> Matters came to a head after a few flour bombs were thrown from the upper tiers [of the McEwan Hall], and when he paused momentarily, from the first floor gallery a block of male students chanted out in perfect unison a parody of a regular joke from a radio comedy show, the Charlie Chester show:
>
> 'Old Joe Cunnin-ing-ham spoke too long!
> Never gave a hol-i-day – Bang on!'
>
> What impressed me at the time was that the students who intervened so wittily and appositely could not have known in advance the contents of the Rectorial Address, but their 'chant' was so neat, and delivered as if they had practised it together for weeks beforehand.

The new Rector was taken aback by this mounting display of insubordination but drew his oration to a close. Following a whispered exchange with the Principal, Sir John Fraser, the holiday was announced.

At this time, the other Scottish universities decided on very different people to honour. Aberdeen chose Eric Linklater, a Scottish novelist. Glasgow chose Sir John Boyd Orr, who campaigned for the hungry of the world and who, as Lord Boyd Orr, received the Nobel Prize for Peace. St Andrews chose Sir George Cunningham, eminent Indian administrator and civil servant.

Andrew Browne Cunningham, who was to be known to the lower deck as "ABC", was born in Dublin of Scottish parents and educated at Edinburgh Academy and as a naval cadet. His father was Professor of Anatomy at Edinburgh University. He served in the Boer War and the First World War.

His career was in the doldrums during the 1930s. But officers senior to him retired or died unexpectedly and he was promoted quickly. During the Second World War he was Commander-in-Chief of the Mediterranean Fleet. His ships defeated the Italian navy several times, the most important being at the battles of Taranto in 1940 and Cape Matapan in 1941. Three of the biggest Italian cruisers were sunk at Matapan in a few minutes. But the British Mediterranean Fleet under his command from 1939 to 1943 lost nearly 200 ships to U-boats and to the Axis powers' warplanes. Moreover, the decisions of the British high command to invade Crete and Greece were disastrous.

Cunningham commanded Allied naval forces in the invasions of North Africa, Sicily, and the Italian mainland. In 1943 he was the officer who accepted the surrender of the Italian fleet. He was briefly the head of the British naval mission in Washington, where he won the respect of the Americans as the Allies planned the final stages of the war.

Cunningham retired from the navy in 1946 and was Lord High Commissioner to the General Assembly of the Church of Scotland in 1950 and 1952.

I am indebted to Dan van der Vat for advice about Cunningham.

PART II

1948 ONWARDS

Actors, Celebrities, and Television Personalities Prevail – and a dramatic period of student power

COMIC ACTOR BREAKS TRADITION
OF ALMOST A CENTURY

Edinburgh University

ALASTAIR SIM, *actor (1900–1976). Elected 1948.*

This was the end of an era. The politicians and the military men were, generally, out. From this election, the rectors were to be from different and more colourful walks of life: a priest, the discoverer of penicillin, television 'personalities', a professional foot-baller, and two students from the university.

Alastair Sim was an acclaimed actor, mainly in comic parts. His supporters, in the campaign for votes, said that he was *militantly non-political.* His rival was a Conservative politician: Harold Macmillan, who was to be Prime Minister; but Macmillan was not then well known to the public. Voting was 2,078 to 802: turn-out was almost 50 per cent. Macmillan's supporters claimed Sim won because the women preferred him.

The only politicians that were in the future to be chosen by the students were Jo Grimond in 1960 and David Steel in 1982. They were, however, not the usual kind of politician. They were leaders of the Liberal Party, which in their days had very few MPs but which appealed to the idealism of youth. Grimond and Steel had Scottish connections also.

The election was held three years after the country rejected Churchill and returned Labour to power. Macmillan's backers said that "at this time, when Socialism is causing so much disaster to the country," the university should show its support for the Right . . . "If you value Freedom and Liberty, room for improvement of Social conditions, you will vote MACMILLAN," a leaflet said.

Five of Macmillan's backers hid his supplies of food in one of the rooms in the Old College and stayed there after the building was closed down for the night. They came out at two o'clock in the morning, climbed on to the roof, and put up a poster, fifteen yards long, saying "Macmillan for Rector" along with two large photographs of him.

One of the guilty, Dr Iain Cowie, recalled years afterwards: "We slipped out of a window into Chambers Street at 3 a.m. into the arms of two patrolling policemen. However, after giving explanations we were let go."

Sim's supporters claimed that Macmillan had persuaded a possible candidate not to run: this was Lord Burghley, an Olympic gold and silver medallist and a popular figure. "On 14th October Macmillan spoke to Burghley and on 15th October Burghley announced his withdrawal."

Sim's rectorial Address was remarkable. His audience was as difficult as audiences can be but he used all his professional skills and triumphed.

Sim's wife Naomi wrote:

> We had been warned that by tradition the students made such a racket that not a word could be heard of their new Rector's Address. Even so, I was unprepared for the noise in the McEwan Hall. Every one of those 2,500-odd students seemed to be yelling at the top of his voice, and this sound was punctuated by hooters, rattles, trumpets, and exploding squibs.
>
> While all this was going on, the Vice-Chancellor and Senate, with the new Rector bringing up the rear, had come in procession down the central aisle and taken their seats on the platform in perfect calm and dignity (as if this appalling racket as an everyday occurrence and perfectly natural behaviour for students) before Alastair, now robed, moved to the lectern.
>
> He told me afterwards as he stood there waiting to speak there was a dreadful moment when he felt one of his knees give slightly and wondered if he was going to fall, but I couldn't have told for he seemed pleasant and quite relaxed. Out of curiosity, I suppose, the students allowed his first words to be held, and that was their mistake for he quickly made them laugh and with their enjoyment came interest and they were hooked. . . . When it came to the end it was impossible not to know that it had been a huge success.

It has been said that part of the text was written by his friend James Bridie, the distinguished Scottish playwright.* Bridie later said that of all the eight rectorial Addresses he

---

*One of Bridie's plays, *What Say They,* is about rectorial high jinks at a fictitious Scottish university.

had attended, this was the only one he had heard. One of Sim's biographers wrote: "As one reads [the Address], one can hear it being spoken, in the inimitable Sim manner, the clipped words, the sardonic intonations, the crocodile smile. His own character appears in every line: 'I admit that even to this day I enjoy being called an artiste, and if anybody likes to qualify it with some such adjective as "great," "incomparable," "superb," then you can rely on me to finish the ritual by reacting with becoming modesty'."

Among the topics of his Address was his early career:

> I tried my hand at children's theatre, here, in Edinburgh. What a field of constructive work was here, I thought! The unformed, the uninhibited minds of children would prove to be rewarding soil for my enthusiasm.

> I was determined that it should be no namby-pamby affair, this children's theatre of mine, nor too goody-goody either, or wishy-washy, or airy-fairy ... It was to be a grand, rollicking, rumbustious and thrilling entertainment. Excellent! I see no reason to alter these views of what a children's theatre ought to provide.

> Everything went smoothly and gaily and according to plan, until I myself made an appearance on the stage ... I may have been an ogre; I have tried to forget. I know I expected gales of laughter, possibly swelling to a cheer. Instead there was a sudden deathly hush. Then thin, isolated wails of misery came from the body of the hall. These grew, and spread, and I was aware of a stampede of mothers leaving the hall with their unhappy offspring, between angry mutterings and reproachful backward looks."

Sim was not only an actor but also a director of plays. He was born and brought up in Edinburgh, left school early, and studied briefly at the university. He took up teaching, set up his own school of drama and speech, and became a lecturer in elocution at New College, the divinity college of the university. His first part in a play came late, when he was 30, but he went on to make a big name in film comedies and comedy-thrillers.

Sim turned to more serious work in 1940. He worked closely with James Bridie, who helped to found the Citizens' Theatre in Glasgow and was an eminent figure in Scotland's cultural life. Sim played in and directed several of Bridie's best plays: *Mr Bolfry, Dr Angelus,* and *Mr Gillie.* Their partnership was very fruitful for them and for the theatre.

Sim, at the time of his election by the students, was playing in Bridie's *The Anatomist* at the Westminster Theatre in London. His win was announced before the curtain went up and the audience cheered.

Sim received the honorary degree of LL.D. from the university at the end of his term and was awarded the CBE in 1953. He refused a knighthood, saying it would be ridiculous to be called Sir Alastair.

He went on more successes in film and plays. Perhaps he will be best remembered for his part as the headmistress in the film comedies about St Trinian's School.

His opponent in the rectorial election, Harold Macmillan, was first elected to Parliament in 1924 and had a crucial job during the Second World War as a British government representative in North Africa – a job that he did with tact, skill, and acumen. When he stood for the rectorship he was comparatively obscure. He was to be Prime Minister from 1957 to 1963.

Sim's supporters said of Macmillan in a pamphlet that he was an ambitious, clever Scot destined for future office. To describe Macmillan as a Scot is perhaps stretching the facts. His grandfather Daniel Macmillan was born on the Isle of Arran in 1813, but moved to England in 1833. Daniel Macmillan was the founder of Macmillan's the publishing house. He was Harold Macmillan's only link with Scotland.

Harold Macmillan was born in London and educated at Eton and Balliol College, Oxford; he married a daughter of the Duke of Devonshire, and he never lived in Scotland nor held a Scottish parliamentary seat.

Nevertheless he played the Scottish card in a message to the students. "My family is of Scottish descent. My grandfather, like so many Highland lads, left his native croft at a tender age, to seek his fortune across the Border. It would indeed be a proud day for my family and myself if I were to find myself, a hundred years later, as Lord Rector of the University of the capital city of Scotland."

Macmillan was to be Prime Minister from 1957 to 1963. During his premiership the cartoonists were to depict him as both an Edwardian figure and as "Supermac," a figure with extraordinary powers.

A distinguished historian, Robert Rhodes James, has written that Macmillan's in-laws, a very grand family, so disliked him that there was intense family competition not to sit next to him at meals. They and many other people thought he was stupendously boring. And, wrote Rhodes James, "his teeth were malformed, his clothes were scruffy and poor, and he had a moustache that was in sore need of attention."

A GREAT SCIENTIST DEFEATS MANY OTHER STRONG CANDIDATES

SIR ALEXANDER FLEMING, *discoverer of penicillin (1881–1955).*
Elected 1951.

Alexander Fleming, the discoverer of penicillin, is one of mankind's greatest benefactors. In the year he was elected, the field of candidates was exceptionally strong. Apart from Fleming, it comprised a brilliant novelist, an eminent poet, an international religious leader who was also a diplomat, a notable humorist, a much-loved entertainer, a man distinguished in Edinburgh public life, and a leading member of the Scottish bar. The field of eight candidates was one of the biggest ever.

Fleming was awarded a Nobel prize, a knighthood, fellowship of the Royal Society, and almost thirty honorary doctorates. His obituarist in *The Times* wrote that he "remained quite unspoiled by the publicity and acclaim that came to him, and no one was more aware than he of the indispensable part played by other investigators in the development of penicillin." He loved gardening, painting, and motoring. Fleming is buried in St Paul's Cathedral.

Let us now consider the other candidates.

The novelist

The novelist Evelyn Waugh had at this time published most of his greatest works, including *Decline and Fall* (1928), *Vile Bodies* (1930), *Scoop* (1938), and *Brideshead Revisited* (1945). Some of his most brilliant writing is in *Scoop*, his novel about a mature columnist Henry Boot who is mistakenly sent abroad as a war correspondent. Boot's column contains a phrase much loved by journalists and others, the immortal: "Feather-footed through the plashy fen passes the questing vole."

Waugh had also written a biography of Edmund Campion (1540–1581), Jesuit and martyr, and the *Sword of Honour* trilogy of novels based on his war service in Crete, Yugoslavia, North Africa, and Italy.

Waugh became a Roman Catholic in 1930 when he was twenty-seven. He was put up for the rectorship by Roman Catholic students among others. Waugh wrote to his principal backer, Bruce Cooper:

> As soon as I received your very kind invitation to stand for the Rectorship, I wrote to my income-tax accountant to ask whether election expenses were admissible as professional expenses against tax. His answer is: no.
>
> I have also written to my agents & publishers. I have not had their answer. My fear is that they would not be allowed by their accountants to charge these expenses as legitimate advertising. These things are sharply watched.
>
> So it seems that I must pay out of taxed income. This means that for every £10 I give you, I must earn £60. I can therefore only offer a minimum sum. It is plain . . . that money is not an important consideration. What is the least you can manage on? I hope you will understand my parsimony in this matter. I will guarantee £75. Can you do it on that? . . . [In the end, his publishers, Chapman and Hall, paid.]
>
> I have never voted in a general election as I have never found a Tory stern enough to command my respect . . . I should think the best election line would be not my worthiness but the conspicuous unworthiness of the other candidates . . .

His backers put out a leaflet saying that he was the leading satirist of the twentieth century. Waugh told the students:

> I am a Scot of the diaspora. Less than two hundred years ago my great-great-grandfather took part in that most successful action of Scottish Nationalism – the conquest of England by peaceful penetration. Since then we have always looked upon ourselves as Scots . . . [This ancestor was the Revd Alexander Waugh (1754–1827), a DD of the university and a preacher of fervid and impressive eloquence, who moved to London and throve there. Evelyn Waugh was playing the Scottish card in a mild way; at other times he adopted, in an exaggerated way, the manners of a crusty English gentleman.]

I have never gone into public life. Most of the ills we suffer are from people going into public life . . . I have paid such taxes as I find unavoidable. I have learned and practised a very difficult trade with some fair success.

It seems to me essential to your repute among the great Universities of Christendom that you should choose a man connected with the Arts. I am opposed by a poet. If he writes better than I, please vote for him. But do not, I beg, choose anyone connected with commerce . . . Don't choose a man in public life. Don't choose a pure clown. That is not in keeping with your great history.

One of Waugh's backers, Raymund McCluskey, has written:

The real rectorial rivalry rose alas from a Catholic-Protestant dimension. The opposite candidate was Sydney Goodsir Smith [see below]. The Waugh group were almost all Catholic students who met regularly at the Dominican Catholic university chaplaincy in George Square. (Our HQ for the campaign was the Greyfriars Bobby bar at the top of Candlemaker Row.) It fell out that S. G. Smith's supporters came from across the religious divide.

There was one seriously physical clash between the rival groups when they met at the narrow lane at the rear of the Old Quadrangle. We all got tore into each other about six or eight a side and broke each other's poster boards but not each other's skulls. Pat Nuttgens, the mildest of men, was given a rather bad knock.

We in the Waugh campaign went on to have reasonably successful careers . . . of undetected crime. Mr Waugh let us keep the balance of campaign funds for an excellent post-rectorial party.

Bridget Nuttgens, née Badenoch, wrote of this election:

I tended Pat's bleeding head when he staggered round to my father's house and made him up a bed on the library sofa.

We considered that we ran an extremely good campaign, although this was not appreciated by the run-of-the-mill Scottish students who, when adjured to vote for Evelyn Waugh, frequently replied: 'Who's she?'

Penguin were at the time producing paperbacks of Waugh's novels, and we made facsimile copies of the orange cover, substituting a lamp of learning for the little penguin symbol under the title which read

THE RECTOR

EVELYN WAUGH

The false covers were inserted into rows of his novels laid out in bookshops.

Some of our band narrowly escaped arrest by the police on suspicion of trying to steal lead from the roof of the McEwan Hall on to which they had climbed to erect a banner. Deciding that votes were likely to come from the Arts Faculty we waylaid Professor [John] Macmurray on his way to the 'ordinary' Moral Philosophy class. One of us, Patrick Reyntiens [later a leading artist in stained glass], dressed up in a gown and announced to the class he was substituting for the Prof and would continue with Macmurray's philosophical Theory of Apperception, about which there was only one essential thing to remember which was to VOTE FOR EVELYN WAUGH.

I think it was shortly after the election that Waugh came up to Edinburgh to give a talk and, since Bruce [Cooper, his principal backer] had read somewhere that his favourite drink was green chartreuse, some supporters scraped together their pennies to entertain him sumptuously.

True to character he brusquely rejected our advances, and we ended up, *sans* Waugh, sitting on the floor (less far to fall) of Bruce's flat in Marchmont and drinking the lot.

The poet

Sydney Goodsir Smith, his backers declared, was a real creative genius. He would be able, as an Edinburgh man, to work in the students' interests as their spokesman. Smith has also been described as "an outstanding polymath, combining the roles of poet, playwright, broadcaster, author, translator, painter, critic, and wit." He was an accomplished pianist and wrote a comic novel.

Though born and brought up in New Zealand, Smith went to Edinburgh when his father was appointed a professor there. His father, Sir Sydney, was professor of forensic medicine at the university from 1928 to 1953 and was to succeed Fleming in the rectorship. The name Goodsir was inherited from his mother's side. He studied at Edinburgh and Oxford universities

"Sydney Goodsir Smith," wrote Hugh MacDiarmid, the poet:

> has won recognition at home and abroad as an outstanding figure in the Scottish Renaissance Movement. His prose work alike as a literary critic and as an imaginative writer is of first importance. He is, moreover, a vital and vivacious personality, whose brilliant gifts and lively disposition have won him hosts of friends at home and abroad. A scholar, a lover of all the arts, a great wit, a well-informed Scot with all his country's best interests at heart and above all a passionate concern for freedom and a hatred of every sort of cant and humbug, he typifies all that is best in the Scottish National Awakening now in progress.

Other messages of support came from Edith Sitwell, poet; Neil Gunn, novelist; Duncan Macrae, actor; and Sorley MacLean, poet in Gaelic.

Smith's campaigners said that he "with straight-faced drollery or exuberant fun, must have come nearer to killing more of his friends than any other man living."

Smith was described as the best poet in Lallans after MacDiarmid. He also wrote a play in verse, *The Wallace*, which was staged at the Edinburgh Festival in 1960. The play so aroused patriots that at the end of one performance some people in the audience rose and sang *Scots wha hae wi' Wallace bled.* The actor Iain Cuthbertson, who played Wallace, said the language of the play was "eminently speakable, once one had a firm grip of one's dentures".

Smith's greatest work is *Under the Eildon Tree,* a love poem. The following example of his work (reproduced by permission of Calder Publications, London) is about the decline of the fishing industry:

> Ae boat anerlie nou
> Fishes frae this shore,
> Ae black drifter lane
> Riggs the crammasie daw,

Aince was a fleet, and nou
Ae boat alane gangs oot.
War ir peace, the trawlers win
An the youth turns awa
Bricht wi baubles nou
An thirled tae factory ir store;
Their faithers fished thir ain,
Unmaistered; – ane remains.

[ae = a or one; ainerlie = only; lane: alone; ir = or; crammasie = crimson; daw = dawn;
aince = once; alane = alone; bricht = bright; thirled = bound or constrained; ane = one]

The religious leader

The Aga Khan, forty-eighth head of the Ismaeli sect of the Shia community, was properly called Aga Sultan Sir Mohammed Shah KCIE, GCSI, GCVO, and GCMG – he was four times a knight. The first knighthood was awarded by Queen Victoria and the last by Queen Elizabeth II. He was a notable owner of racehorses, winning the Derby in 1930, the Two Thousand Guineas, the Derby, and the St Leger (the triple crown) in 1935, and the Derby in 1936, 1948, and 1952. Success like that needs a lot of money.

He captured the imagination of the public in 1946 when he was weighed in diamonds to celebrate his diamond jubilee. The ceremony was held once in Bombay and once in Dar-es-Salaam. The Aga Khan at that time weighed 17 stones 5½ pounds (about 126 kilos). Diamonds were borrowed from the London Diamond Exchange for the ceremonies and were taken to the ceremonies by warship and flying boat. When the scales balanced, the worth of the diamonds was £640,000. His followers gave that amount of money to him and he gave the money to good causes and public works. The diamonds were returned to their owners.

The Aga Khan took a leading position among Indian Moslems as a whole. The *Dictionary of National Biography* says of him:

> Shrewd, active, a connoisseur of the arts, a good scholar, a citizen of the world, an experienced and courageous politician, a hardworking religious leader alive to the importance of the education and physical fitness of his community, with great material resources, he was for long a major figure in Indian politics, and in his time, helped by his broad minded and constructive approach, he gave service of great value to his community and to the Commonwealth.

He paid the expenses of his own campaign in the rectorial election. If he had been elected, the university might have benefited from his wealth and generosity.

The entertainer

Jimmy Logan, who came from a show-business family, was at an early stage in his long career as a comic, dancer, and singer. His debut in films was in 1949. For many years he appeared in pantomime in the winter and revue in the summer. He also worked in radio and television and in straight drama; wrote and produced *Lauder*, a one-man show in honour of Harry Lauder; and ran the Metropole Theatre in Glasgow from 1964 to 1972. He appeared in nine Royal Command performances.

Logan said, before the election: "Whatever happens, no matter how many votes I poll, even if I should fail miserably, I shall regard this nomination as an honour that cannot be excelled even by a Command Performance."

The humorist

Stephen Potter's many books are parodies of academic writing and mock the pretensions and devices of ordinary life. They include *The Theory and Practice of Gamesmanship; or the Art of Winning Games without Actually Cheating* (published in 1947), *Some Notes on Lifemanship, One-Upmanship, and Supermanship, with a summary of recent researches in gamesmanship* (1950), and *Oneupmanship, being an account of the activities and teaching of the Lifemanship Correspondence College and of one-upmanship and gameslifemastery* (1952).

These books were very popular and gave a number of words to the English language. He also published scholarly works on D. H. Lawrence and Coleridge and was a writer and producer for the BBC.

The lawyer

John Cameron was a former Dean of the Faculty of Advocates and was to become a judge of the Court of Session. He was educated at Edinburgh Academy and Edinburgh University. He served in the First World War, as a midshipman, and in the Second World War, commanding the last vessel to leave Dunkirk and later serving on destroyers. He received the DSC for bravery during the Normandy landings. He had held many public appointments. He stood, said his backers, as an independent candidate, "holding the firm conviction that more can, and should, be done in Scottish Universities towards bringing staff and students together both in and out of lecture rooms." His backers at the election wrote that he had "that certain air – call it panache, gallantry, or what you will."

Cameron was to become a member of the university Court when a judge on the Court of Session; during that time he battled with the Rector, Gordon Brown.

The public figure

Sir Andrew Murray, former Lord Provost of the city, was educated at Edinburgh schools (Daniel Stewart's and George Watson's) and became a town councillor only six years after leaving school. He went into insurance and later was the chairman of six large companies.

Murray was knighted as Lord Provost and visited many countries as holder of the position. He took a big part in the city's development: slums in the Old Town were cleared while its character was preserved; and council estates were built in the suburbs. He helped to found the Edinburgh Festival in 1947. He was a candidate for Parliament as a Conservative and as a Liberal, without success.

Murray stood for the rectorship as someone who would be a working Rector. His backers wrote of "the energy and enthusiasm he has displayed throughout a public life devoted to the service of others" and of his "warm interest in student activities, his heart and his pocket for ever open in response to appeals from the student body." When he was Lord Provost he had "an aura of popularity unsurpassed by any predecessor."

Other people were suggested as runners in 1951 but did not agree to run or were unable to do so. They included Alastair Sim, the retiring Rector; Dr George MacLeod, leader and founder of the Iona Community (a vibrant evangelical wing of the Church of Scotland); Kenneth Horne, radio comedian; and Mohammed Mosaddegh.

Mosaddegh was Prime Minister of Iran and held strongly nationalist views. His Oil Nationalisation Act of 1951 was aimed at the Anglo-Iranian Oil Co. Mossadegh became the target of invective – indeed hatred – in Britain and other Western countries.

He wrote to his supporters in Edinburgh: "Being a profound believer in the instrumentality and efficacy of knowledge in the correction of human frailties arising through egotism and materialism, I earnestly believe that institutions of learning, such as the University of Edinburgh, must play a great part – so sorely needed – for a better understanding between the Ancient East and the Modern West."

Mosaddegh's supporters withdrew his candidature, saying they were forced to do so because of "a trivial and unexpected technicality". They hoped that the publicity they had already received would be of some help in furthering the cause of world peace. Mosaddegh was to be ousted from office in Iran in 1953 – the CIA and MI6 wanted a change of regime. The Shah took over power.

Fleming's backers at first were mainly medical students; a powerful bloc as was shown from time to time in the history of the rectorship. His backers sent an envoy to London to get his signature of acceptance to being nominated. They soon panicked. They had heard that the Aga Khan's faction was plotting to kidnap their envoy on his return to the city at Waverley Station and seize the vital document. Fleming's men acted quickly and efficiently: they whisked their man away from the train at London and took him to Edinburgh by car.

Their campaign had the most effective of the posters: it said simply FLEMING. Non-medical students joined the cause.

Voting was as follows: Fleming, 1096; the Aga Khan, 660; Cameron, 373; Waugh, 237; Smith, 227; Murray, 170; Potter, 124; and Logan, 73. The Aga Khan wrote to his supporters: "I am not at all disappointed and feel that my old friend Fleming deserves it more than anybody to have our gratitude for his wonderful discovery. I owe my life to penicillin, so you can well imagine my feelings."

The usual noisiness prevailed at the installation. There followed the usual outbursts of rage and bursts of outrage. Someone who was present at the installation wrote to the Principal: "I am a Scot but I am utterly ashamed of your students' behaviour . . . How you, sir, and your colleague Lord Provost James Millar can sit and smile while such buffoonery and rudeness goes [sic] on is scandalous. Look at your faces – and his. He is silent, enduring."

A letter to the editor of the Edinburgh *Evening News* said: "Edinburgh, world-famed centre of education and culture, must hang her proud head in sorrow and shame . . . God help Scotland if yesterday's behaviour is a sample of the mentality of our future educated men."

The Rector himself wrote to the Principal:

> I admit that I went to Edinburgh with some trepidation and it was only after the McEwan Hall ceremony that I really felt comfortable. It was not only for my own sake but I should have hated to see flour and soot strewn about that lovely hall.
>
> I wonder, though, why they elect someone and ask him to give an address

when they refuse to hear it. It seems a pity that one should take so much trouble to prepare an address which is not listened to – something cheaper would suffice. There is a well-known saying about pearls and swine.

I do not really mean that. I was annoyed for only about five or 10 minutes at the beginning of my address and then I was quite happy and spent the pauses in thinking which bits I could cut out without quite disjointing the story . . . I have come back South with enormous satisfaction that Edinburgh University is a good place and I am proud that at last I am part of it.

He also wrote:

It was a very exciting experience and after [the age of] 70 you don't want too much excitement. I remember when I first read a paper to a [learned] society, in 1907. My knees shook, but they were concealed behind the lecturer's desk, and apparently my face did not give me away so all was well. My knees have not shaken since - until I got up to deliver my address in Edinburgh, amid a Babel of noise. This time, though, I had on a long gown, and nobody noticed. I soon got used to the clamour.

When he had finished, people from the audience carried him shoulder-high to the Union amid a tremendous noise of shouting, song, drums, mouth-organs, and trombones. There they all had tea.

Fleming's Address was on the subject "Success". He described what he held to be the most successful careers in history – those of Pasteur and Lister – and said that what was needed was a conjunction of luck and genius. And he spoke of team-work; but much was also to be said in favour of lonely research.

He was once asked how to cure a cold, and said: "A good gulp of hot whisky at bedtime – it's not very scientific, but it helps."

Fleming was born near Darvel, Ayrshire, the son of a farmer, went to Darvel School and Kilmarnock Academy, and moved to London when he was thirteen to live with his brother. He took a job as a shipping clerk but continued his education by going to classes at the Regent Street Polytechnic.

Fleming later came into a small legacy, which made it possible for him to start the study of medicine when he was twenty. He won many prizes and a scholarship at St Mary's Hospital medical school, London. He joined the Territorial Army and was a private in the London Scottish Regiment from 1900 to 1914. He was a good marksman and was in the college rifle team. That brought him to the attention of the person who ran the bacteriological laboratory at the medical school and he was taken on there as a researcher. During the First World War he served in the Royal Army Medical Corps and was mentioned in despatches.

In 1922 Fleming discovered an anti-bacterial agent, naming it lysozyme. Fleming was carrying out research at St Mary's Hospital, in 1928 into the virus that causes influenza. Some of his cultures were kept in covered plates; he had to take off the covers so that he could see what was going on. Spores of a mould drifted on to one of his plates and grew into a colony about half an inch (1.2 cm) across. That was not a rare thing to happen. But the colonies of bacteria around the mould "appeared to be fading away. What had a week before been vigorous staphylococcus families were now faint shadows of their former selves." Fleming took note.

The discovery of penicillin was imminent. He wrote a paper in 1929 which "covered nearly the whole field, realised most of the problems, and made considerable progress in solving them." But Fleming's first samples of penicillin were unsuitable for medical use: they were too weak. A lot of work had still to be done.

Progress stopped for eleven years. Two experimentalists, Howard [Lord] Florey, a bluff Australian, and [Sir] Ernst Boris Chain, an excitable German Jewish émigré, took up the work. With the help of money from the Rockefeller Foundation they worked out a way of manufacturing *penicillium notatum* so that it could be used. The three shared the Nobel prize for medicine in 1945. But they lost the patents to America, where a strain of penicillin with higher yields was developed

MEDICAL STUDENTS SWING THE VOTE

Edinburgh University

SIR SYDNEY SMITH, *professor and forensic scientist (1883–1969).*
Elected 1954.

Sydney Smith owed his victory to the mass vote of medical students. He became professor of forensic medicine in 1928 and Dean of the Faculty of Medicine in 1931, retiring from both posts in 1953, the year before the election. A medical background was not his only advantage. He was also the candidate likeliest to look after the interests of the electorate.

This was another rectorship that was marred by squabbles: the university authorities were petty and heavy-handed and the students were keen to maintain what they saw as tradition. One dispute was about the painting of slogans during the election campaign. Somebody painted "Vote Sydney Smith as Rector" on a fence at the veterinary school. Police questioned the slogan-writers but left the matter to the university.

Five students were summoned to appear before the Principal and Deans' Committee. They were accused of defacing university property and were each fined £3. If they did not pay within ten days they would be "sent down" for the rest of the term. This sentence aroused anger among the body of the students. Painting slogans was an ancient tradition. Students thought that the Principal, Sir Edward Appleton, had acted harshly. A meeting of students was called and a whip-round was held to pay the fines.

A student was quoted as saying: "Are we to be prevented from putting up posters and everything else? That seems to be what they intend to do. We might as well not have rectorials. It seems they want to make it too darn sticky for us to do much at all." Sir Edward, put on the defensive, said he did not mind notices and slogans as long as they were removable. Any suggestion that the authorities wanted to damp down the traditional exuberance was "pure invention".

Backers of Smith saw their chance. They put out 2000 copies of a leaflet saying: "There has been a sharp deterioration in the staff-student relationship . . . Students are becoming increasingly aware of the need for a strong representative on the university Court, to bridge the wide gap between themselves and the university authorities." One of Smith's backers also took the chance to take a dig at three of the other candidates, who were in the entertainment business. "Rectorials are becoming a farce. It is time we had an active Rector, working for the students, and not comic turns."

Some students went to the Principal's house at night and painted on the garden wall, in letters two feet high, "Syd [i.e. Sydney Smith] for Principal." The slogan was not about the election of the Rector but about the Principal's attitude. The slogan writers tipped off journalists, who phoned Sir Edward's home at midnight. Lady Appleton said: "I hope those responsible realise how silly it is. After all, it is not what one would expect after Edinburgh University has been raised above all others by having the first gentleman of the land [the Duke of Edinburgh] as its Chancellor."

Six medical students went to the Principal's house during the night and tried to remove the slogan with turpentine and scrubbing brushes. They worked for fifteen minutes without success. One of the students said: "The slogan is ridiculous, but apparently the paint is good."

The other squabble was about where the installation was to take place. The McEwan Hall had always been used for installations since it was built in the late nineteenth century but the university authorities were still upset by the rows about the painting of slogans; they apparently feared rowdyism and vandalism in the hall. Moreover, the Old Quad had been damaged – though not seriously – on election day during the rectorial "fight" with the traditional soot and garbage. When it was all over, the combatants joined forces and cleared the mess away – a remarkable break with tradition.

The authorities decreed that the installation could not be held in the hall. This decision was taken by the university Court and the meeting was chaired by the Rector himself.

The president of the Labour Club wrote:

> The administration appears to regard the student body as an irresponsible social group which has to be coerced into civilised conduct, while students are increasingly suspicious of the reasons which have prompted the administration's actions . . .
>
> The university authorities have a duty to preserve the buildings and

general amenities of the university, but it is generally believed that this duty could have been fulfilled in a less tactless way. As it was, the authorities appear to have committed themselves to the view that all university property is absolutely sacrosanct – even when it is only a piece of wooden hoarding serving no more useful purpose than that of surrounding a portion of undeveloped land.

The Students' Representative Council put pressure on the university. In the end the Court allowed the hall to be used. Fears about rowdyism turned out to have been unjustified: the installation and Address were comparatively quiet. Smith was, however, annoyed by interruptions at several points and rebuked people in the audience.

He received a rebuke himself in a letter to the editor of the *Student* magazine, signed "Disgusted": "He talked for approximately 45 minutes . . . I cannot see why he could not refrain from speech during the National Anthem. I do not think that his 'aside' to his neighbour could have been of vital importance. In conclusion, sir, I feel that charges of ill-mannered and irresponsible behaviour levelled with a nauseating and monotonous regularity at the students of this university will be better founded when charges of disrespectful behaviour cannot be levelled at our so-called administrators."

Here again was a strong field of contenders, but not nearly as strong as in the previous election.

Peter (later Sir Peter) Ustinov, playwright, actor, director, writer, and entertainer. Ustinov said he was surprised and delighted to get as many votes as he did (see below). If he had been a student, he said, he would have voted for Smith – "a local figure of high standing". Ustinov was to stand again, in 1963, and was to be twice Rector of Dundee University and Chancellor of Durham University.

Barbara Kelly, actress and entertainer, was famous for her appearances on a television game show, *What's My Line?* She and her husband, Bernard Braden, were a golden couple of television during the 1950s. Their programmes included *Breakfast with Braden, Bedtime with Braden,* and *On the Braden Beat.*

Barbara Kelly's invitation to stand came from people in the Faculty of Science and she replied appropriately:

> I spent three years in Chemistry and it was finally decided to give me a final examination consisting of one question. I was asked to give the formula for sulphuric acid, and my answer was 'I don't know.' The examiners decided that this answer was substantially correct in that I really didn't know, so everyone was happy. They got rid of me from chemistry and discouraged me from carrying on. As for physics, I'm dead against them, preferring to let nature take its course.

She also said in her letter of acceptance: "I am considered sweet tempered, with lots of character, most of it weak."

Kenneth More, actor, by the time of the election had appeared in several well-regarded plays and in films such as *No Highway, Genevieve,* and *Doctor in the House.* He was named Best British Actor in the BAFTA film awards of 1954. His career was to continue to flourish and he was awarded the CBE in 1970. One of the painted slogans put up by his supporters simply said: "Ken More," which is a good exhortation, in the Scots tongue, to Scottish students.

General Sir Colin Barber KBE, CB, DSO joined the Cameron Highlanders in 1916 and served in France. When the First World War finished he served in India for twelve years. The Second World War took him back to France. He was, when the election came, the General Officer, Scottish Command, and Governor of Edinburgh Castle. He was a good golfer and shot and, being just under 6 feet 9 inches tall, was nicknamed 'Tiny'.

Supporters of Smith carried their campaign almost to Barber's stronghold. They crept at night onto the grassy slopes below the castle and planted forty-eight giant candles there. The candles, lit at eleven o'clock at night, spelled out "Syd" in letters 15 feet high. The message burned for an hour and could be seen from all along Princes Street, until police were called and put the candles out.

Barber's forces painted slogans at the Old Quad, saying Barber's the Gen Kid, Barber's Good for You (a play on the slogan Guinness is Good for You), and Good Mornings Begin with Barber (a play on the slogan Good Mornings Begin with Gillette.)

Smith's people fixed a huge campaign slogan onto the highest point of Salisbury Crags in Holyrood Park. Whoever did it was lowered by ropes from the top of the Crags and bored four spikes into the rock, 12 feet down. The spikes held a white sheet with "Syd" in red letters 9 feet high. It was a custom over many generations to put posters and placards in the most inaccessible positions.

The result of the election was: Smith 1097 votes; Ustinov, 739; Kelly, 402; Barber, 378; and More, 95. Smith's supporters held a celebratory dinner for him in the Wee Windaes restaurant on High Street. Toasts were made to the Rector, the returning officers, the university, the Sydney Smith Society, and the chairman of the society. It was said to have been a most convivial event.

Smith has been described as a burly, cheerful man who had great charm and who disliked humbug. He was a natural academic politician. Smith was born in New Zealand; both his parents were British immigrants. He qualified as a pharmacist in New Zealand when he was twenty-three, began to study medicine, and finished his medical studies at Edinburgh. He returned to New Zealand for a while, taught and practised forensic medicine in Egypt for eleven years, and returned to his old university as a professor. He wrote a standard textbook on forensic medicine and his reminiscences, *Mostly Murder*. Smith was often in conflict with the established experts in forensic medicine, such as Sir Bernard Spilsbury, who until then had been unchallenged.

Smith was an expert witness in many notable trials, such as the Ruxton case. Dr Buck Ruxton of Lancaster had strangled his wife in a fit of jealousy and killed their young nursemaid to prevent her seeing the body. He dispersed the remains in countryside near Moffat, Dumfriesshire, some in a ravine. The bodies were badly mutilated but Smith was able to identify the victims. This case aroused enormous public interest. Ruxton was hanged in 1936, although 10,000 people signed a petition for clemency.

Scotland has produced many great forensic scientists. They include James Marsh, the first person to use toxicology in a jury trial (it was a case of arsenic poisoning); Robert Christison (see pages 20-21 and 31-3), for fifty years a professor at Edinburgh University; Henry Faulds (1843–1930), who suggested fingerprints as an aid to detecting criminals; and John Glaister and his son, also John, who between them held the regius chair of forensic medicine at Glasgow University from 1899 to 1962.

Professor Keith Simpson, a pathologist who appeared many times in trials for murder, was of Scottish ancestry. Indeed the greatest forensic scientist of all, Sherlock Holmes, has honorary Scottish nationality. His creator, Arthur Conan Doyle, was born in Edinburgh and qualified as a doctor there. Conan Doyle based the character of Holmes on Dr Joseph Bell, who was one of his medical teachers.

ROWDYISM AT INSTALLATION SHOCKS THE ESTABLISHMENT AGAIN

Edinburgh University

JAMES ROBERTSON JUSTICE, *actor and naturalist (1905–1975).*
Elected 1957 and, most unusually, re-elected 1963.

James Robertson Justice was an actor in British comic films, especially noted for his roles in *Doctor in the House* and its sequels. His other films were *Whisky Galore, Moby Dick,* and *Scott of the Antarctic.*

The ceremony of installation after his first election was full of incident. The Duke of Edinburgh was present as Chancellor of the university; he was unused to such goings-on. The *Scottish Daily Express* said that the Duke ran a gauntlet of "tissue" paper – the *Express* really meant lavatory paper but was too genteel to use that term. The Duke smilingly kicked away a bag of flour that burst at his feet. Missiles aimed at the platform party found their targets but also hit people in the front rows. Stink bombs landed all around. The Bishop of Edinburgh, the Rt Revd Kenneth Warner, was struck on the collar by a tomato. He said: "I am running out of handkerchiefs". The royal Duke as he left the hall was sprinkled with water.

As Robertson Justice moved forward to start his address, the *Express* said, a tomato struck the lectern just beside his hand. He looked up contemptuously in the direction from which it came, and his trained bass voice cut through the din and silenced it. He sneered at them for their damp squibs, their tomatoes, and their paper throwing.

The burly, bearded rector tamed the strident students who tried to interrupt him. After getting the rough edge of his tongue a few times most of the hecklers subsided, and his speech was listened to with enthusiasm and long periods of attentive silence. One tactless interruption brought this response from him: 'How can we kill the blight of ignorance without the spray of education? And who is to administer the spray but the teachers, those heroic members of a dedicated but depressed profession, who are given nothing better than a few leaky garden syringes with which to spray the blight on 20 million orange trees'. He also said:

> . . . The mass communications industry, or at least that part of it which is run purely for private profit, squeals like a wounded hare when any . . . censorship is suggested, and it is, I am bound to admit, difficult to draw the line. But the unwarranted intrusion into private grief and the completely irresponsible pursuit of the private vendetta savours more of degeneracy and licence. How is the teacher to cope with this debauching of the public's emotions?
>
> It is the same with the great part of radio and television. We are constantly bombarded by products of an alien culture to the extent that we are in danger of forgetting that such a thing as indigenous culture ever existed in this country.

The audience's behaviour, and the far worse behaviour of Glasgow students at their own installation at about the same time,* deeply upset the university authorities. It was decided that the academics and administrators would boycott the next installation. They did not want to be associated with boisterousness, nor did they want to be targets of missiles.

James Robertson Justice in the film *Doctor in the House* and its sequels played the part of Sir Lancelot Sprat, a domineering, gruff, and exhibitionist surgeon. This fictional background ensured many votes from the medicals.

Robertson Justice (the name is sometimes hyphenated) had many interests. When Edinburgh awarded him an honorary degree the citation said he was "film star, journalist, engineer, farmer, sailor, policeman, racing motorist and bird-watcher." His entry in *Who's Who* did not mention his films but said he had had "some three score jobs in different parts of the world". His main interest was birds, especially falcons, and preserving wildlife. When he was Rector he spoke in favour of the Campaign for Nuclear Disarmament and against closures of railway lines in Scotland.

Nobody seems to know for sure where he was born – was it Dundee, or Wigtownshire, or in the north-west of Scotland, or somewhere else? He went to an English public

---

*A few days after Robertson Justice's installation, Rab Butler, the Home Secretary, was installed as Rector of Glasgow University and the behaviour of the audience was dreadful. Butler and the platform party were pelted with flour bombs, tomatoes, lavatory paper, and eggs and squirted with foam from fire extinguishers. A flying cabbage knocked out a press photographer. The speech was drowned by uproar. Many dignitaries walked off the platform. Butler stood and took it – nobody knew why he did not walk off too. Newspapers all over Britain and all round the world carried the story and photographs. The university was shamed. The Principal, Sir Hector Hetherington, said that graduates of Glasgow might find it hard to get jobs.

school and Bonn University where he took a doctorate in natural science. His family hoped he would enter the diplomatic service but he became a journalist with Reuters, the news agency. He served with the International Brigade in the Spanish Civil War and in the Royal Navy during the Second World War. He was a Labour candidate for Parliament in 1950 but was defeated.

The way Robertson Justice started in acting was very like one of the enduring legends of the theatre. He was occasionally a chairman of music hall shows at the Players' Theatre Club, London, where amateurs and resting actors perform. He was noticed there by a film director in 1944 and was given his first part – a small one but the beginning of a big career. Of impressive and unmistakeable appearance, after his role in *Doctor in the House* he tended to be type-cast.

The first term, 1957–1960

This was the biggest field ever. Robertson Justice was opposed by no fewer than nine candidates.

Sir Walter Mercer, medical man, was strongly backed by the medical students. Mercer went to school at George Watson's College in Edinburgh, studied at Edinburgh University, became professor of orthopaedic surgery at Edinburgh in 1948, wrote the textbook *Orthopaedic Surgery* and many articles, was President of the Royal College of Surgeons of Edinburgh, served on innumerable committees, and was heaped with honours by his colleagues. In the early days of the election campaign he was strongly tipped for victory.

Sir Alexander Gray, economist and former civil servant, was professor of economics at Edinburgh from 1935 to 1956. He was also a poet and translator of poems from European languages. He wrote of Scotland: "This is my country / The land that begat me. / The windy spaces/ Are surely my own. / And those who toil here/ In the sweat of their faces/ Are flesh of my flesh/ And bone of my bone."

Bertrand Russell, philosopher, mathematician, writer, Nobel prize winner, and campaigner against nuclear weapons. He had stood in 1923 when the Conservative Prime Minister, Stanley Baldwin, won.

Malcolm Muggeridge, journalist, who was to become Rector in 1966. One of his backers was David Simpson who, with two other backers, went to meet Muggeridge off the London train at Waverley station in central Edinburgh. Mr Simpson wrote of this encounter:

> We discovered a large and hostile crowd, who had apparently gathered to express their displeasure at the tone and content of an article which Muggeridge had recently published in an American magazine. His subject was the Royal Family, and his attitude was less than wholly respectable. The extracts gleefully reported in the British Press contained criticisms so mild by modern standards that today they would pass unnoticed. Likewise, the 'hostile' crowd would in those days have probably expressed their disapproval by nothing more violent than booing.
>
> However, the police were taking no chances, and had taken Muggeridge off the train at Dunbar. They drove him to Compton Mackenzie's flat in Drummond Place where he was staying. So we went there, and spent a

thoroughly enjoyable evening listening to the conversation between these two great characters, occasionally joining in ourselves. The conversation was lubricated by copious quantities of Grant's 'Standfast', a brand of whisky then sold in a distinctive three-cornered bottle. In return for lending his name to the advertisements for the whisky, Mackenzie had been given by the distillers a generous supply.

Lionel Daiches, lawyer and broadcaster, was another contender.

Jacqueline MacKenzie, actress and presenter of travel and magazine programmes on television, worked for Border Television during the 1960s. She was also known as Jackie Forster after her marriage. She was to come out as gay in 1969 and she later worked with groups such as Lesbian Archives, the Minorities Research Group, organizations for gay medical workers and gay social workers, and the magazine *Sappho*.

Trevor Huddleston, a member of the Community of the Resurrection, missionary and campaigner against apartheid, wrote *Naught for Your Comfort*, a best-selling book on racial conflict in South Africa, published a year before this election.

Edwin Muir, poet, had also stood in 1939.

Charles Martin, the final contender, was a former chairman of the Labour Club and a student at Moray House Training College.

Voting was: Robertson Justice, 1003; Gray, 688; Mercer, 581; Russell, 550; Muggeridge, 246; Huddlestone, 160; Martin, 77; Muir, 61; Daiches, 30; and Mackenzie, 25. Daiches's nomination form was signed by 30 people and Mackenzie's by 23. Turn-out was high at 65 per cent.

The second term, 1963–1966

In the 1963 election there were four other candidates.

Julius Nyerere had been made prime minister of Tanganyika when it was granted internal self-government in 1961. Nyerere had been a student at Edinburgh University in 1949, on a Government scholarship. He was the first person from his country to study at a British university. At Edinburgh, under the influence of Fabian socialists, he developed ideas of grafting socialism on to African communalism. Nyerere was President of Tanganyika when it became a republic in 1962, and of Tanzania, formed in 1964 from the unification of Tanganyika and Zanzibar.

Nyerere, when in high office, was lionized by the liberal left of the West for his style of African socialism, but his critics accused him of being a priggish autocrat whose ideals failed to bring his people prosperity.

Peter Ustinov, playwright, actor, director, writer, and entertainer, who was to be twice Rector of Dundee University and to be Chancellor of Durham University, had also stood for the rectorship at Edinburgh in 1954.

Yehudi Menuhin, later Lord Menuhin, virtuoso violinist and educator, was another distinguished candidate.

Sean Connery, actor, was to become the most famous Scot in the world. At this time, however, he had made only one notable film, *Dr No,* in which he played James Bond for the first time. Connery came bottom of the poll. He was also defeated at St Andrews in 1967, when he was much better known.

In the voting Nyerere, Menuhin, and Connery were eliminated early from the count. Robertson Justice in the end had 1916 votes and Ustinov 1521. Ustinov had also been runner-up in 1954.

Eric Morton has written:

> My MD graduation was in the . . . McEwan Hall. This was enlivened by the presence of the actor James Robertson Justice, who was Rector at the time and who sat immediately above me in the centre of the assembled senate . . .We had a long time to wait to observe the large number of students who filed up one by one to be duly capped
>
> James Robertson Justice, impressive in his splendid rectorial gown, regularly took snuff . . . followed by a flamboyant flourish with a brightly coloured silk handkerchief. brushing off the surplus. I had plenty of time to observe his facial expressions as the students approached. He never looked exactly bored, but I noticed that every now and then his face would light up, he would smile and his eyes twinkle and it did not take long to realize that the smile occurred only when an attractive young lady graduand approached the platform. Sadly this occurrence was relatively rare, but at least observing his performance made the lengthy ceremony rather less tedious. His obvious reactions as well as his splendid appearance were in marked contrast to the sober faces of the academics who surrounded him.

Dr Morton has also written of the Rector: "He was *indeed* a character and I used to meet him in the Goat Club in New Bond Street . . . it was a perfectly respectable club, for naval officers, with an interesting history. Justice used it largely as a daytime drinking club, as did quite a few personalities in the entertainment world with no naval connections."

Clyde Reynolds has also given us an account events from this time:

> One of the more impressive failures in promoting a rectorial candidate was the attempt to place a banner across the Old Quad the night before the election. Setting out from the Dramatic Society workshops in High School Yards well after the nightly postering campaign had died down, a small band scaled the gates of the Old Quad bearing a long builder's extension ladder, a length of steel hawser, and some U-bolts, and an impressive cotton banner in support of James Robertson Justice. At four something in the morning, all was quiet as they fixed one end of the hawser high up round one of the upper pillars and began to file the existing nuts round, to deter early removal by the servitors.
>
> Having threaded on the banner, they were just raising the light lead rope to hoist the other end of the hawser up the farther pillar when the cleaners arrived; before 5 a.m., not after six as 'reliable' informants had suggested. Immediately, the cleaners woke the Bedellus, who emerged from his lodging by the main gate clad in dressing gown and slippers.
>
> The students made impassioned pleas, but were under no circumstances allowed to complete the project. The Bedellus did, though, allow them to retrieve the steel hawser and other material and leave to return the ladder to its rightful place. He did not ask their names.

JRJ hosted two celebratory breakfasts in Surgeons' Hall for his supporters. A communications breakdown resulted in the first event being supplied with no food, just crates of champagne. They were speedily consumed, someone having sent out for mutton pies and crisps. The repeat a couple of days later satisfied everyone with its lavish quality and most of the stalwarts had to be asked politely to leave before night fell.

LIBERAL PARTY LEADER OF CHARM AND IDEALS

JO GRIMOND, *later Lord Grimond, Liberal politician (1913–1993).*
Elected 1960.

Jo Grimond was leader of the Liberal Party from 1956 to 1967 and again briefly in 1976. Only five Liberals were Members of Parliament when he became leader, but during his term that number doubled. He was a smooth man, with cultured, rather upper-crust tones and a charming quiff. Many people, especially idealistic young people, idolised him as a politician with sincerity and principles. His party also attracted the protest vote against the other two.

Grimond's rectorship was notable for another outbreak of ill feeling between the students and the authorities. The students wanted the installation be held in the McEwan Hall as was the tradition. The Principal, Sir Edward Appleton, and other senior figures banned the use of the hall. They feared a repetition of the students' behaviour when James Robertson Justice, who was Grimond's predecessor, was installed. Behaviour at Robertson Justice's installation was comparatively mild but did upset academics and administrators because the Chancellor of the university, the Duke of Edinburgh, was present. On the other hand, the Duke seemed to enjoy what went on.

A serious row about the installation took place between Appleton and David Steel, Senior President of the Students' Representative Council and former President of the Liberal Club. Steel was also Grimond's campaign manager. (He was himself to become both leader of the Liberal Party and Rector of Edinburgh University.)

Professor John Mackintosh, a distinguished historian and political scientist, who was present at the row, later told Steel: "The great thing about student politics is that it teaches you how to deal with rogues and villains."

In the end the university authorities gave way over using the McEwan Hall for the installation, but the upper ranks of the university hierarchy stayed away. That kind of ill feeling broke out regularly between the university establishment and the students for years. Principal Appleton won the Nobel prize for physics in 1947 and when he was Principal gave a lot of time to his academic specialism. He left much of the ordinary administration to the Secretary of the university, Charles H. Stewart, who tended to be inflexible in his attitude to students.

Steel had a problem – would people behave properly during the election campaign and during the installation and Address?

The status of the rectorship was in danger at this time. A pro-Grimond pamphlet, almost certainly written by Steel, said in the run-up to the election:

> The big issue in this rectorial may be not the election of a Rector for the next three years but the office of Rector itself. The right to elect a Rector is a traditional and intensely democratic one, which must be jealously guarded if we are to retain it in full measure. We, the student body, must ensure in the coming campaign that nothing in our behaviour calls into disrepute the high office of Lord Rector nor antagonises university or civic authorities towards it."

David Steel told a mass meeting of students: "There is nothing particularly funny in inviting a distinguished man to be Rector and then giving him dog's abuse when he comes." He wrote a stern letter to the people who were to attend the installation. "You are advised not to wear a coat if the weather permits." (This was in February.) No coats were to be taken into the auditorium; nor were bags or briefcases: the implication was that coats or bags might be used to conceal missiles.

> Men should wear lounge suits with white shirt, collar, and tie. Dark blazer is a very suitable alternative. Stewards and servitors have strict instructions to refuse admission to anyone who is obviously unsuitably dressed (e.g. leather jacket, tartan shirt, and corduroy bags!) Women should wear appropriate dress, suit, or blazer and skirt. (Polo necked sweater and jeans are definitely out.)
>
> We in Edinburgh University have a chance to rescue rectorial ceremonies from the bad reputation which they have acquired throughout the country after deplorable behaviour at previous ceremonies at this and other universities . . .
>
> The university Court has, understandably, made it quite clear that the use of the McEwan Hall is being granted on trial. If our ceremony is a failure, marred by the actions of an irresponsible minority who will not see reason,

then future rectorial ceremonies will be simply emasculated versions in the Upper Library [an elegant hall, but a very much smaller venue] with admission only to the invited students, such as S.R.C. members. That would be quite wrong. This is not an occasion for the privileged few but a real student occasion when we welcome our elected representative.

That is always supposing that there will be another rectorial. For with the appointment of a Royal Commission on the Scottish universities still in the air and a fairly widespread feeling against the institution of the rectorship itself, this ceremony could have a major effect for or against the rectorship. If we wish to retain the democratic right unique to Scottish students to elect the chairman of the governing body of the university then we must show that we respect the office.

The ceremony went off beautifully. It was described as one of the most restrained ever to be held. Two thousand people were admitted to the hall. Stewards were ready to detain anyone going in by the wrong door or sitting anywhere except in the seat shown on his or her ticket. The stewards were told to throw out anyone behaving in an unruly way.

Leading figures in the university boycotted the ceremony. The Principal, Chancellor, members of Senatus and the Court, and others held their own little ceremony for Grimond in the Upper Library of the Old College, where Grimond was "installed" as Chairman of the university Court and as Vice-President of the General Council (the body of all the graduates). It was a snub to the students and to tradition.

This left the ceremony in the McEwan Hall short of senior figures. But the Students' Representative Council recruited sympathetic members of the academic staff, including Professor Mackintosh, to fill out the academic procession.

Grimond said in his rectorial Address. "Put five professors of science into a room [a voice: 'Shoot them'] and what do they talk about? [A voice: 'Women!'] Nuclear fission? Not a bit of it. They talk about the politics of the faculty. They gang up. They plot against the humanities." Students should not disparage politics, which was to him an integral part of human existence. "I urge you all to become politicians, Liberals preferably, but if you can't manage that even Labour or Conservative politics are better than none. I urge you because politics are important, because politics are rewarding, but, most of all, because politics are one of the greatest, most natural, and most enjoyable of human activities."

After the ceremony Grimond was chaired to the Union building, appeared there on a balcony, and went on to the Old College in a horse-drawn carriage. Ahead of him went a pipe band.

The Students' Representative Council noted that there had been no painting on university buildings during the campaign and no damage to persons. "For the first time in many years no students have been arrested by the police, or subject to disciplinary action by the university authorities. All this makes us feel that the rectorship has been given a new lease of respectable life in the eyes of the public."

Grimond's opponents in the election were Roy Thomson and Philip Noel-Baker.

Roy Thomson, later Lord Thomson of Fleet, was born in Toronto, Canada; his father, a barber, was Scottish. Thomson bought many newspapers and radio stations in Canada and the United States. He moved to Britain in the 1950s, buying *The Scotsman* in 1952.

He held interests in Scottish Television and North Sea oil. Thomson was to acquire the *Sunday Times* in 1959 and *The Times* in 1966.

His supporters denied he was a dictator in control of a vast newspaper empire and that he was interested only in making money. Nor was he narrow-minded and with some axe to grind. He was, a leaflet said, a philanthropist who had recently given a large amount of money to the university and who had founded a social and welfare centre in Lanarkshire.

"He likes success and likes to share his success with others." He gave his editors much more freedom than they had before. Thomson's backers also said: "He has sufficient business acumen and experience to advise the Court on the vast sums of money to be spent in the next few years."

Philip Noel-Baker, Labour MP, had been awarded the Nobel prize for peace the year before the election. Noel-Baker had had a brilliant academic and athletic career at Cambridge University. He was a Labour MP from 1929 to 1931 and from 1936 to 1970, Secretary of State for Air from 1946 to 1947, Secretary of State for Commonwealth Relations from 1947 to 1950, and Minister for Fuel and Power from 1950 to 1951. Noel-Baker held academic posts and wrote important books on international problems. He campaigned for peace through multilateral disarmament.

Admiral Lord Mountbatten, statesman, naval commander, cousin of the Queen, and the last Viceroy of India, declined to stand. Hastings Banda, nationalist leader in Nyasaland and later President of Malawi, also declined.

Some law students asked Charles de Gaulle, the President of France, to be a candidate "as champion of a great sister democracy". He would, they said, be an ideal representative and nothing but good could come from "this renewal of our 'ancien alliance'."

They added: "We were indeed happy to read of your success in the National Assembly this week and wish you every possible success there in the future." The letter ended: "Vive de Gaulle!" and "Vive la France!" Days of negotiation followed, involving the French consulate in Edinburgh, the Embassy in London, and the Elysee Palace. The story ran in the *Daily Mail*, the Edinburgh *Evening News*, the *Glasgow Herald*, and the news on the Scottish Television channel.

Bill McDowall, who was one of the students wanting de Gaulle, took notes at the time and has preserved them. McDowall and his colleagues asked the Students' Representative Council if a non-British person could be nominated. David Steel, as President, said he was sure a non-British person was ineligible.

In fact, Glasgow had elected Raymond Poincaré, President of France, in 1914 and St Andrews had elected Fridtjof Nansen, Norwegian explorer, biologist, patriot, and philanthropist, in 1925. The rules about rectorial elections were roughly the same for all the universities.

Steel was at that time strongly critical of the French government. He was in a tricky position. When pressed for concrete evidence that non-British people were ineligible, he referred the matter to the assistant Secretary of the university. The assistant Secretary said he saw "no barrier" to a non-British person being nominated. Mr McDowall says that no obvious rule for or against a foreign candidate was to be found but points out that Steel was organizing Grimond's candidature and would be unhappy to see a strong candidate like de Gaulle in the running. It is also possible that other students – not Steel – were against foreigners such as de Gaulle and Thomson.

Steel had another matter on his mind. The French government had in effect summoned for service in the armed forces the Vice-President of the Union Nationale des Etudiants Français, Dominique Wallon. As a student, Wallon was entitled to have his military service deferred. Steel wrote to the French Ambassador in London to protest:

It is with deep concern that I learn that your government has cancelled the legitimate military deferment of M Wallon, presumably because of his strong opposition to your government's policy in Algeria.

This Students' Representative Council has had occasion in the past to protest about the apparent connivance of your government at violations of fundamental human rights against student leaders in Algeria, but I am more profoundly disturbed to see that your country appears to have reached new depths of political degeneracy in the treatment of its own nationals by setting aside the rule of law and replacing it by arbitrary exercise of authority based on political expediency.

I must earnestly urge you, as representative of your country in Britain, to convey the revulsion of the student community here at this victimisation of a student leader in France, and ask you to make representations to the highest authority to have this decision reversed and to permit M. Wallon the normal period of military deferment.

It is not known how the French Government reacted.

The election result was Grimond 1907 votes, Thomson 847, and Noel-Baker 544.

Emeritus Professor J. Forbes Munro has recalled his time as a member of the Students' Representative Council and of the Liberal Club, which was strong at that time.

The board on which the result was published was thrown down into the Old Quad, where the announcement was made. My friends and I seized it and paraded it around town. We brandished the board outside the *Scotsman* offices on North Bridge, intent on making sure that the mouthpiece of Edinburgh's middle classes was aware of the outcome.

On the day of the installation there was a Rector's Breakfast at the Beehive Restaurant in the Grassmarket, a university dinner in the Upper Hall, and an SRC dinner and the Rectorial Ball in the men's Union – all in the space of a couple of days. At the Ball I had the pleasant task of looking after the presidents of the other SRCs in Scotland and their partners (more senior members of our SRC executive had to look after even more distinguished guests) and it was the only time in my life that I had an unlimited bar tab to be used at my discretion. Fortunately I did not go completely mad with it.

Grimond wrote in his autobiography: "[A] byproduct [*sic*] of becoming an MP was the Rectorship of two universities – Edinburgh and Aberdeen." (He was defeated at St Andrews in 1967.) Grimond had some thoughts about what a Rector's job was – it was not, in his view, his duty to be a working Rector. In any case, he, as leader of the Liberal Party and an MP, could hardly have had the time to attend to the business of the university. Grimond also had some thoughts about professors and students:

The modern world is more inclined to hand its hat to professors than to take it off in the street when it meets them. Vice-Chancellors are perpetually in committee or incommunicado . . .

Although at first sight more sophisticated, today's students are often more naive than my generation. Fewer have ever been away from home. [He spoke as a former undergraduate of Oxford University.] The battering they receive from television hardly equips them to think for themselves . . .

I usually attend[ed] the sittings of the Court of both Edinburgh and Aberdeen Universities. Appleton was the Principal when I was Rector of Edinburgh. He endeared himself to me by drawing me aside and enquiring anxiously: 'I trust you are not going to be a working Rector?' I reassured him. But I turned up two or three times a month, giving small parties as well as attending the Court. I found Edinburgh stimulating but exhausting. There was a tension about it – admirable on the whole but perhaps a strain for Rectors and some of the students.

Grimond's family was in the jute business in Dundee, a centre of the industry. He was born in St Andrews and educated at Eton and Oxford University and became a barrister. He did not, however, work for long as a barrister.

He served in the Second World War and when it ended joined the staff of the United Nations Relief and Rehabilitation Administration (UNRRA), which helped people from the newly liberated countries. Grimond moved on to work for the National Trust for Scotland but his heart does not seem to have been in that job. He had a private income and wanted to be in Parliament.

Grimond married into the ubiquitous Bonham Carter family. His wife's grandfather was Henry Asquith, the Liberal Prime Minister from 1908 to 1916.* Grimond won his parliamentary seat, Orkney and Shetland, in 1950 and, charismatic and popular, became leader of his party. Small as the Liberal Party was, it nevertheless was divided on ideological grounds. One group wanted to veer right and another to veer left. Grimond's aim was to make the Liberals a real radical alternative to the Conservatives.

Grimond's biographer Michael McManus wrote: "Taken at face value he would have been a perfect Tory. He had the right background and qualifications, a private income and the natural manners of the ruling class. Yet, as he once told John Strachey [a leading Labour politician]: 'apart from ideological differences, I knew that if I became a Tory I should always be tacking up against the wind from the right'."

One of his most noted speeches was to the Liberal Assembly in 1963: "In bygone days, commanders were taught that when in doubt, they should march their troops towards the sounds of gunfire. I intend to march my troops towards the sound of gunfire."

One commentator has written: "Jo Grimond was the Prince Charming of British politics. Intelligent and witty, extraordinarily handsome and of ample private means, he exuded effortless superiority. . . . He was also vain and lazy. True, his vanity prompted short bursts of intense activity and on form he could be a stirring orator. His laziness meant he was incapable of sustained effort."

*One of Asquith's daughters married Asquith's private secretary at No 10 Downing Street, Sir Maurice Bonham Carter, nicknamed Bongie, and one of the children of that marriage was Laura who became Grimond's wife.

RECTOR QUITS IN ROW OVER DRUGS AND SEX

MALCOLM MUGGERIDGE, *journalist and television sage (1903–1990).*
Elected 1966.

Malcolm Muggeridge was a pundit on television and radio and a well-known journalist. He was not only a celebrity but also an iconoclast, for he had encouraged, indirectly, the spirit of rebellion.

His iconoclasm was attractive to the voters at the university, but he came to reject his own early dissident ideas. He assailed the liberalism of the 1960s and condemned what he saw as the collapse of morals. He took an especially strong line on drugs, abortion, and contraception. The views that Muggeridge put forward about morals were out of touch with feelings among young people. Those who voted for him got more than they bargained for, as it turned out. He stirred up controversy over "bad" behaviour by students and resigned from the rectorship to great publicity – publicity which harmed the university. His term of office lasted less than a year

Muggeridge resigned over the issue of drugs and sex, or , to put it more circumspectly, over an article in the *Student* magazine about the taking of LSD and a call by the Students' Representative Council for the contraceptive pill to be available to students on request. The rows that followed shocked genteel Edinburgh.

Muggeridge's sermons on sex were mocked by an anonymous poem in the satirical magazine *Private Eye:*

> You are old, Father Malcolm, the young man said,
> And your hair has become very white
> And yet you incessantly talk about bed
> Do you think at your age it is right?
> In my youth said the sage, as he shook his grey locks,
> I behaved just like any young pup
> But now I am old I appear on the box
> And tell others to give it all up.

Both in his early years and in his prime, Muggeridges's private life was marked by cynicism, alcoholism, depression, and adultery. Muggeridge graduated from Cambridge University and went to India as a teacher. His early adulthood was spent in Egypt as a lecturer and in Russia, India, and London as a journalist. He was the first Western reporter to write truthfully about the sufferings of peasants under Stalin.

During the Second World War he worked for Intelligence and after it for the *Daily Telegraph.* He was editor of *Punch* from 1953 to 1957. He was a moderately successful journalist. Although he was famous for his appearances on television, he said he had no television set at home and never watched his own performances. Muggeridge as a pundit was nicknamed "Saint Mugg". He did not shrink from criticizing Winston Churchill and the royal family – criticism that was sensational in that era of deference.

As the 1960s progressed Muggeridge became more and more worried by the "permissive society". He said: "The orgasm has replaced the Cross as the focus of longing and the image of fulfillment." "Bad" behaviour by students was a wonderful chance for him to preach yet again his well-known message about sexual promiscuity.

Muggeridge announced his resignation from the rectorship at a place and on an occasion that he chose with care. The place was the pulpit of St Giles Cathedral in Edinburgh – the High Kirk of St Giles, as it is properly called (the Church of Scotland having no bishops and no cathedrals). St Giles, on the Royal Mile between the castle and Holyrood Palace, is at the heart of Scottish life. The occasion was a service to mark the beginning of the university's term. He had given a warning that his speech would be very controversial, so reporters and television cameras were there. The speech or sermon or blast against "immorality" was, as we shall see, emotional and theatrical. Muggeridge achieved his publicity.

At the beginning of his term as rector, some student activists, a closely-knit group of politically-motivated men and women, opposed him, saying Muggeridge was just a famous face from London looking for prestige and publicity. They wanted a working Rector and engineered a confrontation with him.

Muggeridge, in turn, reacted with forthrightness and flair. The other main actors in the drama were the Principal, the Students' Representative Council, the *Student* magazine, and the newspapers. Public opinion was also an influence on what went on, when, for example, the controversies spilled into the correspondence columns of *The Scotsman.* This fuss aroused resentment among the students as a whole. The president of the Students' Representative Council accused Muggeridge of twisting the facts, throwing mud, and doing a lasting disservice to the university.

Muggeridge, before he took office, wrote to the president of the SRC: "The Rector's job, as I understand it, is to work with you and your colleagues. If ever I felt for any reason that my relations with the SRC precluded full cooperation I should at once resign . . . If the job's usefulness as providing a liaison between you and the university authorities were to be limited or precluded I should resign." This means, in plain language, that he would not automatically follow the SRC's policies. That view was to collide with the views of some activists and of the people who ran the *Student* magazine.

The drugs scandal

The article in the *Student* about LSD was written without capital letters and in type that was small and extended across a fairly wide page. Reading it is hard. It gave advice on when and how to take the drug and when not to take it. Here is an extract:

> . . . any one is justified in borrowing from the advances of pharmacology in an attempt to come to grips with his own potential. the following points of advice are basic to anyone considering such a step. educate yourself, i.e. unlearn; this is a long and painful process. books can help a great deal, especially thin ones. leary's 'the psychedelic experience' and huxley's 'doors of perception' are standard texts and clearly written. 'the psychedelic experience' is the oldest voyage in the world, and the literature is vast. read and think, unlearn, choose at least one close friend to be with; someone in who you can place complete trust. this person should preferably have had experience on inner travel – and should certainly know what sort of experiences you are likely to meet. he should not be there in any game-playing role. to be able to guide someone on their first trip demand a great deal of anyone – and few people are able satisfactorily to meet this demand.

And so on.

This article provoked outrage. The Rector said:

> When I taught at the Egyptian University in Cairo in the late 20s it was taken for granted, by one and all, Egyptians and Europeans, Leftists and Rightists, young and old alike, that hashish was an unmitigated blight, affecting, particularly, students and the professional classes. In the classrooms it was perfectly obvious who were the addicts; they were useless academically and in every other way – bemused, hopeless figures for whom one could do nothing . . .
>
> We were capable of every absurdity from Lenin to D. H. Lawrence worship, but a plea for freely accessible hashish would have been greeted with universal derision. Anyone advocating the legalisation of hashish would have been put in a padded cell. Yet precisely this has happened . . . To me, it is as if the B.M.A. should recommend reviving Indian suttee or binding up female feet in the old Chinese style, or Royal Academicians break off their deliberations to advocate female circumcision, or the licensing of African witchdoctors to practise in the Home Counties . . .
>
> The CIA may well have thought it worthwhile to promote acid-head propaganda along with their cultural activities. Minds bemused with LSD and pot are unlikely to think too much about Viet Nam or racial matters; every trip away from reality is an aid to brain-washing.

The Principal, Professor Michael Swann, wrote an open letter to the students, saying in part:

> I don't suppose anyone objects to the law where hard drugs such as heroin are concerned . . . Nor, when they have read what my colleagues in the Medical Faculty have to say about the true facts of LSD, do I imagine that anyone will think that this particular drug should become a free for all . . . Some people imagine that drugs can give them a heightened consciousness, and somehow make life more significant.

But a chemical, he said, could not impart into one's brain something that was not there before. The drugs shuffled around the connections of the immensely complicated machinery inside our heads:

> But shuffling round the connections, even of an ordinary wireless [i.e. a radio] set does not, alas turn it into a hi-fi, and at best it will produce only distortions and whistles.

The executive committee of the Students' Representative Council, publisher of the *Student* magazine, suspended the editor, Anna Coote (when she left the university she took up a career in mainstream journalism).

Muggeridge spoke to a crowded meeting in the university Union. He would resign, he said, if the students backed legalization of drugs. "This is an issue, which if it were to be the case that I felt a majority of students in this university really were in favour of what would seem to me to be a completely monstrous change, then I would feel it impossible to go on representing you. It would be something that I could not possibly tolerate or stomach. I would regard it as a piece of sheer insanity."

Stephen Morrison, the Students' Representative Council's director of publications (and later a senior executive in television), said that the students felt their Rector was a reactionary and not an independent thinker. He called a meeting of the whole Students' Representative Council, which reinstated the *Student*'s editor.

The sex scandal

The next row was over a motion passed by the Students' Representative Council saying: "That this Council believes that the Student Health Service should make it its policy to provide information concerning the contraceptive Pill and the Pill itself, if requested by any student." Again, the reaction was one of shock and outrage. Muggeridge told a packed audience in the university Union: "I would say myself that people who are going to be promiscuous should have as many birth pills as they will accept. I think it is most unfortunate if the promiscuous produce children – for the children particularly."

He quoted one of the Beatitudes: "Blessed are the pure in heart, for they shall see God," and he added: "In that Beatitude there lies infinitely more promise than could possibly be provided by the fantasies of narcotics or erotics." He was later to add that the pill might well prove more destructive to civilization than the H-bomb and that widespread use of contraception was calculated to lead to mental disturbance and moral confusion.

John Kidd, a member of the City Council, described Edinburgh University students as sluts and said pill-happy students were supporting prostitution. Some students from the Divinity Faculty at New College spoke out. "We personally agree with the declared view of the Church of Scotland that sex outside marriage is wrong . . . the security of marriage is based on . . . an exclusive sexual relationship." Pre-marital intercourse lowered the Christian view of marriage and invited instability, they said.

The Student Representative Council's stance was soon rather undermined. Doctors from the Student Health Service said the SRC's call implied that the Student Health Service had refused to see patients who came from advice on birth control. "This is NOT the case, and rarely a day passes without one or more students coming to see us about this matter. In each case advice is given after careful consideration of that individual's health and need. In a number of cases the Pill is prescribed." They said that no doctor would accept a direction from any authority that he was obliged to prescribe the pill.

Soon afterwards a clinic giving advice on contraception to unmarried people was opened in the city. In any case a woman who was refused contraception by the Student Health Service was free to register instead with a general practitioner.

Muggeridge decides to quit

The next issue of the *Student* challenged Muggeridge to support the Students' Representative Council's demand about contraceptive pills, telling him:

> We believe the motion [by the SRC] is an example of the new progressive spirit. And we welcome it. We welcome it because, like yourself, we regard this whole subject as a sordid one. We do so, however, for different reasons. We see the sordid elements as the back-street abortions, the unwanted children, the failure in examinations, the mental illnesses, and the righteous interfering moral hyenas."

The *Student* specifically told the Rector:

> You have . . . a moral responsibility to the students you have been elected to represent. This entails a duty to present an official student view no matter how violently you disagree with it. You will remember that you stated in the Union on your last visit that you would resign if you disagreed with any view that the Students' Council asked you to put it forward. You said that you would resign and stand for re-election to see if your views were contrary to those just of an 'energetic minority' of the majority of Edinburgh students. You also stated that the Pill was as disastrous to society as the Bomb. We ask you, our Rector, do you agree with the Students' Council motion? OR WILL YOU RESIGN?

Above the article was a caricature, showing Muggeridge's face as a skull. Some people thought the caricature was excessive and repellent.

A week after the publication, the president of the Students' Representative Council, Nick Chalmers, distanced the SRC from the articles in the *Student*, writing: "The SRC's request was in no way a demand for sexual licence. The SRC's feelings on casual lust are the same as Mr Muggeridge's. The SRC feels that decisions relating to sexual behaviour have been, and always will be, a matter for responsible individual choice." The SRC, he said, had asked the Rector or his Assessor to transmit to the university Court a decision of the SRC. "The SRC has never asked the Rector or his Assessor to endorse or approve of this request."

The President went on: "The SRC has made it very clear to Mr Muggeridge that the newspaper *Student* represents only the views of those that write it." So far, so good. But Chalmers went on:

He [Muggeridge] has consistently ignored this fact, as he has ignored the SRC's outright condemnation of the newspaper's expressed views on drugs. Instead, he has chosen to paint a picture of student leaders clamouring for sensual debauch. He must know that this picture is blatantly untrue.

The SRC is involved in a dispute with a master propagandist on his own grounds. Mr Muggeridge has chosen to throw mud, and undoubtedly some of it will stick. However, the SRC feels that by his masterly misrepresentation of the issues involved, Mr Muggeridge . . . has done a lasting disservice to Edinburgh University and to the students who elected him as their Rector.

Muggeridge was "nursing his wrath". The Principal held a dinner for about twenty people the night before the service was to be held in St Giles; sitting beside Muggeridge at the dinner was Vice-Principal John (later Sir John) Crofton.

Sir John recalled later:

I was astonished to find that all he could talk about was the wickedness of Edinburgh students, their primary interest in sex and drugs, their general absence of morality. Nothing about student militancy. It was all about marijuana, heroin, and condoms. Of course I was deeply shocked at such misrepresentation. I came back as hard as I could on the students' side.

If I remember there was general discussion after dinner, with Malcolm playing the same old record stuck in the same old groove. He was quite impervious to other views. Was this genuine or was it a guileful plot to gain publicity? I suspect that it was, consciously or unconsciously, the latter.

The whole matter boiled over when Muggeridge gave the sermon at the service at St Giles.* He told a packed congregation:

The students here in this university, as in other universities, are the ultimate beneficiaries under our welfare system. They are supposed to be the spearhead of progress, flattered and paid for by their admiring seniors, an elite who will happily and audaciously carry the torch of progress into the glorious future opening before them.

Now, speaking for myself, there is practically nothing they could do in a mood of rebelliousness or refusal to accept the ways and values of our run-down, spiritually impoverished way of life, for which I shouldn't feel some degree of sympathy, or at any rate understanding. Yet, how infinitely sad; how, in a macabre sort of way, funny that the form their insubordination takes should be a demand for pot and pills; for the most tenth-rate sort of escapism and self-indulgence ever known . . . The resort of any old, slobbering debauchee anywhere in the world at any time – dope and bed.

The feeling aroused in me by this, I have to confess, is not so much disapproval as contempt, and this, as you may imagine, makes it difficult, in fact impossible, for me as Rector to fulfil my functions.

Muggeridge later added, in an interview with a journalist: "The whole university system, both here and in the United States, is in a most appalling mess. It would be better to send any would-be student to Europe – Germany or France – so that they can learn a

---

*The text of the address in St Giles was published as a sixteen-page pamphlet by the Church of Scotland and sold 23,000 copies. The address was also sold on audiotape.

few languages . . . If a girl in this country goes to university and does not comply with this sex thing she thinks she is a failure." And he said in a television interview : "The main requirement for a candidate [as Rector] is that he should ceaselessly, foolishly, obscenely, flatter the students."

After the resignation, Fr Anthony Ross, chaplain to the university and future Rector, said that the problems of students ought to be met by counsel and constant work, not by gestures from uninformed absentees.

Principal Swann came out strongly in support of Muggeridge. The Principal described the article in *Student* as "nauseatingly disgusting" and said that he found it difficult to contain his anger. "That two students at this university should so treat a distinguished man, duly elected by the student body as their rector, I find deeply disturbing." He named the students: Morrison and Coote.

The Principal said that when the "vast clouds of smoke" that obscured everything had drifted away:

> . . . there will be rather a lot of damage, and everyone, the just as well as the unjust, is liable to be more than a little blackened. And let there be no doubt about it, there is quite a lot of damage, and a lot of people are looking decidedly off-white. I can even put a cash figure on the damage, for amidst the avalanche of letters we have received are a few cancelling gifts or legacies promised to the university. Well! . . . the new mixed Union and more student flats will just have to wait a bit longer. [The Principal talked about a cash figure but did not give it.]
>
> Worse than the damage to our purse is the damage to our reputation, and this I dare say you can estimate as well as I can. If more than the tiniest handful take or have ever taken drugs, I should be surprised – and I speak with some inside knowledge here. And I am equally sure that casual sexual intercourse is far less widespread among students than the general public imagines, or than many students, for a variety of reasons, would like to pretend . . .
>
> Why then, you may well ask, did Muggeridge imply that Edinburgh was one vast heaving mass of 'dope and bed'?

The answer, Principal Swann said, lay in the full context of Muggeridge's address in St Giles's. Muggeridge had said that the demands by the Students' Representative Council and the *Student* magazine were not for truth, or beauty, or anything like that, but for "pot and Pills." "Muggeridge, in short, was right – and if the student body don't want to be thought in favour of 'pot and Pills' they have got to say so much more loudly, clearly, and vigorously than they have done. By resigning, Muggeridge simply forced these issues to everybody's attention." The Principal ignored the SRC's distancing itself from the articles that appeared in *Student* and he ignored the SRC's condemnation of casual lust.

A few months after Muggeridge resigned, Swann said in a speech: "From time to time throughout the session, we have been troubled by this journal [*Student*], for which comment has been quite indubitably free but for which facts have by no means always been sacred." He said the article on LSD got the dose five to ten times too high. "We are fortunate that no one was foolish enough to take this advice, or *Student* might have had a permanent psychosis, if not a death, on its conscience."

Backing for Muggeridge also came from the Church of Scotland's moral welfare committee, which said it hoped that Muggeridge's outspoken declaration of his moral convictions would encourage other laymen when they had the opportunity to uphold the highest Christian standards of behaviour. *The Scotsman* published many letters saying that the SRC and *Student* were not representative of the student body as a whole. Some of the adjectives used in the letters to describe the SRC and *Student* were 'arrogant', 'irresponsible', 'incapable', 'bureaucratic', and 'absurd'. The whole episode was remembered at the university for many years.

The election

Muggeridge had three opponents in the election.

John P. Mackintosh, Labour MP for Berwick and East Lothian, who also stood in 1971 (see page 173).

Lord Birsay, who was chairman of the Scottish Land Court, a judgeship which carried the status and title of a law lord.

Quintin Hogg, Conservative MP, had held many ministerial offices, including First Lord of the Admiralty, Minister for Education, Minister for Science and Technology, and Secretary of State for Education and Science. He had also been chairman of the Conservative Party.

He renounced his hereditary peerage of Viscount Hailsham in 1963 so that he could be a candidate for the leadership of the party but the job (and the prime ministership in the future) went to Alec Douglas-Home. He was to become a life peer in 1970, returning to his old nomenclature of Lord Hailsham.

Muggeridge was the first successful candidate to be famous through television. The voting was clear for Muggeridge, but the other candidates all polled well. Muggeridge received 1689 votes; Mackintosh 1152; Birsay 1096; and Hogg 1014. Muggeridge took just over 34 per cent of the votes.

The installation

Muggeridge's Address had some passages that probably surprised his academic audience.

> I belong to what is a tiny minority who look with utter scepticism on the assumptions commonly made as to the beneficial consequences which will automatically flow from more expenditure on education, continuing expansion of universities, raising of the school age and other proposed developments aimed at keeping more and more school children and students at educational institutions for longer and longer.
>
> If one ventures to point out that places like California, where more is spent on education per head of population than anywhere else in the world, are also famous in literature and in life for crimes of violence, moral depravity of every kind, and a high rate of lunacy, even by twentieth-century standards, one lays oneself open to a charge of obscurantism, if not downright Fascism.

PROTEST, STRIFE, AND REBELLION ON CAMPUS

Edinburgh University

KENNETH ALLSOP, *journalist (1920–1973). Elected 1968.*

Students, especially in Paris, were clamouring for revolution in 1968, the year Allsop was chosen. They were against the capitalist system, American action in Vietnam, compulsory military service in the United States, and traditional authority in general.

Paris was torn by demonstrators seeking to bring down de Gaulle and the old regime that he represented. Young people rioted at the Democratic Party convention in Chicago; the police attacked them with batons and tear gas. Workers in Prague took to the streets in the struggle against the Communist regime. Five buildings at Columbia University, New York, were occupied, the President's office there was ransacked, and the Dean of College held prisoner for twenty-four hours. The most dramatic episode in Britain was when thousands of protestors besieged the United States Embassy in Grosvenor Square, London.

Demonstrations and sit-ins were held at the London School of Economics, North London Polytechnic, Essex University, and other British universities and colleges. Emissaries of revolution travelled from campus to campus. Posters of Fidel Castro and Che Guevara decorated the walls of students' rooms.

In Britain, feeling was especially strong against apartheid. The Springboks, the South African national rugby team, toured Britain during 1970. People all over the country protested wherever the Springboks were playing. Edinburgh students put on a big demonstration at Murrayfield, the national rugby stadium. Edinburgh students also had a specific issue: the university's shareholdings in companies that were doing business with South Africa.

Kenneth Allsop as Rector was caught up in the controversies. And he supported the Edinburgh students' demands for a much bigger part in the government of the university, as we shall see. These were not the only issues. George Foulkes, who was a recent president of the Students' Representative Council, said the university was an "undemocratic, impersonal organism out of sympathy with the needs of present-day society." He said that, among the overstressed staff, alcoholism, psychiatric complaints, and other ills abounded; and, among students, loneliness and depersonalization.

Allsop was a noted journalist for newspapers and magazines and was famous for his appearances on television, covering current affairs. He was a supremely polished and authoritative figure, yet sympathetic. He was not simply a celebrity come from London to give a speech and disappear.

Allsop was to recall the many differences he had with the Principal, Professor Michael Swann (who was to be knighted and still later to become a life peer) over students participating in the government of the institution. Allsop said: "I thought he misread the situation in society at large. People generally are calling for more participation. His fears about student intrusion were out of harmony with my own views. Professor Swann is immensely capable, sophisticated, and likeable, but he is a man who likes to be in charge."

Swann turned in 1969 to Professor John (later Sir John) Crofton, former Dean of Medicine, and asked him to be Vice-Principal, to handle the unrest and to take a major responsibility for student affairs. Sir John later said:

> He thought a clinician like myself might be the most effective person to handle these disturbed characters . . . I liked and admired Michael.
>
> I had far more trouble with conservative colleagues than with militant students . . . SRC meetings, which occurred in the evening, at that time went on and on and on with vast numbers of speeches. The wild characters largely existed as nocturnal predators and slept during the day. Ordinary sensible students drifted away to bed. By the time the vote was taken in the early hours the nocturnal characters were liable to have a majority over the residuum of moderates.
>
> I learned from this experience and played it in reverse. When there were difficult wild students on a committee . . . I arranged the meeting for 9 a.m. The 'wildies' would seldom turn up. This was their time for coma.
>
> Of course there were lots of enormous student public meetings demanding the resignation of everyone in authority or complete abolition of all curricula – real Cultural Revolution stuff. Indeed some of them regarded

themselves as Maoists, though they didn't wave little Red Books or overtly quote Mao . . . They could, of course, be extremely offensive. Michael [Swann] – and even worse his wife Tessa, a sensitive musician – would get obscene telephone calls in the middle of the night.

Charles Stewart, Secretary of the university, told Crofton that some of the wilder students were from broken homes.

George Foulkes, who was Allsop's Assessor on the university Court, has recalled: "Swann treated Allsop with appalling disdain. He did not appreciate Allsop's fine academic ability and saw him merely as a common journalist." Sir John Crofton has written that Swann was superb at handling staff. "But to my surprise he proved poor at handling students . . . in fact he tended to be pompous with students and resistant to their aspirations. I think he must have sensed this personal lack but, with his usual skill, had decided that I could help to correct this deficiency."

An anti-apartheid group sent a petition to the university during Allsop's term of office asking the university not to invest in companies linked with apartheid. The university responded, in an extraordinary statement:

> Such suggestions sound attractive to anyone concerned about the evils of apartheid, but they are unrealistic. Most large British firms have South African subsidiaries, and virtually all British firms have some trade with South Africa, as does the Government. In the last resort, moreover, virtually all Government money comes from such industrial concerns.
>
> This suggestion, if taken seriously, therefore, would mean the university closing down the Appointments Office and the declining of all U.G.C. and most other sources of income. [The U.G.C., the University Grants Committee, distributed government money to universities.] It would also mean that students, including the signatories [to the petition], must decline their Government grants . . .
>
> The university does not have directly, or so far as it is aware indirectly, any interest in companies known to be active in the support of apartheid.

The phrase "known to be active in support of apartheid" was carefully chosen. It was equivocal. The protesters were targeting not those companies that actively supported apartheid but the companies that simply did business in South Africa.

Then came an explosion. The *Student* magazine wrote that it had a document, said to be from the university's stockbrokers, showing the university did indeed have holdings in firms that did business in South Africa; the holdings totalled £522,850. "This disclosure," said the *Student*, "follows a university Court statement drawn up by the Principal and approved by the Court" – the statement by the Court trying to imply the contrary.

A series of strong letters appeared in *The Scotsman*. Two former Rector's Assessors wrote about "unfair and damaging pressures brought to bear on the Principal and Secretary" [of the university] by the "irresponsible expression of what purports to be student opinion".

The writers said that the Rector and his Assessor appeared to act as the mouthpiece of whatever small group happened to be paramount in the Students' Representative Council. "To do so is to misunderstand the nature of their special obligation to the student body as a whole . . . At the present time their duty . . . must surely be to moderate so far as they can the unfair and damaging pressures about which such authoritative concern is being expressed. It is very much to be deplored that instead they seem intent on leading and exacerbating them."

This letter was signed by W. V. Stevens, Rector's Assessor 1952–1957, and Sir Edmund Hudson, Rector's Assessor 1961–1963.

Allsop replied:

> How generous of Sir Edmund Hudson and Mr W. V. Stevens to draw upon their experience as Rector's Assessors at the university from, respectively, seven and 17 years ago so as to instruct me upon my duties as Rector. However, they, too, must take some tuition: in tempering their language and also in verifying their information.
>
> First as to their language: I am nobody's mouthpiece, nor am I 'intent on leading and exacerbating' mischievous and malign agitation, as they imply, and they would be well advised to exercise more prudence in future about making such public allegations.
>
> So I would suggest that they are mistaken in supposing that my sensibility of student outlook is limited to being rehearsed in my attitudes by a tiny band of puppet-masters . . . While I wholeheartedly supported the SRC's insistence that the university dissociates itself from the money-making out of a base and inhuman system of exploitation, I did refuse to support their demand for the Principal's resignation, which seemed to me absurd and disproportionate . . .
>
> Actually, I was already aware, without their sermonising, that my loyalty lies with the university as a whole, which is precisely why I am at this moment acutely concerned that its reputation should appear to be contaminated by implication in squalid business dealings and by equivocation about their true nature.

He spoke of a cleverly conducted campaign by the university authorities, organized with brigadier-like strategic skill at deploying the counter-attack and spreading a smoke-screen.

In the end the university Court climbed down, in tortuous language. It declared: "The Court, by a large majority, while still firmly opposed to the political policy of apartheid, has decided in an area of admitted difficulty to apply the dividing line based on the criterion of active and direct support."

Allsop told a press conference that he had been aware of the strong feeling that either the Rector or the Assessor should be a student. There were difficulties in having a student as Assessor – lack of continuity of office, too much personal involvement in university affairs to permit objectivity, and the need for time to do the job. But Allsop said a traditional Assessor seemed too often to be "a middle-aged man rather remote from student life" and inaccessible to students, who probably did not know who he was nor how to get to him.

Allsop's Assessor, George Foulkes, was a former president of the Students' Representative Council and a former President of the Scottish Union of Students; he was thought to be the youngest Assessor, at twenty-six, ever to be appointed. Foulkes was to become a Labour MP and a Minister.

The appointment did not please everyone. Foulkes took part in an anti-apartheid protest when the Springboks team was in Edinburgh. A letter to the *Student* magazine asked if Mr Allsop was aware that his Assessor had taken part. Allsop replied that he was not aware of it. "Nor, as a matter of fact, am I aware what Mr Foulkes had for breakfast yesterday, of his opinion of Kingsley Amis's new novel, of whether or not he sympathises with the power station workers' unofficial strike, or indeed (although I would be ready to make an educated guess) how he voted at the last General Election." Allsop said that he did think that anyone holding such a position as the Assessorship "should first undergo gelding surgery."

The election

There were four other candidates in the rectorial election.

Stephen Morrison, a twenty-one-year-old student of politics at the university. He stood as a student-for-Rector candidate and claimed to have the support of student presidents from twenty universities or university colleges. He had the backing of a newly formed group of students and graduates called the Student Rector Campaign.

The group said that it wanted a non-violent step towards truer democracy, similar to electors in a Highland constituency choosing one of their own number to represent them at Westminster instead of an absentee landlord. Backing for the campaign came from Tam Dalyell MP, who was to become Rector of Edinburgh in 2003.

Morrison has been described as being very left-wing at this time, a revolutionary and rabble-rouser. He went on to a distinguished career in television.

Alastair Sim, actor, had been Rector from 1948 to 1951. This time around, "he feels strongly about the whole process of educational reform . . . he is interested in student representation. . . . Alastair Sim has a remarkably young and active mind – a belief that youth should be heard far more often than the Establishment permits."

A. S. (Alexander Sutherland) Neill was one of the greatest educationists of the twentieth century. He was born in Kingsmuir, Angus, and studied English at Edinburgh University, where he edited *Student* "and was noted as a wit, writer, and sketcher". The *Scottish Biographical Dictionary* says that his Summerhill School, which he set up in Suffolk in 1927, was:

> a co-educational progressive school which 'began as an experiment and became a demonstration'. It was an attempt to provide an education free of the authoritarian overtones of other progressive schools. He held with Freud that 'emotions are more important than intellect.' Like many progressive schools, Summerhill became a school for children, especially American children, from higher income groups. Many pupils were 'difficult,' and Neill spent a lot of time giving psychotherapy, at first called 'Private Lessons.' He was the most extreme and radical of British progressive schoolmasters and a great publicist, producing over 20 books.

Neill's manifesto reflected his views on schools. He wanted total reassessment of the education system, participation by students in the planning of courses and lectures and in all policy-making committees of the university Court, and classroom democracy – if students wished it.

Tom Hutton, a freelance writer, was a recent graduate and had as a student been active in the student community. He was a working Rector candidate. "I can regulate my time to suit myself. I am also resident in Scotland within easy reach of the capital. I feel that conservative as the students of Edinburgh undoubtedly are, they are not stupid. To have another disaster with a candidate to whom the position clearly means nothing would be to imperil the rectorship fatally."

There were non-runners. The most eminent was Alexander Dubcek, who was appointed to the top Government post in Czechoslovakia in early 1968 and brought in many liberalizing reforms, for example the abolition of censorship and an increase in freedom of speech. This was called the "Prague Spring." The Soviet Union sent its armed forces to occupy Czechoslovakia in August 1968. Dubcek was removed from his post in 1969. He was to the West a great hero. But he declined to stand for the rectorship because he did not want to get involved with the West at that time.

Others who declined to stand were Garfield Todd, the former Prime Minister of Rhodesia (Zimbabwe) and Robert Kennedy, the United States politician.

One student nominated Majid Jahangir, but the papers were not accepted. The Students' Representative Council said they were invalid because the nominee had not signed them. The nominee was a beaver at Edinburgh Zoo. Terry Windsor, one of the beaver's backers, said the beaver was hard working and had been living for longer in the city than any other candidate.

The keynote of the Allsop campaign was "Ken no Mug" – that is, Kenneth Allsop would not be the same as his predecessor, Malcolm Muggeridge, whose term of office was damaging to the university as a whole.

Allsop received 2162 votes, Hutton 967, Sim 780, Morrison 592, and Neill 387. Turnout was 58 per cent.

The new Rector's supporters welcomed him at Turnhouse Airport with a bunch of flowers and other presents. Eight girls wore long black boots, black miniskirts, white jumpers, and black floppy hats. On the hats were the letters OKA – a combination of OK and the Rector's initials.

Allsop was invested as Rector by the Duke of Edinburgh, the Chancellor of the university. The Rector spoke in his Address about the demonstrations and other political agitation in universities.

> I do not consider that rough stuff and slogan-chanting constitute good convincing argument. On the other hand, what I find almost as disturbing as the violence which many protestors readily resort to, are the hysteria and resentment too often echoing from the other side of the great divide, which now seems to be delineated at about the age of 25. I do not mean condemnation of violence alone, but the eagerness to condemn youth and fervour and indignation and concern.
>
> I am not attracted to those who march so as to bring their boots down on others' faces and who protest by howling down the opinions of the opposition. But I am equally dismayed by the increasing volume of resistance to the principle of protest from those who see it as vexing – a nuisance and irritation – or worse, as a menace to the status quo and which, therefore, should be quelled by direct force or indirect threat.

After the Address, the junior president of the Students' Representative Council spoke to the meeting. She was Sheila McKechnie, a third-year student of politics and history. Miss McKechnie was the voice of militancy and rebellion on this occasion.

She said that the Principal had referred to a "politically motivated minority" at the university – that is, the protestors. She said, however, that changes were long overdue and "if things continue in the same vein, it will not be long before we are a politically-committed majority . . . The difference between the London School of Economics and Edinburgh may not be as fundamental as many students and staff would like to believe." The London School of Economics was at the centre of militancy for left-wing students for much of 1967, 1968, and 1969. Sit-ins, "demos", and meetings of protest and defiance constantly interrupted the normal business there.

She blamed violence at the LSE on the intransigence of staff. "How long will it be before what seems to be the exception at the LSE becomes the rule at Edinburgh?"

Of behaviour at the installation, Andrew Troon of *The Scotsman* wrote:

There seems to have been some worth-while development in stink-bomb technology. They now, apparently, can be made to explode soundlessly so that you get no warning until you are enveloped in the odour.

Paper aeroplanes are smaller but more effective than heretofore, with delta-wing shapes predominant. Wise pilots made use of the thermal qualities that existed over a portion of the audience who whiled away the waiting time in song.

One flour bomb alone was seen. It was dropped from above as the Rector and Chancellor made their way out of the hall. Not a great deal of activity has been noted in flour bomb research and development since the last rectorial installation, for this one missed and wasted its self-raising properties on an empty expanse of floor.

Allsop's career began on the Slough *Observer* in 1938. He served in the RAF during the Second World War, was wounded, and lost a leg. He was constantly in pain from this. After the war he worked with newspapers again and joined Independent Television News in 1956. During his writing career he worked for the *Sunday Express,* the Press Association news agency, *Picture Post,* London *Evening Standard, Punch,* the *Daily Mail, New Statesman,* and *Observer* among others. His hobbies were ornithology and United States history and sociology. In 1973 he took his own life with an overdose of barbiturates. Some of his associates said the pain from his war wound might have overcome him. He also suffered from an excruciatingly painful complaint of the kidneys.

RECTOR CAMPAIGNS AGAINST 'ELITIST' UNIVERSITY AUTHORITIES

JONATHAN WILLS, *postgraduate student (1947–) Elected 1971.*

Jonathan Wills was a student when, in a revolutionary election, he won the rectorship, the first student to do so. As soon as he was elected he said: "This is the turning point in the campaign by students for participation in university government."

Wills said during the campaign: "What we want is the replacement of the present elitist and paternalistic system by a democratic, responsive, and responsible one . . . University government is unrepresentative. Further, we have a system in which confidentiality is used to cover up incompetence." He had one target – the university Court.

Wills has said that in his campaign he had an excellent confidential source in the administration's office. This was a person who detested the "secret, arrogant, and dictatorial ways" of the Principal, Professor Michael Swann, and of Charles Stewart, the Secretary to the university.

This Rector's term and his successor's were notable for many clashes between the Rector and the senior academics and administrators. The university was reluctant to recognize that representation of the students at high levels was inevitable; and that resistance to change only made matters worse.

Nevertheless, Wills's predecessor, Kenneth Allsop, said:

I think the concept of the Court being a crusted bastion of reaction . . . is quite wrong. The Court is a rather fluid body which has a continuous turn-over of new people, people lapsing, people coming in, so that what we have has not got the situation of a totally remote and elitist body . . .

They are not all of one mind by any means. They are a highly persuadable body. It does not, as many think, have its mind made up to resist all change.

Not a bit. In my experience the Court is very amenable to argument.

Wills, when he was a student, drew brilliant cartoons for the university magazine and was well-known on campus. Backing for his candidature came from the SRC and the *Student* magazine, which during this era was run by left-wingers. Wills was never of the far left: he was in fact the "broad left" candidate. He had been a fringe member of the International Socialists, a left-wing group, but quit. Wills saw himself as a reformist and as spokesman for his voters. He has said: "I have always been a democratic socialist."

Senior academics and senior administrators held that the only proper link between students and the Court was the Students' Representative Council. They did, however, say he could "present his personal views".

When elected, Wills said he would not take part in the usual paraphernalia of the rectorial installation and Address – no robe for the Rector and no hymns. "The Principal and his party can wear tiaras if they like."

All members of the Senate and the university Court were invited to the ceremony but hardly any went. Principal Swann was said to have another engagement. Wills said that Swann "probably felt I would be making a personal attack on him, which I wasn't." The platform party consisted only of the Rector and the President of the Students' Representative Council, Allan Drummond.

A spokesman for the university said that in some ways Wills had chosen a bad time to hold his installation and Address (a Wednesday afternoon) because Wednesday afternoons were a time for faculty meetings.

Very few students turned up either. The usual number for installations had been 2000 but this time only 400 showed. The audience was the quietest in memory. The *Student* said in an explanation: "The only notice that appeared in the University was a small announcement of an academic holiday . . . The Principal's policy was to draw as little attention as possible to an attack on his system of administration. This went to the lengths of not attending. It was up to the SRC and the Rector to publicise the event and here they failed."

The Chancellor of the university, the Duke of Edinburgh, was invited but did not attend. Buckingham Palace said: "No slight was intended. The Duke makes up his diary of engagements many months in advance and he only got three and a half weeks' notice for this installation. The invitation simply arrived too late." The Palace also said that the royals family "prefers to keep January free from official engagements" and spend that time quietly at Sandringham.

Wills told the *Scottish Daily Express*: "I think the Duke needs a rest. After all, he has just got a big pay rise so he might as well spend it enjoying himself. The Royal Family probably considers it has better things to do. I am completely indifferent to the Royal Family."

What Wills had said in his interview with the *Express* was raised at the next meeting of the university Court by Lord Cameron, a judge of the Court of Session, a former Dean of the Faculty of Advocates, and a very grand figure. Lord Cameron said that it was a most regrettable remark to make for publication.

Wills said he had made a poor joke which he regretted. But for other remarks he made no apology. To him as a republican the monarchy was irrelevant and he saw no reason why a Greek prince should be Chancellor.

He said in his rectorial Address that half the students ignored the elections for the Students' Representative Council and did not vote at rectorial elections.

> These people are the secret weapon of the administration, who represent their apathy as thoughtful dissent from radical policies. Every time a student representative puts forward a faintly radical proposal, the administration produce electoral statistics to show that the proposer has the support of only one forty-seventh of the electorate. And of course [on the Court] the co-opted members and the Principal's and the Chancellor's assessors have the support of 100 per cent of their respective electorates . . .

Wills said that most students were not conscious that the academic machine could be challenged and modified:

> They saw no prospect of change from academics who profess to be liberals or even socialists but who refuse to extend their democratic notion to their own institutions."
>
> The real power of the chair . . . is the power of obstruction. I can if I really want to get nasty and run the meetings on strictly procedural lines. In the last resort I can adjourn meetings . . . The message is simple: as long as the Court remains an undemocratic institution I will make sure it is run undemocratically in the interests of students.

He also said of the Court's membership: "For all the charm and joviality of individual members, they all seem to be in the same social and political clique. Now it may be a very nice clique and for all I know many aspiring academic politicians may have ruined their health and family life trying to enter it, but I am impertinent enough to wonder why these people are allowed to occupy these comfy leather chairs on ten Monday afternoons a year."

Wills attended his first meeting of the university Court wearing corduroy trousers, suede shoes, and a roll-neck pullover with leather patches at the elbows. He said after that meeting: "My Assessor and I had a very frank, indeed blunt, exchange of views with the other Court members." Only one thing had marred the open nature of the discussion: ". . . an unfortunate tendency of some members to speak to me as if I were a little boy. I dare say they will get used to me in time." That did not happen.

Wills has also said: "I held in great contempt Swann and Charles Stewart [the Secretary to the University] for good reasons, not least their gross personal offensiveness."

At his first meeting he put forward a series of proposals, including: "Student observers to be allowed at meetings; the Rector to be a member of the committees on staff and finance; and the Court to give up its role of hearing appeals in matters of discipline. All were turned down."

Wills as chairman

Wills was so tenacious in discussions at the Court that the Principal was moved to say early in Wills's term of office: "Each of the last two meetings, under the Rector's chairmanship, lasted for over four hours, of which more than three were taken up with student matters – largely constitutional and other contentious matters, put on the agenda, some at the very last minute, by the Rector himself."

One member of the university Court, Sir William Murrie, a retired senior civil servant, said that he could repose no confidence in Wills as a neutral chairman. He wanted important business dealt with efficiently and with despatch. So long as the Rector remained in the chair he could not see this happening.

The Court refuses full access to its politically sensitive files

Wills asked the Court to let him see certain files: he was interested in how the university was financed and in its relationships with other institutions. The files were mainly about military and industrial matters. The companies, organisations, and subjects named in the request included the Ministry of Defence, NATO, United States Advanced Research Projects Agency, United States Army and Air Force Contracts, and US Information Service. Subjects closer to home were Access to Confidential Information, Military Aid to the Community, and Unsatisfactory Students. No doubt Wills suspected that "unsatisfactory" did not refer to academic performance. But the subjects of the other files were of great interest to left-wingers.

Sir John Crofton, who was Vice-Principal from 1969–1970, has recalled that the Principal found a file labelled "Jewish students." Did this file have sensational matters? It proved to hold letters from rabbis about examinations being held on Saturdays.

Lord Cameron, a member of the Court who was to be a vigorous opponent of Wills and Wills's successor, Gordon Brown, said that members could not demand to see files and that the Rector appeared to have misconceived his powers and his functions. Other members said Wills's request "was more reminiscent of authoritarianism, dictatorship, and an atmosphere of suspicion in which neither the university nor society could flourish".

One member said that to give way would lead to "the same sort of inquisitions that were common in Nazi Germany and Stalinist Russia." Wills thought that the remark was a gross insult and has said that the person who made it later apologized "but this was not minuted of course".

Wills told the Court: "I have no intention of muck-raking through anyone's private files. I merely contend that I cannot perform efficiently as president of the Court without unrestricted access to information." He was not interested in publication of information in the files. He wanted background information. "They [the Court] have assumed that inspection is the same as publication. To suggest this is a little impertinent, and I am sick of being misrepresented deliberately."

Files, the Court decided, would not be available if they had confidential material; or if publication of them would harm third parties; or if publication would be prejudicial to individuals. The vote was twelve to two with one abstention.

The Court refuses to open up its minutes

Wills and his successor occasionally called "general meetings" of students. Wills put to the Court a motion "mandated" to him by a general meeting. That called for copies of the Court's minutes to be freely available in the university library. The Principal said that some items were essentially confidential, so that only bowdlerized minutes could be published. Bowdlerized minutes would merely shift to other areas the suspicions of those who were in any case pathologically suspicious.

General meetings gave the Rector nothing more than the "feeling" of a small spectrum of the student body and then only one which was politically active. The Principal said these motions were the negation of good government. "Mandation" was unacceptable. The Students' Representative Council was the only correct means of communication between the student body and the Court.

The principal said that the Rector had aligned himself with the most partisan general meetings, and he could no longer be regarded as an impartial chairman.

Wills challenged, at one meeting of the Court, the accuracy of the minutes of the last meeting, and produced four pages of amendments and corrections. The Court accepted only a few minor amendments; the others were dismissed as either irrelevant or not the sort of thing the Court traditionally recorded in its minutes. The Rector asked for a shorthand writer to be present at future meetings but the request was turned down.

Wills has said: "Stewart and Swann routinely concocted minutes of meetings and organised cabals to ensure that their version of the minutes was approved. That is why they refused to have a professional note-taker present."

But members of the Court spoke of their private code of personal secrecy which enabled them to speak "in a less inhibited way" than they would if verbatim records were taken and names were attached to statements.

The university's investments in 'slavery'

Campaigning against apartheid began during the previous rectorship, and was still going on. Wills acknowledged that the university had sold its shares in South African companies but added that of the 100 companies in which Edinburgh University had shares, fifty-two were "up to their armpits" in South Africa. The university should consider the morality of "investments in slavery".

Court removes students' president from its meetings

The Court was at this time allowing the president of the Students' Representative Council, Allan Drummond, to attend its meetings. But Lord Cameron wanted Drummond to be excluded. Drummond was one of a group of people who had held a sit-in at university property in support of striking miners. He gained access to the property by a ruse. Lord Cameron said his conduct was irresponsible and unworthy of his office. Sir William Murrie invited Drummond to apologize for the conduct of which he was accused, but Drummond did not do so.

The Court decided at this point to exclude Drummond; but Wills invited him to stay. Drummond declined. The minutes record: "At this point the Rector pointed out that it had been a nice little meeting. On being asked to withdraw the statement he stated that he had no intention of withdrawing it or apologising." Lord Cameron expressed his "extreme distaste for the offensive way the Rector had conducted the Court business since assuming the chair". Lord Robertson, who was another judge of the Court of Session, agreed. The Rector said he was disgusted at the "vilification" of Drummond.

The Court banned Drummond but also asked the Students' Representative Council to send another senior office-bearer in his place.

Wills wrote a report in the *Student* magazine of what went on at this meeting. Members of the Court thought that the report was misleading and in part false and that Wills had broken a promise he would keep the Court's business confidential. Three people present, including the two judges, declared that the Rector was unfit to be chairman if he did not stick to rules of confidentiality.

The minutes record that Wills said the article had been written in the heat of the situation. He hoped he would in future stick to confidentiality. Several members of Court said they believed that the Rector made up his own rules as he went along and therefore his statement was difficult to accept. Wills has also said: "I did not give any commitment to confidentiality if I did not consider it warranted by the circumstances."

'Keep out the merchant banker'

A seat on the Court was vacant: the Principal put forward the name of Ian Noble, of Noble Grossart Ltd, merchant bankers. Wills said he had nothing personal against Mr Noble, but he felt the Court had no need of merchant bankers. He wanted a delay in filling the vacancy. The Court decided to co-opt Mr Noble right away. The Rector strongly objected.

The election

There were four other candidates at the election.

John P. Mackintosh, Labour MP for Berwick and East Lothian, was a significant figure in Scotland's progress towards devolved power. He had stood in 1966. He said: that relations between the students and the Court were "in such a sorry state" only because of the Court's monolithic mishandling of crises. "After all, this is basically a benevolent university." The Court, he said, "shouldn't imagine I can be bullied or frightened". His backers said he was able to command honourable regard from the Court as well as the students. He thought a student Rector would be overwhelmed by having to cope with both academic work and the political experience of the Court.

In the rectorial election Mackintosh was supported by a mixture of people and groups: the executive committee of the Conservative Club, a former president of the Labour Club, former Rector's Assessor George Foulkes (who had been President of the Students' Representative Council and was to become an MP and a Minister), and the Union's management committee. The International Socialists said they would not take part in the campaign, as student politics were a distraction from the real struggle of the workers.

Mackintosh was an academic until he became an MP, teaching history and politics at Glasgow, Edinburgh, Ibadan (Nigeria), and Strathclyde. He produced studies of British and Nigerian politics and government. He captured the parliamentary seat of Berwick and East Lothian from the Conservatives in 1966 and resigned his professorship at Strathclyde. He later became professor of politics at Edinburgh.

Of him it has been written: "He intended to be an inspiration in the growing struggle for devolution. His premature death [in 1978] removed a major force in the Labour attempt to bridge the counter-pulls of unionism and nationalism."

William (Willie) Rushton was a well-known actor, comedian, cartoonist, broadcaster, and writer. He appeared in the television programme *That Was the Week that Was*, which satirized the "establishment". He was one of the co-founders of the satirical magazine *Private Eye*.

Paddy Dresser, another student, claimed that the whole rectorial system was lunacy, and the students should vote for the biggest lunatic (him).

Ian Simpson, a student in the Faculty of Law, was on a student-for-Rector ticket and was a Conservative; he lacked the support of the Students' Representative Council.

The final count was in favour of Wills with 2096, Mackintosh 1644, Rushton 820, Dresser 133, and Simpson 124. Turnout was 50 per cent.

Wills undertook during his election campaign to resign as Rector after a year because he was nearing the end of a PhD course (it was in geography) and did not expect to stay in the city. Wills did resign after a year.

Wills was born in Oxford and went to school in Warwick and in Lerwick, which is Shetland's capital. After he took his doctorate, he worked for Gordon Brown MP and became a local councillor in Shetland and chairman of the Shetland Labour Party. He was Labour parliamentary candidate for Orkney and Shetland at the two general elections of 1974 and in Shetland for the Scottish parliamentary election in 1999. He worked as an author, journalist, broadcaster, guide to wildlife in Shetland, crofter, and boatman. He specialized in oil, fisheries, and maritime and environmental issues.

RADICAL RECTOR BATTLES
WITH UNIVERSITY'S AUTHORITIES

GORDON BROWN, *post-graduate student (1951–). Later MP and statesman. Elected 1972.*

Gordon Brown's tenure was most extraordinary in the history of the office. He fought for radical ideals and clashed many times with leading figures among the university authorities. There were storms and earthquakes. No other Rector has ever been like him.

Brown was aged twenty-one when he was elected and was taking a PhD. He was the leader of a group of left-wingers active in the Students' Representative Council, the Labour Club, the *Student* magazine, and elsewhere. Some were on courses at the department of politics.

He brought dedication, fervour, and determination to the post. "Gordon was very charismatic," said Carol Craig, a friend of Brown in their student days who became a management psychologist. "He was very unusual, he had a lot of confidence, he was very intellectual, and he was definitely very attractive to people because he had that sense of a young man that was going places, and people used to say that he was a future leader of the Labour Party."

He especially wanted to make the university more democratic by winning a bigger say for the students and for the academic and non-academic staff. The university Court at this time, the *Student* pointed out, included a number of notables from Edinburgh life: "three company directors, two High Court [*sic*] judges, four professors, the Lord Provost of Edinburgh".

Brown's ideas and ideals clashed with the Court's traditional ways and conventional membership. This was a time of considerable student unrest and demonstrations.

Dr Jeffrey Robinson, who was present at the meetings as a member of the administrative staff, has recalled:

> Feelings of that time were typified by rumours that the university had replaced the old wooden doors at the entrance to the offices in Old College with armoured bronze glass because it was easier to take fingerprints from the latter; and that the bank of switches at the receptionist's desk controlled steel shutters which were capable of sealing off the building within seconds.

Old College appeared at that time to be populated by large numbers of blue-uniformed servitors who materialized at the slightest hint of trouble. Dr Robinson has said. "The whole place seemed to have a beleaguered air. It was against this background that Gordon Brown conducted his rectorship."

Meetings of the university Court had become lengthy, difficult, and fractious. People going to its meetings sometimes had to get through a crowd of student activists and be photographed. "Gordon Brown chaired these meetings in a way, I think, designed to make it as difficult as possible for the Court to conduct its ordinary business."

Dr Robinson cited an example:

> The Court meeting of Monday 16 April 1973 started at 2.15 and finished at 7.15. Much of the first half of the meeting was taken up by the Rector dissecting the minutes of the previous meeting and questioning the decisions recorded. This took a considerable time and was conducted against the growing and visible impatience of members (particularly, I recall, some of the lay members) but I imagine that was its purpose.

Another person who remembers this time has said: "Gordon had a high boredom threshold."

Brown knew how to get his message across to the students. The *Student* magazine when he was editor had lots of pretty girls on the cover, showing plenty of flesh. During his campaign for the rectorship, pretty girls dressed up in miniskirts and in T-shirts with the slogan "Gordon for Me", after a Scottish song about the Gordon Highlanders.

He fed information and opinion to the *Student* magazine and talked to newspapers. He issued statements and press releases. The university refused to circulate one of his press releases when he was Rector: he said it was political censorship of the "lowest and most dreadful sort".

Brown revealed what had happened at the Court's meetings, using the Court's minutes. Exasperated, the Court decided in April 1973, six months into Brown's term of office, that the minutes should record only the decisions reached, the votes cast, and the "absolute minimum of narrative necessary to put decisions in their context".

The university Court tries to eject the Rector from the chair

The Court tried to oust the Rector from the chair several times and was foiled each time. The most serious attempt was in 1973, when the proposals were:

> The chair person of the Court to be chosen by members for one year; the post of Rector's Assessor to be abolished; one non-academic member of the staff and three students to be members of the Court; no trade union official in a trade union having a formal relationship with the university to be a member.

Brown said this would have left the university's government in the hands of an oligarchy. Students signed a petition in favour of the Rector staying. Opposition to the ousting came in 1975 from the General Council of graduates, the Students' Association, the non-academic staff, the Edinburgh section of the Association of University Teachers, and the town council. Proposals to change the Rector's status would have to be approved by the Privy Council through an Order in Council, which is a form of delegated legislation. If the idea went ahead, a battle would be fought in Parliament and through the law courts.

Brown's most determined opponent on the Court was Lord ("Jock") Cameron, a judge of the Court of Session who was a candidate for the rectorship in 1951 (see page 145). Four months after Brown became Rector, Lord Cameron told the Court that the conduct of the university's business was being jeopardized by the Rector's occupation of the chair. He called for a rule to be drawn up "separating the office of Rector from the right to chair the Court". The motion was carried by twelve votes to four.

Brown said he wanted to know when and how his chairmanship had harmed the conduct of university business – for example, if he had been incompetent. He challenged the Court to say if it wanted him removed merely because of his views as a student member.

Brown wrote during his term:

> The rectorship is no more of an historical anomaly than the rest of the university's structures of government and indeed the Rector is the only member of Court who is directly elected from within the university. The rectorship was instituted in a new form in 1858 as a means of student representation. That it fell into disuse and has only recently been revived is reason for strengthening the office and not for decapitating its powers . . . It is improper for the Court when it finds the present rules do not suit its own purposes to begin to change them.

A student takes the university to law

Brown's Assessor resigned in early 1973 because he had to give more of his time to studies. Brown told the Court that he was appointing Allan Drummond to the place. Drummond had been president of the Students' Representative Council and, as president of the SRC, had sat on the Court already. But Drummond had organised and led a sit-in at university offices in protest against apartheid. Lord Cameron wanted him banned from again becoming a member. The nomination of Drummond as Assessor, said Lord Cameron, was a deliberate and calculated affront to the Court.

Brown replied that it was intolerable and foolish in the extreme not to accept his nominee. He did not believe the Court would wish to punish Drummond twice for an action "which it had conceived as a crime". He had appointed Drummond because of his unsurpassed knowledge as a student of university business.

The Court decided to reject Drummond, by ten votes to five. This meeting lasted for five hours.

Drummond took the matter to the Court of Session, claiming that the Court had acted illegally. The judge granted an interim interdict (in English law, an injunction) against the university, stopping it from keeping Drummond out.

But the judge laid down conditions. Drummond was not to be involved in disruptive activities in the precincts. Nor was he to incite other students to do so. He was not to describe in public the proceedings of the university Court or the views of any member of that Court put forward at the meetings. The university therefore won its case about "confidentiality".

"Ban universities coming from apartheid regimes"

Edinburgh University was preparing in early 1973 to be the host of the Congress of the Association of Commonwealth Universities (ACU), held every five years. Representative were to come from the University College of Rhodesia and from four English-language universities in South Africa.

Both countries had white minority rule. Brown believed that Edinburgh University, by being the host of the ACU and indirectly the host of Rhodesian and South African academics, was condoning apartheid. The Principal, Professor Michael Swann, said that the Rhodesian University College would remain a member of the association as long as Rhodesia was part of the Commonwealth; and said that South African universities were not members of the association but sent observers. "This is a gathering of liberal universities."

Brown wrote to the education ministers of Commonwealth countries, as "the elected President of the Court of Edinburgh University." He asked about the ministers' attitude to Rhodesian representation at the Conference "and your course of action if the Rhodesian invitation is not withdrawn and Rhodesia not expelled from the Association." The inference might be that the Commonwealth universities should boycott the conference in Edinburgh.

Principal Swann in his turn wrote to the education ministers saying that Brown's views were not the official views of the university. Swann also said that the Rector, in describing himself as "the elected president of the university Court," had given the wrong impression. "He may be thought of as the Principal by some countries where the Rector of the university holds an executive position."

He also said that the Rector wrote without even the Court's knowledge and without its permission. A leading figure in Scottish public life and former Rector of Glasgow University, Lord MacLeod of Fuinary (the Revd George MacLeod), wrote to *The Scotsman:* "If a Rector addresses anyone from the office of the Rector, is it really true he must have the backing of the university Court? By corollary, does the Principal of a university have the backing of the Court for every communication he may care to send from the office of the Principal?"

Brown later said that his letter to Commonwealth countries had been a request for information. The Rector was president of the Court, he said, but the letter was clearly from him and not from the Court.

The Court in the end declared it did not intend to dictate to the ACU "whom it may or may not invite to its own deliberations." The ACU's meeting went ahead.

The row about investments in South Africa

Edinburgh University, under pressure from anti-apartheid campaigners, had sold its investments in South African companies. But Brown revealed that the university still had investments in sixteen companies doing business in South Africa, including such names as Rio-Tinto Zinc, a mining conglomerate, Barclays Bank, and Reed International, a paper and publishing group. All the companies had been blacklisted by the Anti-Apartheid Movement.

About thirty people, organized by the Students' Representative Council, picketed a meeting of the Court, and called on the university to declare its policy on South African investments. A steward of the picket said: "Mostly the Court members just barged past and wouldn't even take our leaflets, let alone talk to us."

Brown wants community represented, not the city's "establishment"

Workers' power and links between the university and the community were on the minds of Brown and his friends. That was the root of another conflict. At one meeting of the Court it was proposed that two co-opted members should be re-appointed: Robert Pringle of Nuclear Electronics, a company with links to the university, and Roger Young, headmaster of George Watson's College, a boys' school. The Rector ruled their nominations were out of order.

Brown at the next meeting nominated Helen Crummy, secretary of a tenants' association, and Ray Wolff, president of the Edinburgh Trades Council. They were, he said, "genuine representatives from the community." Brown wanted to put out a press release saying that he was going to nominate Crummy and Wolff as members of the Court. The university's Secretary, Charles Stewart, told the information officer not to put out Brown's statement because, he said, the agendas and minutes of the Court were confidential. Stewart has been described as an extremely able administrator, but "a bit of a stickler".

Brown said: "It is paradoxical again that a university which purports to stand for free speech should resort to the crudest forms of censorship and secrecy - pathetic when most of what happens at Court is no more secret than the six o'clock news. "The Court believes it can silence a Rector through imposing confidentiality when it cannot get him to agree, by consensus, to what they are doing." The Court, however, decided that all of its business was confidential and backed the Secretary's vetting of the press releases.

Brown's secretary released the information directly. Brown told the Court that the university Secretary had vetted other press releases from him. Court business, he said, should be public, with minor exceptions such as the personal affairs of staff. The Court held a secret ballot of its members – most unusual. Pringle and Young were elected; both of Brown's candidates were beaten. Brown said afterwards it was rather damaging that the Court could not recognize the need for change by co-opting new members. The Court showed that it had neither the capacity nor the desire to reform itself on a more representative basis, he said.

He also said: "There are vast areas like adult education and community work where the Court draws little on expertise." The *Student* magazine wrote of "the old boy network." Brown wrote in a paper *to* the Court that the Court was so obviously balanced on the side of the influential classes in Edinburgh that that the idea of community representation had become a farce.

Academics' expenses "too high", says Rector

Brown criticized the payment of academics' expenses when they went to conferences. "If by any chance they are indispensable to the conference, then the conference organisers should pay their expenses. Fifty thousand pounds is sufficient to pay a year's salary for 10 academics or 15 manual workers." This viewpoint showed that he lacked a full knowledge of how conferences are financed and run.

The University said that the costs were 0.3 per cent of the university's budget. Members of staff were almost invariably expected to contribute towards their expenses. The Court decided that no cuts were to be made.

"Staff and students should elect the Principal"

The Prime Minister, Edward Heath, offered Swann the chairmanship of the BBC's governors in 1973, although Swann was not Heath's first choice. Swann did not hesitate to accept; the post was a glittering prize; and he disliked the hurly-burly of student activism.* He said he was astonished at the offer, but he was very ambitious and had let it be known in London that he was available for some top job.

Brown told a general meeting of students that that the choice of Swann's successor should fall on a "Left-winger," not a "Right-winger" – someone approachable, not someone remote. "It is useless to elect a Principal who is not acceptable to students and staff – because that is making for trouble." He called on students to submit nominations. "We want a student veto on the choice of the new Principal.

"If one is choosing a Principal, it is a good test of the chap that he is prepared to work with students right up to the top and accept them as fully participating members of the Court. I'd be quite happy to work with the new Principal as long as he doesn't write for the Black Papers." The Black Papers, of 1969–1970, were radical right-wing commentaries on education. Swann contributed to them.

The Rector and his Assessor produced a long paper about the role of the Principal. It was frank in some passages. "Principals should be free to return to their studies without being bound to administrative responsibilities for life. . . Since there is no provision, financial or otherwise, for a Principal to return to his studies, the tendency is for younger academics not to be interested in the job." The memorandum suggested a fixed term, perhaps five or seven years. "There is, it seems to us, a fairly clear argument for *election* of

---

*He was to spend seven years at the BBC and they were counted successful. Swann became Provost of Oriel College, Oxford, in 1980 but resigned after a year: he was used to important public affairs and found college life detailed, narrow, and dull. The college in its turn did not like the amount of time he spent on outside interests. He became a life peer in 1981 and went on to hold many public posts. Swann was a biologist of great distinction but gave up that work in the early 1960s.

future Principals, jointly by the staff and students of the university." The town council and the graduates should also have a voice.**

The election

Brown said in his campaigning that the key issues were the size of grants and fees, facilities, and housing. He said he wanted the university Court to discuss the broad issues of policy so that "a clear picture of the university's role in the community could be formulated." He also campaigned on students' rights and for greater democracy. Brown's opponent for the rectorship was Sir Fred Catherwood, who was perceived as an "establishment" figure: the two camps were very far apart.

Catherwood was educated at Shrewsbury School and Cambridge University, became a chartered accountant, and held many posts in industry such as the managing directorship of British Aluminium.

He was director-general of the National Economic Development Council from 1966 to 1971. This was an umbrella organization for Government, employers, and trade unions, aiming to reconcile all three over workers' demands for rises in pay. He was to be chairman of the British Overseas Trade Board from 1975 to 1978. Catherwood was also to be a member of the European Parliament from 1984 to 1994 and its vice-President from 1989 to 1992, and President of the Evangelical Alliance from 1992. He published several books including *The Christian in Industrial Society* (1964) and *The Christian Citizen* (1969).

Catherwood said that he had a record of success in representing the views of others in top-level negotiations. He was both willing and able to bring the views of the mass of students – not just the vociferous minority – before the university Court.

He promised to put through one major reform a year. Catherwood also said that Brown would not be able to cope with the university Court's "bureaucrats". The SRC had voted in principle for a student as rector but Catherwood said that did not deter him from standing. He was not necessarily prepared to regard the Students' Representative Council as a representative body. Catherwood's backers said he would represent all students. He promised to hold polls to find out students' views on major issues and he would go to Edinburgh regularly and often. Catherwood's backers said: "Wills [the outgoing Rector] has failed."

Voting was Brown 2264, Catherwood 1308. Turnout was 38 per cent. The Principal was not pleased with the result, and stayed away from the formal announcement.

One unusual part of the run-up to the voting was a "spoil your vote" movement, a protest about the way that Brown was chosen as the "student candidate." Neither the

---

** The *Committee of Patronage*, about half a dozen people, was given the task of looking for Swann's successor. Lord Cameron, the chairman, and Charles Stewart thought that the selection and nomination should be by the committee alone. But other members disagreed. Soundings were in fact taken of senior people throughout the country. Sir John Crofton, a former Vice Principal, who was on the committee, has said: "Most of our advisers felt that the best person would be Fred Stewart, the Professor of Geology, who had been chairman of a Research Council Committee and had done a marvellous job in cooling the many prima donnas in many disciplines and actually getting things done. His wife . . . felt he could never stand the sort of student militancy to which he might be exposed and firmly turned [the job] down."

Students' Representative Council nor the *Student* magazine, it was claimed, had put across enough information about how to nominate someone for the post. The implication was that Brown, the SRC, and the *Student* had hijacked the nomination. A total of 199 votes were spoiled, or about 5.6 per cent of those cast.

Brown polled 63.4 per cent of the votes cast and 23 per cent of the whole electorate. Swann said: "There is a good deal of uncertainty among the students as to whether they want a Rector or direct student representation on the Court. They won't be allowed both by the Privy Council." The Principal at the end of Brown's term was Sir Hugh Robson, who thanked Brown for his services as chair of the Court and "recognised the dedication which he had pursued his aims". On behalf of the Court he offered Mr Brown his very best wishes for the future.

Brown and Scotland

Brown took a degree in history. When he became Rector he was working on his PhD thesis about the Scottish Labour Party; his work on that subject later led to him write a book on Jimmy Maxton, the Scottish independent socialist, "Red Clydesider", and chairman of the Independent Labour Party from 1926 to 1940.

Brown was Rector and aged twenty-four when he edited the Red Paper on Scotland, a radical tract. Scotland's problems, it said, arose from the uneven and uncontrolled development of capitalism and called for a centralized state under workers' control. The Red Paper was especially important in its support for devolution. The Labour Party in Scotland at that time detested the movement for devolution. Other topics covered by the twenty-eight contributors were the literary tradition, community democracy, and ownership of land in the Highlands where "0.1 per cent of the population own 64 per cent of the land".

After taking his doctorate he was a lecturer in Glasgow College of Technology and became a journalist and current affairs editor for Scottish Television. In 1983, he was elected MP for Dunfermline East.

ELECTORS TURN AWAY FROM THE ACTIVISTS

MAGNUS MAGNUSSON, *television personality, celebrity, and journalist (1929–). Elected 1975.*

Magnus Magnusson had been for three years a well-known face on television. His main opponent was backed by activists and left-wingers who wanted a student as Rector.

The issues were: did the electorate want another activist like the two previous rectors? Should confrontations between the Rector and the university Court be brought to an end? Should the Rector lose the right to chair the university Court?

Opinion in the electorate swung against the activists. Voting was: Magnusson 2414, Allan Drummond (the student activist candidate) 1731. Other candidates trailed. The ordinary electors seemed to have had enough of activism, but still to cherish the right of the Rector to chair the university Court.

The university "establishment" believed that the two previous holders, Jonathan Wills and Gordon Brown, had wrongly stirred up trouble, had impeded the work of the Court, and had embarrassed the university. People in the upper ranks – academics and administrators – were eager, as at many other times, to remove the Rector from the chair.

From this time, the activism of 1968–1975 was in decline. Moreover, the students had representatives on the Court, the Senate, and committees. No longer was the rectorship the rallying-point for dissent and discontent. Numbers at the university grew from 9368 in 1970–1971 to more than 20,000 at the end of the period covered by this book: the community was larger and less united than before. Students became less interested in politics and politicking, more interested in getting good degrees.

The election

Magnusson campaigned for a "moderate" approach but also endorsed some of the beliefs of the activists. His supporters said the voters should choose Magnusson if they wanted "effective SRC representation on the Court as the students' voice; an active lay chairman on the Court as the students' choice; and a three-year working Rector." Not all of these promises were delivered.

Magnusson was well briefed during the campaign. He said:

> The Court has indicated its wish to increase official student representation on the Court, and to revert to an impartial chairmanship by a chairman whose interest is not sectional but impartial; someone who would devote his attention to the interests of the university as a whole, and to the proper functioning of the Court.
>
> The Rector would therefore not be the mandated representative of the students, but the student choice of the best person to ensure that all interests in the university . . . would be heard, fairly and openly. Instead of the politics of confrontation (often, alas, manufactured) which have been such a feature of university government in recent years, there could be a new spirit of co-operation and conciliation . . .
>
> What is quite apparent from the exceptionally high attendances at campaign meetings during the last week, is that the students of Edinburgh University are well aware of the important issues at stake in this particular election. The questions I have been asked have been without exception searching and thoughtful and courteous.

Magnusson's main opponent, Allan Drummond, had been president of the Students' Representative Council, a member of the Union committee of management, and editor of *Student.* He had been Gordon Brown's Assessor on the Court for two years.

Drummond's manifesto said:

> Drummond is committed to chairing the university Court to ensure the voice of the student is heard and listened to. He sees no point in standing for Rector in order to let the present Court take away his right to be chairman.
>
> The Court already has 10 lay (i.e. non-university and uninformed) members out of 19. There should be more students, junior academic, and non-academic staff on the Court. The Students' Association says we need

five students on the Court and Allan Drummond believes that is worth nego-
tiating, without surrendering the Chair of the Court.

Drummond also said: "I believe unequivocally that we as students must be involved at
all levels, and especially at the highest level, in expressing and pressing our views about
change in the university."

During his campaign he criticized what he called the "frittering away" of money by the
university on "private residences, chauffeur-driven cars, and entertainments for senior
staff". He said: "This university is not a large private company which can treat its senior
staff like top executives, particularly when we are facing severe cutbacks in education as a
whole . . . At a time when many students are searching for accommodation the university
has got its priorities all wrong again." Students protesting about lack of places to live had
held sit-ins at three university properties.

Backing for these remarks came from the *Student*, magazine:

> The university is cutting back on library hours and nursery facilities, over-
> loading time-tables, and reducing tutorial provisions while the symbols of
> extravagance still remains [*sic*]. Consider the chauffeur-driven cars, generous
> expense accounts, lavish art centres, and high subsidies to peripheral organi-
> sations such as the University press.
>
> It is grossly unethical in an institution of Higher Education that under-
> paid sections of university staff and the teaching of students should suffer so
> that the university can maintain a lavish and decadent veneer to impress the
> outside world."

There were three other candidates.

David Steel, Liberal MP. He was president of the Students' Representative
Council in 1960–1961 and was a key figure in the election of Jo Grimond to the
Rectorship in 1960. Steel was to become Rector in 1982. He said during this
campaign:

> I do not want to see the rectorship downgraded. There is a good case for
> direct student representation on the Court, but that should not be at the
> expense of losing the right of the students themselves to elect some outside
> person to chair the Court.
>
> The university is now seeking to change the constitution in order to leave
> the Rector as merely one among several student representatives. It would be
> the end of the office as we have known it. A vote for me would be a vote to
> retain the office in its rightful position.
>
> I will appoint either a student or a recent graduate living in Edinburgh as
> my Assessor . . . I am against having as Rector distant figures with no univer-
> sity connection. The present rot in the rectorship set in with the resignation
> of Malcolm Muggeridge, and student elections were an understandable reac-
> tion to that. The time has come to set the rectorship back on an even keel.

Barry Fantoni, assistant editor of the satirical magazine *Private Eye*, said:

> When I was at art college in the late fifties I found a lot wrong. To put
> matters right I founded the first active students' union in the college's
> history, and became its president for three years . . . You won't get far by elect-
> ing a professional chairman. Your representative must do more than sit and

do nothing impartially. Nothing will be achieved through personal confrontation and attack. It's been tried and it's failed. It has failed because nothing is
ever achieved through fighting but a lot of bloody noses . . .

I think I have shown at *Private Eye* that I can address myself to urgent and
serious matters, without getting pompous.

Andrew Cruickshank, a distinguished classical actor, had also played in a popular television series set in Scotland called *Dr Finlay's Casebook,* which ran from 1962 to 1971.
His platform: "Unified control of Scottish education and the universities by a Scottish
parliament; bring Scottish universities up to the level of those on the Continent and into
the twentieth century; widen the university's horizons to make universities a focus for
Scottish community on a social and cultural basis."

Voting was: Magnusson, 2414; Drummond, 1731; Steel, 883; Fantoni, 267;
Cruickshank, 75. Turnout at 55.5 per cent, was comparatively high.

Magnusson gave his opinion about why he won and why the turnout was higher than
usual. He said the students felt that the two student rectors had achieved a great deal, but
to continue any further would be counter-productive. He denied that his success was due
to an "anti-student" vote. ("Anti-student" is a loaded phrase – it implies that he was
against student "rights".)

Magnusson also said: "In the past, to get anything done, the student rector had to use
his right to chair Court meetings as a weapon. I suggested that we build on what they
have achieved, but this time with constructive co-operation. Instead of using the chair as a
bludgeon, I will try to ensure that the kind of issues raised by Gordon Brown are given a
fair hearing in the Court."

During Magnusson's tenure, a deal was done over the status of the rectorship. The
university authorities agreed to the Rector staying in the chair. In return the Students'
Representative Council agreed that students would be banned from being Rector.* The
ban was in one sense an act of retribution. The authorities were also implying that a
student in office might be a trouble-maker. He or she could not be detached and
impartial.

Another big change was brought in during Magnusson's term. The vote in rectorial
elections was extended to all the university's staff, both academic and non-academic. This
was acceptable to left-wing students. It suited the authorities, too, for it diluted the
students' vote. The rector was given extra work, in looking after a bigger constituency.
Perhaps that extra work would divert rectors from being trouble-makers in other matters.
Robin Harper MSP, who was Rector from 2000 to 2003, said that his work as rector was
40 per cent for students and 60 per cent for staff.

The Scotsman said: "The university's student leaders have endorsed the changes. Their
current mood is one of pragmatism rather than idealism and they believe the changes will
provide them with more genuine influence in the university than could be provided by a
student Rector."

Another change was made: three students were to be allowed seats on the Court; a
fourth would attend without voting rights.

---

*The same ban was brought in at Glasgow University in 1977, after the election of John Bell, a student. Bell had
been president of the Students' Representative Council. As Rector he did not choose to chair the university Court's
meetings. He said that when he sat as an ordinary member he had more freedom of action.

Magnusson was born and brought up in Edinburgh of Icelandic parents: his father was Icelandic consul there. He was the first person to be elected who was not a British citizen. Magnusson went to Oxford University, became a journalist with the *Scottish Daily Express* and *The Scotsman,* and moved to broadcasting. His fame came from conducting a television quiz, *Mastermind,* which ran from 1972 to 1997. He also wrote books and translated Icelandic sagas (with Hermann Palsson). He was the second Rector to have made his name through television, but the other, Kenneth Allsop, was the more serious journalist.

Magnusson appointed Drummond as his Assessor on the university Court, but Drummond was sitting his final law examinations at the end of that academic year and resigned after two terms. Magnusson replaced him with William Storrar, one of the students who had campaigned for him.

Magnusson chose as the theme for his rectorial Address "The pen is mightier than the sword." He said: "Together, the picture and the pen represent an overwhelming new power over the sword, either by reinforcing each other or by distorting each other. This is the danger in our new pictorial society that can confidently expect to sell a product with a pin-up without any relation to its function, worth, or value."

It was later said that Magnusson did not get in touch with opinion among his constituents and that he spent a lot of time on travel for television work. An official of the Students' Association, Michael Baron, wrote: "[The Rector] has become the chief apologist for Court decisions . . . The present role of the Rector is that of the Principal's public relations man . . . If Mr Magnusson wants to leave on the same bus as Mr Muggeridge, he is standing at the right stop." (Muggeridge had upset many people on campus and resigned.)

During the next rectorial election, one of the leaflets asked: "What did Magnusson actually DO for the students and staff at University? Did he join in the campaign for improved accommodation, did he support the banning of sexist magazines from union shops, did he oppose cuts in education or social services in general, have you heard him voicing support for the low-paid NUPE [National Union of Public Employees] of the University staff? He hasn't done bloody much, has he?" This leaflet was put out by the supporters of one of the candidates in that later election, Paul Foot, Revolutionary Socialist, campaigning journalist, and member of the staff of *Private Eye.*

But a former high-ranking official of Edinburgh University has said the university authorities thought that Magnusson had been an effective rector and had helped to lay the foundations for the reasonably fruitful staff–student relations of the following decade.

DOMINICAN PRIEST AND APOSTLE
TO THE OUTCAST

Edinburgh University

ANTHONY ROSS *(1917–1993), priest and Dominican. Elected 1979.*

Father Ross was dynamic and charismatic, a scholar, a teacher, and a communicator with all sorts of people: ". . . a tremendous mobilising force in work for the homeless, nomads, the mentally ill, physically disabled, prisoners on parole, and ex-convicts; he established and galvanised institutions to give them a new hope and to confront the world with its want of charity . . . he was the apostle to the outcast."

A candidate from his religious background would in Glasgow have run into sectarianism. That did not happen in Edinburgh.

There were seven other candidates.

Ludovic (later Sir Ludovic) Kennedy was a journalist, broadcaster and writer. His wife, Moira Shearer, was Scottish and a former ballerina. Kennedy was born and brought up in

Edinburgh, studied at Oxford University, and during the Second World War served in the navy. He was prominent in current affairs programmes on BBC television and also devoted himself to defending victims of injustice. He stood for Parliament as a Liberal and wrote several books including an autobiography. He was living in Edinburgh at the time of the election.

Fran Morrison, BBC presenter and reporter, campaigned in Edinburgh for six weeks. Her slogan was "make Fran first". It was pointed out that in American slang "to make" meant something quite different.

Richard Demarco, gallery owner in Edinburgh and arts impresario, stood five times in Edinburgh, a record. He also stood twice for Rector at St Andrews.

Ron Curran was a full-time organizer for the National Union of Public Employees; he wanted equal treatment for academic and non-academic staff, real control by staff and students over teaching and assessments, less professorial power, and the setting up of departmental councils.

Campbell Barclay, BBC Scotland's industrial correspondent, who said that he would be a public relations officer for the university, mediate between the different interests there, and be a welfare officer and ombudsman.

Paul Foot, a writer for the magazine *Private Eye* and a Revolutionary Socialist, was sponsored by the Socialist Worker Society. Foot wanted "to eliminate all crap from society." Foot addressed several meetings during his campaign. His subjects were: why you should be a socialist; Shelley's vital theme of revolution against oppression (Shelley was one of Foot's interests); Toussaint L'Ouverture, black revolutionary in Saint Domingue (later named Haiti); and the politics of the press.

Willie Gallagher was an IRA member who was at the time serving a twelve-year sentence for explosives offences. He was also on hunger strike. His backers said that the evidence against him at his trial was not enough to prove him guilty and that the system of justice in Northern Ireland was flawed. They also said: "Willie Gallagher is innocent", "a vote for Willie Gallagher is a vote for a free society," and "a vote for Gallagher is a warning to the Government that a 'police state' will not be tolerated. No to repression!"

The candidates opposing Ross admitted during the campaign that, if they were not to win, they wanted Ross to do so. Ross's "manifesto" had echoes of the great debate over democracy and students' rights. "He advocates student participation in decision-making at all levels." He appointed as his Assessor Mrs Rosemary Gentleman, administrative secretary in the department of history.

Voting was as follows: Ross, 1791; Kennedy, 1670; Morrison, 694; Demarco, 379; Curran, 348; Foot, 267; Barclay, 246; Gallagher, 162. For the first time staff as well as students had the vote. Turnout was 38 per cent. The victor was chaired round the Old Quad; someone said that it must have made John Knox not merely turn but *birl* in his grave.

Ross's baptismal name was Ian; Anthony is the name he took on being ordained. He was born near Beauly, Inverness-shire, into a Highland family of Gaelic-speaking origin, and was brought up in the Free Presbyterian Church, a fundamentalist and Calvinist church. At Edinburgh University he became leader of the Scottish Nationalist students. He also studied at Oxford University. Ross converted to Roman Catholicism when he was twenty and his family cut him off financially. He entered the Dominican Order (the Order of Preachers) in 1939 and was ordained in 1945.

Ross was Roman Catholic chaplain to Edinburgh University for 16 years until 1974. He was also a chaplain to Stirling and Heriot-Watt universities.

Ross was founder of the *Innes Review*, the journal of Scottish Catholic history; and founder of the Scottish Catholic Historical Association. He was author of *Early Scottish Libraries* (with John Durkan) and of *Dominicans in Seventeenth Century Scotland*.

He worked to help the Scottish Association for the Care and Re-settlement of Offenders; Parole Board for Scotland; Edinburgh Discharged Prisoners' Aid Society; the Samaritans; and the Cyrenian Trust, which helped homeless young people. He was an accomplished speaker on television on historical, literary, sociological, and religious subjects; wrote for the Roman Catholic paper *The Tablet,* and contributed to magazines.

Ross also taught extra-mural classes at Edinburgh, Glasgow, and elsewhere, and in schools in England.

Ross when Rector was the leader of an appeal for money to help overseas students. The Government had brought in higher fees for them, to start in 1980: £2000 a year for non-science subjects, £3000 for science, and £5000 for clinical subjects. Fr Ross said: "The thought that the able scholar from overseas will in many cases now not be able to come to us to benefit from our teaching and contribute his or her own work is repugnant."

A week-long campaign was run for the same cause. A petition with several thousand signatures was sent to the Scottish Office. A debate, an exhibition, ceilidh, and lectures were held.

He was elected provincial, or head, of the British Dominicans in 1983, but at the end of the year he had several strokes. His speech was never fully restored. He died in the loving care of friends in 1993.

His obituary in *The Scotsman,* by Owen Dudley Edwards, author and reader in history at Edinburgh University, said: "He retained his impish humour, his hostility to fashion, and his love of humanity, to the end. He enabled people of all religions and none to find in God and one another love and friendship, where previously they had been alone and afraid."

STUDENT LEADER, LIBERAL PARTY LEADER, AND RECTOR

DAVID STEEL, *Liberal politician, later successively Sir David and Lord Steel (1938–) Elected 1982.*

David Steel was at this time leader of the Liberal Party. Liberals were few in the House of Commons but the party attracted independently-minded people, especially the young.

Steel was an Edinburgh person, for his school was George Watson's College there and he took a degree in arts and a degree in law at the university. When he was a student he was president of the Liberal Club and of the Students' Representative Council and ran Jo Grimond's campaign for the rectorship – Grimond was then leader of the Liberal Party.

Steel said during his own campaign for the rectorship: "At a time when education is going through such national difficulties, having a voice in parliament is a useful asset." He would be an active rector and would chair meetings of the university Court but he would not be a working Rector.

He spoke about the style of rectorship of ten years before – that is, under the ultra-active Jonathan Wills and Gordon Brown. That period, he said, had brought about positive change, and he admired the style of that time, but with improved student representation and welfare provision such an active type of rectorship had been made unnecessary.

At the hustings he was questioned about his promise to chair meetings of the university Court. How could he guarantee to attend meetings if – say – the House of Commons was having important votes? Steel admitted that he would not always be able to attend, but would "do his utmost".

How would he cope if the Liberal Party was in the next Government? He admitted he would have to resign if pressure of work became too great, but thought that was unlikely.

Steel said at the end of his period in the post: "The most satisfying thing for me has been dealing with the individual cases of students who have been unable to get grant payments from the authorities and so on." Of the "working rector" he said: "To some extent, the very extension of student representation [on the university Court] almost did the rectorship out of a job, and it would be a mistake to imagine that there is a task here to be done by the rector as someone who is plodding around on a day-to-day basis."

He was active during the university's celebrations of its 400th birthday, chairing events and promoting publicity; the administration was grateful for his presence and his keenness.

His opponents were John Deason, Marithuma Subramoney, and Willy Roe.

John Deason, an unemployed ex-docker, stood as a campaigner for "the right to work." He was a member of the Socialist Workers' Party and the Socialist Workers' Students' Organisation – both devoted to the revolutionary struggle. Their strategy was direct action, that is, the occupying of official buildings, agitation for strikes, and "challenging the rules in our society". The university at this time was having to cut costs. Deason said: "If we're going to fight cuts we've got to occupy parts of the university. Instead of working with the university administration we're going to attack them, and force them to stop any cuts going ahead . . . our anger can be shown by hitting the bureaucracy where it hurts, by occupying the Old College now." The Old College, an elegant eighteenth-century building, was mainly used for offices.

Marithumu Subramoney ("Subry"), a South African journalist and anti-apartheid campaigner, was nominated by the university section of Amnesty International. He was put under severe restrictions on his civil liberties by the South African government, and his supporters had difficulty in contacting him. A phone call was, however, set up. He said that a victory for him would be important not only for him but for many others. Glasgow University has chosen anti-apartheid campaigners: Albert Luthuli in 1962 and Winnie Mandela in 1987. They were, however, internationally famous.

Willy Roe was a former honorary secretary of the SRC and a former honorary secretary of the Scottish Union of Students. He was a member of Lothian Regional Council, and lived locally. He was a social work administrator. Roe said he would have time to be a working rector. He said that too many decisions at the university were taken behind closed doors: he advocated more access to information, more open government, and more accountability. He campaigned against the university's proposal to close its day nursery – one of a series of cuts in spending. Roe's candidature was backed by the local branch of the Association of University Teachers and by the Students' Association.

Roe was called "a bright young politician on the make, witty, articulate, and genuinely interested in the university."

Voting was Steel, 2337; Roe, 1737; Subramoney, 438; Deason, 74.

Steel had been a candidate for the rectorship of Dundee University in 1968, when the winner was Peter Ustinov, entertainer and actor. Four other people stood. Steel came last.

Steel during his term came under criticism from activists and others. It is likely that some of the criticism was from Roe's disappointed backers: Steel was of the centre and Roe was of the left.

Steel was elected to Parliament in 1965, the youngest MP at that time, and sat for Border constituencies until 1997. He sponsored the Act that reformed the laws on abortion and he was active in the campaigns against apartheid. Steel became leader of the Liberal Party in 1976. The Liberals were in an electoral pact with Labour in 1977 and 1978. He told the Liberal Assembly in 1981: "I have the good fortune to be the first Liberal leader for over half a century who is able to say to you at the end of our annual assembly: go back to your constituencies and prepare for government."

When the party merged with the Social Democratic Party in 1989, Steel declined to seek the leadership. He contested a seat in the European elections in 1989, entered the Scottish parliament as a Liberal Democrat in 1999, and in the same year became the first person to be appointed as the presiding officer of the Scottish Parliament – a historic appointment.

FOOTBALL COMMENTATOR IS THE WINNER

Edinburgh University

ARCHIE MACPHERSON *(1935–), television football commentator.*
Elected 1985.

Archie MacPherson was famous as a face on television. Moreover, his subject was Scottish football. It was this combination that defeated his opponents, who were a leading figure in the Edinburgh arts scene and two politicians – a Scottish Nationalist and a Conservative. MacPherson had also been the head of a primary school in Glasgow for three years and had taken an Open University degree in education.

The runner-up was the Scottish Nationalist and MacPherson's margin was fairly small. The Conservative did poorly – the fortunes of Conservatives in Scotland were in general decline. The figure in the arts was Richard Demarco, who had stood before; he also did poorly.

Nelson Mandela's nomination was rejected by the university authorities because, they said, he had not signed a letter of consent. His backers were angry. They pointed out that the South African Government had not allowed him to sign the document but that he had given his consent verbally. Moreover, his lawyer, who had power of attorney, had signed a letter of consent for him. The letter did not arrive in Edinburgh. Mandela's backers said that the only explanation was that the South African Government had intercepted it.

When the election came, the Mandela for Rector Campaign called on voters to write his name into the ballot paper. His supporters said that a survey they had made of 3,000 students showed 57 per cent for Mandela. His backers wanted the university to reveal the number of write-ins, but the university authorities refused.

MacPherson said after his installation and Address: "I did find it difficult to get people to take me seriously at first, to see there is a distinction between the public image of a man related to sports and broadcasting and the private man who was in the past a teacher. But it didn't take long once I had made a couple of public appearances and speeches."

His work has been praised by Dr Alex Currie, who was Secretary to the university at this time. Dr Currie said: "This was a big task for anyone, and Mr MacPherson was already a busy person. He identified with the job, was liked by the students, had good anecdotes, worked hard, and refused to let the rectorship be hijacked as it sometimes can be." This, as we shall see, was a reference to a question of sectarianism in football.

MacPherson learned to play football when a youngster in Shettleston, a working class district in Glasgow. "I learned one of the basic things of life. How to body swerve. It's served me well over the years . . . Shettleston then was a hard area, but you were always aware of a thrusting ambition among the working-class parents to see their kids get on and get out of it."

He began to commentate part-time on football for BBC Scotland and went full-time when he was thirty-four. He also wrote scripts for educational programmes.

A student journalist asked MacPherson why he wanted the post. He replied: "It would enhance my reputation, of course. Prestige." His platform in the election was that he would argue for students against further cuts and possible introduction of a loan system; present the university's case for more places and a higher grant; represent, at university committee level, bodies such as the campus trade unions and specialized pressure groups; bridge the gap between the university and the local community; and generally look after the community's and students' welfare on issues such as equipment and accommodation.

He spoke, after becoming Rector, about his popular fame and his post in the university, two contrasting areas of life. He told *The Scotsman* newspaper that both right and left, elitists and their opponents, have their own snobberies about people whose fame has come from football. "I think the Scots are a class-conscious and snobbish race, especially in sport, and a strong working-class ethic offends many people; they cannot come to terms with it in our culture. They feel it should be sealed off and set apart, at least until violence erupts on the terracing, then suddenly everyone is interested." Even within journalism, he said, sport is often not treated seriously, though in the US it attracts some of the country's most talented writers. "Yet its great strength is its popularity – which may make it a further source of suspicion."

He spoke to the Edinburgh *Evening News* on similar themes.

With this job [the rectorship] there's the credibility factor for a start. Television personalities can sometimes be easy candidates in rectorial elections. They're an easy invite. But students have had their fingers burned with them in the past and they're wiser now . . .

They've changed now in that all the candidates have to be seen and heard. It is significant that in this one Teddy Taylor [his Conservative opponent] took part in only one husting, dipped his toe in the water, then blew . . .

I went to them all. I also held meetings with groups and individuals, so I found myself being a little too apologetic about my television identity. The fitba' [football] commentator. But I believe a university needs a Rector who's a busy man in a different area. His experience on the outside, dealing with people and situations, can be very beneficial to students."

MacPherson appointed as his Assessor on the University Court another ex-footballer, Alan Gordon, who had played for both of Edinburgh's top teams, Hearts (Heart of Midlothian) and Hibs (Hibernian). "I've chosen Alan because he's a graduate of this university and he works locally. Perhaps also because I can't ever forget Hibs manager Eddie Turnbull's assessment of Alan . . . 'The trouble with you,' Eddie told him, 'is that all your brains are in your head'."

Sectarianism, an evil far stronger in Glasgow than in Edinburgh, made an appearance during MacPherson's term of office. Rangers football club were at that time said to have a policy of not signing Roman Catholic players. The issue was taken up by the Students' Association, the Students' Representative Council, and a "general meeting." They called on the Rector to sign a letter condemning Rangers' policy. This letter was to be sent to all Scottish Football League clubs, Glasgow MPs, and the Secretary of State for Scotland.

Part of it reads: "Despite their denials, Rangers do employ a sectarian signing policy. Such a policy, as well as being a black mark on the excellent international reputation of Scottish football, is both religiously and socially divisive and the ill-feeling caused by it is a potential source of crowd violence at football matches." MacPherson was firm: he said:

I have broadcast criticism of [Rangers'] apparent policy on both network television and radio on four separate occasions . . . All this is old hat to me. All kinds of people have homed in on Rangers before, and therefore I'm used to it all. It happens regularly, and there is no question that it is done with the very best of motives, but there are ways of going about it.

I think that Rangers are, at worst, an anachronism. I don't think they are spreading any moral decay, or whatever. I think you have to be very careful about how you express your attitude to any particular subject.

He did not like the manner in which the student bodies had raised the question with him. A lot of publicity had been created before proper discussion had gone on with him. "I warned against becoming involved with petitions, letters, and the like because Rangers tend to field them better than in-swinging corner kicks and in all honesty they are singularly ineffective."

There were three other candidates.

Margo MacDonald, Scottish Nationalist politician, broadcaster, journalist, and former teacher, was in favour of "working" rectors. The university's branch of the National and Local Government Union backed her. She told the electorate: "I believe security of tenure to be indivisible from academic freedom. I would seek to use the status of the rectorship to promote the case for security of tenure outside the university amongst the wide community, amongst whom my previous experience and present employment allows [*sic*] access to a very wide range of interests."

In 1973 her victory at a parliamentary by-election in Govan was a turning-point for Scottish politics. Govan, in Glasgow, had always been a Labour stronghold. She did not hold the seat for long. Ms MacDonald was deputy leader of the Scottish National Party from 1974 to 1979. She left the party in 1982 over ideological differences but was to be elected to the Scottish Parliament in 1999 as a Scottish Nationalist.

Teddy Taylor, later Sir Teddy, was Conservative Member of Parliament for an English constituency, Southend East, but it was in Glasgow that he grew up and was educated. He was prominent in student life there, being a leading member of the university Union and a skilled debater. Taylor became involved with local politics and was elected MP for Glasgow Cathcart in 1964.

He was tipped to be Secretary for Scotland in a Conservative government. In the general election of 1979 the Conservatives returned to power, but Taylor lost his seat. He found another – at Southend – in less than a year but it was too late for him to become Secretary for Scotland. He was noted in national politics for opposing British membership of the European Community.

He was standing in the rectorial election as a working Rector candidate and said he was an adamant opponent of student loans.

He was asked why he wanted to be Rector and replied: "There is something in it for me and a very big something. It would be a great honour to be a rector of a university of the standing of Edinburgh. It would give me more standing and authority in fighting the battle for higher education."

Richard Demarco, arts impresario, was a regular candidate for the rectorship. His supporters declared: "He runs a gallery . . . which embraces every aspect and facet of the art world. Everyone is welcome there and the place is constantly busy with something that's going on that's always exciting or at least bizarre. He sees art and culture as an alternative and more effective language than politics . . . He's been invited as a guest of fifteen separate countries on culture missions, many in Eastern Europe, and he's just been awarded the OBE for his services to the community. . . . He hates pompousness and preciousness and any kind of arrogance."

All the other candidates were from Glasgow; and rivalry between Glasgow and Edinburgh is a fixture in Scottish life. Demarco said: "Heaven knows what's going to happen to Edinburgh if the great and glorious institution of the University of Edinburgh is in the hands of a Glaswegian." MacPherson, both a Glaswegian and Rector of Edinburgh, said: "I often tell the story of my wee boy saying his prayers one night before I brought him through here [to Edinburgh] for the Commonwealth Games in 1970. He finished with: 'By the way . . . cheerio God . . . we're going to Edinburgh now'."

The count was: MacPherson, 2472; MacDonald, 2262; Demarco, 555; and Taylor, 326. Turnout was 35 per cent.

THE FIRST WOMAN TO ACHIEVE THE HONOUR

Edinburgh University

MURIEL GRAY, *broadcaster, journalist (1959–).*
Elected 1988.

Muriel Gray was often described as "the outspoken television presenter". She described herself as someone who talks for a living.

It has been said that Muriel Gray made her name by being opinionated, rude, passionately enthusiastic and outraged, a post-punk presenter on television programmes, with an inquisitive face and a mouthful of insults. She was twenty-nine years old when elected and was not like the usual people on the university Court – middle-aged, middle-class men from a background different to hers. She related well to other members but sometimes showed her irritation at meetings by drumming her fingers on the table.

One of the ways she helped the university was to appear at the open days that were held for school leavers. Her presence, in the words of a senior official, gave the place "street cred" and delighted the young people. She worked hard at that task and the university learned from her.

The message she gave to the young people was: if you want to get into the media, get an education first. It was a message that she put across also in her rectorial Address.

Ms Gray did not, however, always have a happy relationship with the university authorities. She spoke in a radio programme about the end of her term: "I have been in Saturday jobs where people I have worked with were more polite to me when I left. I was never said 'cheerio' to. Nobody sent me a note of congratulations when I married a year or two later, or when I later had a child." The impoliteness, she said, was astonishing.

A dinner was traditionally arranged for the departing Rector, but her secretary at the university told the authorities that the date they suggested clashed with a possible commitment to film in London. "It was never re-arranged. I had a couple of letters from some of the nicer members of the Court, thanking me for my contribution. And that was it.

"Once you have been Rector and completed it you are a complete non-person. They say: 'We have used you and got everything we can from you. Now go away and don't mention the fact that you have anything to do with this university'."

Ms Gray said that she achieved something for students in individual cases, but "absolutely nothing" in broad political terms. She said it was unfortunate in a sense that she was the first woman to be Rector. "I do not think I was a particularly sparkling one." That was a bad sort of thing to happen, because women coming later "might be tarred with the brush of not being up to the job".

She said in an interview with *Student* magazine when she was elected:

There's no getting away from it . . . the biggest dickheads in the world are students, and I can say that quite categorically because I was one – I was that dickhead . . . The middle-class students are obviously the most objectionable, the ones who sort of see it as the next step from school.

But I would fight with my life to make sure everyone in the country had the right to go on to higher education . . . Middle-class students will always end up going to university, It's the way of life. I think it is the working-class sections of society who are going to suffer in the next few years. But I imagine to the year million dot that students will always be a bit prattish.

She argued, in another interview during her tem of office, that failing to attend ceremonial engagements "is not the acid test" of being a Rector.

Those parts of Rector are a piece of piss. It is incredibly easy and pleasant to go along to the graduation ceremony, the opening ceremony, doing this and that. The hardest part of being Rector is going along to tiny playgroup openings and having a surgery like I do here. I'm dealing with staff problems and student problems . . . The job absorbs more of my life than I would say is healthy . . .

I didn't go into these elections trying to be elected. I even tried to stand down at one time in favour of [Albertina] Sisulu [a South African who was an anti-apartheid campaigner] and was morally blackmailed into it by people who wanted a working Rector, which is what I am.

Her rectorial address said:

> The child from a tower block must – not should – receive exactly the same education as the child from a mansion . . . if we carry on down the path we seem forced to take at present, I foresee a grim future – the creation of an underclass, where the sprawling big deprived housing estates of Britain will be seas of frustration, of wasted talent and ingenuity, full of those who never had the opportunity of enlightenment or joy. And all because they were born to parents without wealth . . .
>
> You must imagine I am delighted to be the first woman rector. Well to be frank, I am not. I am absolutely horrified. Since the suffragettes secured the vote for women some 70 years ago, am I alone in thinking that women in positions of power and respect have taken a remarkably long time to appear, and indeed show no signs of increasing. After all, even in this university there is yet to be a female Principal, there are yet to be an equal number of professors to men, even this platform, groaning under the weight of so many distinguished gentlemen, could do with being a great deal heavier with the weight of distinguished ladies.

She recalled her own hurt and incomprehension at being treated as a second-class citizen, "apparently through my inability to grow a moustache". Many women, and she included herself, had been forced to adopt the less attractive male mannerisms, like aggression and manipulation, in order to be taken seriously. "There's little point in cataloguing the multitude of tiny incidents, the lost opportunities, the patronisation, even the fear, that chips away at a young woman's confidence and self-esteem when being confronted with the blatant and unchecked sexism that I have encountered, and still encounter, throughout my life."

She spoke of Edinburgh University's admissions policy. Were English students gaining places at the expense of Scots? "What seems to be clear is that somewhere along the line, the successful culmination of five or six years of Scottish secondary education is being seen by some as quite simply not good enough."

The trend was to continue. By 1997, the proportion of students from Scotland was to be 42 per cent and from the rest of the United Kingdom 48 per cent; the others came from overseas.

Gray studied at Glasgow School of Art, worked as a designer, and at that time was in a rock band. A new television channel, Channel Four, started a programme about pop music. She was taken on as a presenter. Her television career was launched and she went on to present other shows. She has also had a parallel career in writing for newspapers. She was declared Columnist of the Year in the Scottish Press Awards 2001 for her work with the *Sunday Herald*.

Muriel Gray has written several "horror" novels: *The Trickster; Furnace; The Ancient;* and *Trash*. She helped to start and run a television production company. She said she "gets grumpy and miserable if she can't be up a mountain every few weeks." Another of her books is about walking and climbing: *The First Fifty – Munro-bagging without a Beard*.

There were three other candidates.

Richard Demarco was a frequent candidate for the rectorship.

Albertina Sisulu was a campaigner against apartheid. Other anti-apartheid campaigners had been chosen as Rector at Glasgow University – Albert Luthuli in 1962 and Winnie Mandela ("The Mother of the Nation") in 1987. But Sisulu did not fare well in this election.

Sisulu has been described as the "real" mother of the South African nation. She campaigned for decades against apartheid and was repeatedly imprisoned, banned, put under house arrest, or detained by the apartheid regime, and separated from her children and Walter, her husband. Walter Sisulu was the first full-time secretary of the African National Congress; he was sentenced to life imprisonment in 1964 on charges of treason and was freed in 1989.

Christopher Lipscomb was a student of biology at Heriot-Watt University in the city.

Voting was: Gray, 2358; Demarco, 1486; Sisulu, 844; Lipscomb, 175. Turnout was 30 per cent.

SINGER WITH A LEADING ROCK BAND

Edinburgh University

DONNIE MUNRO, *musician (1953–). Elected 1991.*

Donnie Munro was singer with the Scottish music group Runrig,* which was originally folk-based but which moved to a rock-oriented sound. The group had deep roots in the Gaelic-speaking world. He was probably the first Gaelic-speaking Rector.

Runrig had an almost unrivalled following in Scotland by 1987 and was successful all over the United Kingdom by 1991, when Munro was elected. It has been said that Donnie Munro was regarded by many young Scots as their spokesman.

His rivals for the post were a leading figure in Edinburgh's arts scene, a Labour MP and a writer of popular fiction. It was said that Mrs Thatcher was asked to stand but refused.

*Runrig is the name of a system of holding land in the Highlands and Islands. Dr Munro has said that the word was thought suitable because it was linked with the cultural background of the band's members. *Chambers English Dictionary* defines runrig as "single holdings made up of detached pieces: land or a share of it so held."

A survey claimed in 1993 that a vast majority of Scots believed that moral values and the behaviour of young people had declined in the previous ten years. Munro said: "I remember reading a passage about young people's declining morality and lack of respect for their parents and elders; it was written by a seventh century monk." If there had been a decline, he said, it could be blamed on social factors. "We have witnessed a diminishing of collectivist morality because of the promotion of this nonsensical notion of the individual, devoid of any intrinsic sense of corporate responsibility."

During this rectorship an old issue emerged again. The university at this time had equal numbers of students from Scotland and England, with 10 per cent from overseas. But in 1980 more than 70 per cent had been from Scotland. These figures meant that the university was being anglicized. The university said that the change came about because of an increase in applications from outside Scotland, many of the applications being from very able students. Observers said that to some extent universities take on, in the public eye, the reputation of their cities. Edinburgh's outstanding attractiveness as a city may be why Edinburgh University became so popular among young English people.

At this time a letter to the editor in *The Guardian* said that the high proportion of English students at Edinburgh and St Andrews universities "is roughly analogous to fewer than half the undergraduates at Cambridge being English and the bulk of the remainder being from the US. Would English people contemplate such a situation with equanimity? I fancy not, especially if half the faculty were also American, and many of them scarcely troubled to conceal their ignorance, indifference, or contempt for the English." It was signed by Douglas Graham of Hamilton, Lanarkshire.

The Principal, Sir David Smith, accepted that the fall in the number of Scots was dangerous to the nature of the university. He said: "We want to see the balance change." A working party, including the Rector, suggested quotas to make sure that at least half the students were from Scotland. This idea was not put into action.

Munro was the most nationalist of the candidates, not in a political sense, but as an icon of culture. He did not stand on a "political ticket" but was a prominent Labour supporter.

There were three other candidates.

Richard Demarco, impresario of the arts, was a prominent figure in the Edinburgh scene. This was Demarco's fourth attempt to be elected, and this was the time he came the closest to winning. His campaign manager said he had been campaigning vigorously in the final two days. "One more day and we would have won." When he lost the election he was visibly moved.

Iain Banks, writer, whose campaign was muted, did not appear to take his candidature very seriously: he thought that being Rector would be "a bit of a hoot". He was born in Dunfermline and he studied English at Stirling University. His output of books is prolific. He writes science fiction under the name Iain M. Banks and his fiction under the name Iain Banks. Glasgow University, announcing he was to be awarded an honourary D. Litt., described him as an ambassador for Scotland's literary culture and an original voice in Scottish fiction.

Maria Fyfe, Labour MP for Maryhill, Glasgow, and lecturer, resigned from the Labour front bench in protest against Labour's support for the Gulf war of 1990–1991.

Voting was: Munro, 1427; Demarco, 1243; Banks, 338; and Fyfe, 313.

Munro appointed as his Assessor the Revd Iain MacDonald, who was a full-time student in the Faculty of Divinity; after a year he was an assistant minister at an Edinburgh church. Mr MacDonald has said:

> I had worked with him as a member of Runrig's management team and as press officer with the band. I have always had the utmost respect for his integrity and also his work-rate so it was an easy choice to get involved in the rectorial election campaign. We teamed up again later when I was his campaign manager for a UK parliamentary election and then a Scottish parliamentary election.
>
> Donnie surprised a good many people in how good a chairman of business he turned out to be. He introduced some informality to the proceedings while retaining a bit of dignity and a business-like approach. He was excellent at bringing people into the debate and making sure that quieter voices were heard.
>
> I have no doubt that there were those who thought he'd be some out of touch rock star who could be easily marginalised but they soon discovered differently as he researched and prepared very thoroughly for meetings.
>
> The hardy annual of removing Rectors from the Court chair was raised, fought, and soundly defeated.
>
> Donnie and I met regularly with interest groups including staff and student unions, local MPs, other Rectors, Assessors, etc through the Scottish Rectors and Assessors Association.
>
> Munro helped to bring more women on to the university Court and tried to make its membership more genuinely reflective of the community it served. He also sought to recruit students from marginalized groups which had historically not produced entrants to higher education.

Dr Martin Lowe, Secretary of the university at that time, has said: "Donnie Munro was hugely liked. He was sensitive, caring, and hard working. He was gentle and humorous."

Munro received an honorary doctorate from the university in the year his term ended. His citation for the degree said:

> Runrig's music, which reflects the inspiration of language and culture, gives expression to ideas beyond the small definitions of an inward nationalism and celebrates a culture which looks outward and recognises its place in the wide fabric of true internationalism.
>
> During the rectorship he touched the lives of many in the university as patron, chairperson, or as open advocate for groups as diverse as students with special needs, AIDS sufferers and their families as well as community groups . . . and Greenpeace and Amnesty. It is as an environmental campaigner that many have come to know him . . .
>
> Donnie Munro gave the role of Rector new vigour. Few have expressed the ideals, hopes, and politics of a generation at the same time. This he continues to do as part of that cultural phenomenon: Runrig. We honour Donnie Munro, as a great Scot, as an important citizen of the wide world as well as one of the most significant contributors to modern Scottish culture.

Munro was born and brought up in Uig, Isle of Skye, went to school in Portree, the capital of Skyc, and studied at Gray's College of Art, Aberdeen. He worked as a teacher of art and went into the music business, running Ridge Records, an independent label. He and his band sold well over 3 million albums and had a Europe-wide following, especially in Germany and Scandinavia. He also produced two best-selling videos and Runrig put on many live performances in major venues. Munro also appeared often on radio and television, wrote columns for Scottish and United Kingdom newspapers, exhibited at the Scottish Gallery of Fine Art, Edinburgh, and lectured in Australia.

Munro went on to work for the University of the Highlands and Islands, having the title of Rector; but that was a different kind of rectorship. The region has one fifth of the land mass of the United Kingdom; the University of the Highlands and Islands serves a population of 370,000. The university, dreamed of for more than 300 years, will foster the diverse cultures and languages of its people partly through a network of other institutions and the use of advanced "distance learning technologies".

He also became director of development at Sabhal Mòr Ostaig, the international centre for Gaelic language and culture.

RECTOR SAYS THE UNIVERSITY ADMINISTRATION "OUT OF TOUCH"

Edinburgh University

MALCOLM MACLEOD, *medical practitioner (1966–). Elected 1994.*

Malcolm Macleod, when he was candidate, was a junior hospital doctor. He was president of the Students' Association in 1988–1989, a post that gave him a seat on the Court, and from that he had experience of the way the university worked. Macleod as Rector sometimes did not get on well with the university authorities. He said that some distinguished people in the upper levels had a "regrettable tendency to respond defensively to complaints and to deny the possibility of fault before the matter has been fully investigated."

He has also said:

> Early in my chairmanship of the University Court we [he and senior officers of the university] instituted a thorough review of the way we dealt with

business – 45 minutes on where the car parks would be leaving five minutes to discuss student housing. This was largely because we dealt with the stuff in the order it came up from subcommittees.

We changed that. We had a pre-meeting in the Secretary's office to decide the most important matters and prioritise them on the agenda. We took a whole load of rubbish off the agenda (like renaming the chair of management studies as the chair of management). We put that in a section we agreed automatically if no one raised it prior to the meeting. Meetings became more effective and were shorter by about 30 to 60 minutes.

Senior members of the administrative staff were also closely involved in the changes. "My greatest achievement as rector was the introduction of a campus-wide ban on smoking. I suspect that over the years lots of people will lead longer, healthier lives at least partly as a result of what at the time was quite a bold action of the Court under my leadership."

He has written:

I instituted a weekly 'surgery' on Saturday mornings which ran for the duration of my rectorship. The main issues were: (1) post-graduate supervision; (2) appeals on grading of post-graduate degrees; (3) sorting out students who were doing the wrong course because their parents had talked them into it (medicine instead of geography for instance); (4) unfair dismissal of staff.

In general the campus advisory services (run in large part by the Students' Association) managed very well all the problems about debt and emotional upset.

I got referred the stuff that was more difficult, or had a university administration aspect to it. At an operating level the university was very good at sorting out problems. At an administrative level they could be very thrawn and unsympathetic because they did not want to set a precedent."

Macleod had been in office for six months when he was awarded a fellowship by the Medical Research Council. His specialism was neurology. He registered as a part-time student for a PhD and at the same time became an employee of the university. The authorities had in 1975 brought in a rule that students were not allowed to stand for the office; nor were employees. This did not apply to a Rector who became a student or an employee. The university authorities decided to close the loophole and decreed that a Rector who became a student or who joined the staff would have to stand down. The process was started during the last meeting of the Court which Macleod attended: his tenure was ending.

Macleod has said: "I think their changing of the rules was part of an ongoing attempt to devalue the position [of Rector], to remove alternative power sources on the Court." Macleod recalled the remark by a professor to David Steel when Steel was President of the Students' Representative Council in 1962: "The great thing about student politics is that it teaches you how to deal with rogues and villains."

Of plans to reduces the status of the Rector he said he would view it as rather ironic if senior university officers sought to widen their own powers at the expense of democratically elected representatives. The Rector, he said, was able to bring a fresh perspective as someone outside the closed circle of university management.

Macleod presented to the university Court a document in which he said: "The vast majority of staff . . . feel isolated from the rest of the university and misunderstood by Old College [the administration, which was housed in the eighteenth-century Old College, also called the Old Quad]. There are times when staff feel wilfully excluded from discussions, and some staff feel new management structures have led to an over-centralisation of power in a few hands in Old College."

Top-up fees were another issue. Universities in the United Kingdom wanted the Government – at that time Conservative – to either give them more money or allow them to charge higher fees. Macleod spoke in his Address about top-up fees. Edinburgh, he said, had always striven for excellence. "It is essential that this university is not so expensive that only the rich can attend. That would be our destruction, and a betrayal of what is best in our history. Entry to this university must never be determined by anything other that academic merit." The Court at Edinburgh has, however, not come out in favour of top-up fees; nor has any Principal publicly taken that view.

The Scotsman ran an article in favour of student loans. The article contained, Macleod said, little common sense and was full of Conservative ideology. "Higher education has suffered greatly from that triumph of Conservative ideology over commonsense and practical politics which has characterised our Government for the last 15 years."

Macleod was not shy of voicing his opinions when he was Rector; of an approaching general election – "Soon we will have the chance to 'downsize' and rationalise the Conservatives." He was speaking to a rally of university staff, protesting against an "insulting" pay offer of 1.5 per cent; of money – "The maximum [student] grant is worth less than half what it was 30 years ago and, as parents are to contribute more and more, then those from poorer backgrounds are less likely to be able to complete their studies . . . Universities derive much of their strength from local communities and from the coming together of people from diverse backgrounds, and that is now at risk." Higher education had been neglected since the Conservatives came to power in 1979. This had been driven by a dogma that "privatisation is good".

His supporters during the election campaign said: "It is clear that the constant increase in staff workload cannot go on. The welcome expansion in student numbers must be matched by adequate resources if standards are not to suffer . . . Nowadays it's easy to run for Rector without regard or respect for the responsibilities of the position. Malcolm is running because more and more we need an involved Rector."

MacLeod had six opponents.

Tony Slattery, entertainer, included in his campaign statement: "Yes, I live in London, but I'm only an hour or two away, and it would give me immense satisfaction to be of service to the students." He said during the campaign: "My politics are the politics of bewilderment." But, he added: "I'm very close with the people in the Campaign for Real Ale, so that should result in an adequate supply of guest beers. And I know a lot of film distributors, so I can get free films from them." He was asked, after the result was announced, if he would stand again. He said: "You are asking me to predict what I will be doing in three years' time. I might have changed sex then – to a man." Slattery was to be voted in as Rector of Dundee University in 1998 in succession to Stephen Fry, actor and author.

Lloyd Quinan, actor and TV weather forecaster, was supported by the Scottish Nationalist club. He warned the students during the campaign that the reputation of their institution was being eroded, and needed a thespian weatherman to sort it out. He was later to work in television and theatre as a director, producer, and director. He became a MSP for the Scottish National Party. He lost his seat in 2003 and joined the Scottish Socialist Party, saying: "The party I joined in 1974 no longer represents the vision of Scotland I believe in. The leadership have let the party down."

Sara Parkin, former chairwoman of the Green Party, was supported by the university's Green Society, Liberal Democrats, and Third World First. She was born in Aberdeen, trained as a nurse in the Edinburgh Royal Infirmary, and was a research fellow in the university in the 1970s. "To the office of Rector I can bring 20 years of political, broadcasting, and campaigning experience . . . my current work includes advising the Engineering Council." She wanted "to strengthen the voice of Rectors by establishing a Scottish Rectorial Council."

Brian Cox, actor: "Dr Brian Cox has established himself as one of the greatest Shakespearean actors of our time. Remembered best for his film Manhunter in which he played Hannibal Lector and for the National Theatre tour of King Lear . . . Brian Cox has three main areas of interest – fighting for larger grants for students and against the potential cut of society funding, trying to address the decline of standards and intensity of education, and guiding arts courses on a more focused and practical nature." His acting career was at this time mainly in television and film.

Richard Demarco, arts impresario, who was standing for the fifth time, said that the election was about Sarajevo, the next millennium, Leonardo da Vinci, and making the Science Faculty more lovable – though not necessarily in that order. It was always an honour to be asked to stand but afterwards he said he was disappointed by the result. "The students are only concerned about everyday things. There is nothing in Malcolm [Macleod]'s rectorship which suggested altering the world at large."

The candidature of Marmalade, a three-legged tabby cat, was disallowed. Marmalade's flat-mate, Adam Thomas, a law student, said: "We went through the official channels, but the application was rejected because the pawprint wasn't clear enough. That seems really petty to me."

The order in the first count of votes: Macleod, Slattery, Parkin, Quinan, Cox, and Demarco. The final score, after redistribution of votes, was: Macleod, 3014; Slattery, 1855. More than 5000 students and staff voted; turnout was 29 per cent

Macleod's campaign was described as one of the slickest and most professional that senior staff could remember. He lacked celebrity status before the election, but more than made up that for in his drive and fervour. His manager was Douglas Alexander, whom Macleod appointed as his Assessor. Alexander went on to become a Labour MP and Minister.

He has said:

> The central premise of Malcolm's campaign, which found favour with a wide cross-section of the university community, was that as a junior hospital doctor he had seen what the Conservative government was doing to the National Health Service and was determined to do what he could to protect the university from the kind of hostility and under-funding that had characterised the Conservatives' approach to the Health Service.
>
> We undertook the election aware that a number of higher profile 'celebrity' candidates would be the principal opponents. In many ways,

therefore, Macleod's campaign reflected a harking back to an earlier era, when the capacity of the candidate to undertake representational work on behalf of the university community featured prominently.

We took our campaigning directly to the widest cross-section possible of the university community. Malcolm met with, and spoke personally to, thousands of students and staff members. He worked tirelessly.

RECTOR'S MESSAGE TO SCHOOLCHILDREN: GO TO COLLEGE

Edinburgh University

JOHN COLQUHOUN *(1964–), professional footballer and sports journalist. Elected 1997.*

John Colquhoun said before the election: "With my media profile, I believe I can highlight problems and promote the university." He saw the rectorship as "a mediating and representative position, a voice and support for staff and students." He was active in the Labour Party and was backed by the Labour Club, but said his position was unbiased and non-political.

When he was elected, he said: "There have been some prestigious former rectors and I have a lot to live up to." He had sleepless nights before his first meeting of the university Court: it is hard for an outsider to tackle, without experience, a big job in a huge organization. Nevertheless, Colquhoun did chair the Court's meetings, not handing over to the Principal.

He spoke about his rectorship to journalists from *The Scotsman:*
> My first Court meeting in Old College was nine days after I had been elected.
> I found it very nerve-racking. [Someone who was there said his hands were
> shaking.] It was full of academics and lay members who are well respected on
> the committee. It is a different world to changing in a dressing room with a
> group of men between 16 and 35. There is a different kind of humour, a
> different kind of outlook on life. It is more businesslike, more serious.
> Football is not really real life but I suppose neither is academia."

The other candidates were Dr John Hargreaves and Dave McBryan.

Dr Hargreaves was prospective parliamentary candidate for the Scottish National
Party and a computer analyst. The *Student* magazine described him, before the election,
as a heavyweight compared with the other candidates. "Unfortunately, this is his biggest
drawback: for 'heavyweight' read 'dull'."

He said before the election: "I'm persistent and diligent. You need someone who is
prepared to stand up to a large bureaucratic body, and I've learned skills like that . . . I'm
not a celebrity, but you don't need a big name to be Rector, you need someone who will
respond positively to the job."

His nomination for Rector prompted accusations of a publicity stunt but such accusations are easy to make. The *Student* magazine said: "His posters describe him as a 'New
Scot' – fatuous phrase (meaning he's English) . . . Under a tedious exterior he is an intelligent and experienced man with all the right qualifications for the job. Having been active
within Unison [trade union] and the SNP, he knows about representation."

McBryan, a recent graduate of the university and a pub quizmaster, was sponsored by
the Hugger Buggy Jaffa Cake Appreciation Society, which "exists to raise money for
charity by excessive consumption of the eponymous comestible". His "surgeries", he said,
would be held in the afternoon "to cater for the hung-over contingent on campus".

Voting was Colquhoun, 1321; McBryan, 739; Hargreaves, 207. Turnout was 10.8
per cent.

Colquhoun left school at sixteen and trained as a painter and decorator. But he
always wanted to be a professional footballer, like his father, and he joined Stirling
Albion, part-time at first. When playing there he scored fifty-one goals in 112 games.
Celtic paid a transfer fee of £65,000 for him in 1983. One observer said that Celtic
"made the mistake of playing him on the wing rather than as a striker". He moved to
Heart of Midlothian and with Hearts he scored eighty-two goals in 424 games. When
playing for Hearts in 1988 he was capped for Scotland. He had spells with Millwall
and Sunderland, returned to Hearts, ended his football career with St Johnstone, and
retired from playing in May 1998.

When he was Rector he visited schools to take a message to the pupils: they ought to
think seriously about going to college or university.
> It is a sad fact that of life that youngsters will listen to sports and music per-
> sonalities more than they will listen to academics. If I can set up an organisa-
> tion where sportsmen and women and musicians get youngsters listening
> and then the academics move in, it would be helpful . . . When I was at school
> I felt that university was not for the likes of me.
>
> We need to brush away the mystique of university education. There are

parts of Edinburgh University people think you cannot walk on because it is hallowed ground. You feel as though you should take your shoes off at the door. But everybody owns it. . . .

The Hearts players are quite proud of me. They see it as striking a blow for thick footballers. We are always portrayed as Neanderthal men who have never grown up. We don't need to grow up. At thirty-three, I am still playing a child's game.

He said he joined the Labour Party at seventeen. "I read *The Ragged Trousered Philanthropists* by Robert Tressell about a guy called Frank Owen who like me was a painter and decorator. He wrote the book in the early 1900s. It is about the plight of the workers but the conditions he wrote about were still prevalent. It affected me."

A journalist, Susan Dalgety, wrote that he was "an articulate man with strongly-held political views, not to mention quite handsome. Since hanging up his boots, he has proved to be an asset to Scottish life. He takes his role as rector of Edinburgh University very seriously and is determined to improve life for kids from working-class areas. He is also a man of principle."

His installation was quiet. A student wrote: "No-one was expecting barn-storming oratory . . . But he spoke with a startling passion and conviction, highlighting the middle-class dominance of higher education."

APPENDICES

How rival groups of students fought each other

We have a detailed account of the fighting between rival groups in the run-up to the elections. It is by a leader of the group supporting the candidature in 1908 of Sir William Osler, a distinguished medical man. Osler was standing as an independent to break the monopoly of the politicians, but he was defeated. The letter was addressed to Osler.

One of the traditions of the Rectorial here is that each party must struggle to raid and wreck if possible the committee rooms of their opponents. That our party would destroy this tradition, by not taking rooms and fighting like the political parties, was one of the first and most strongly pushed objections against us. We did not hesitate to make capital out of this allegation.

Within about a week of the start of the campaign we had entirely wrecked the Liberal rooms and left them uninhabitable. We unscrewed all their doors and took them down to the Osler fort and made barricades of them so that when the Liberals came to attack us they had to batter down their own doors. We had no furniture when we started the campaign, but we had too much by the end of the war.

We had a lot of difficulty with the Conservative rooms as the police would not allow any fighting about them, owing to the value of the neighbouring property ... At two o'clock, twenty of us stripped for fighting, left the Osler garrison and crept through the streets with ladders, axes, and crowbars, etc., towards the Conservative rooms. We found that one of the shutters of their windows appeared to be unfastened. Our ladders were too short to reach it, but we crept on to an adjoining house roof and from there clambered along a narrow ornamental ledge which ran beneath their windows. Ten of the men remained in the street below with overcoats stretched out to catch any of our men as they fell. We managed to put nine into their rooms before the night guard awoke.

Terror and the fierceness of our onslaught overcame them, and they capitulated. Just as our men were entering the window an Inspector arrived with about thirty or forty policemen. He wanted to stop us, but I promised that if we made any disturbance or did anything which he disapproved of I would call off our men at once. As I had kept my word with him in a former fight about a similar matter, he consented to allow us to go on.

During the next half hour, our men wrought their will. Every room was completely wrecked; chairs, tables, piano, etc etc were reduced to matchwood. The whole of the place, inside and out, was painted over with the legend, VOTE FOR OSLER. We then came away bearing some of the spoils of war which we deposited in the Osler fort.

Day and night since the campaign started we have had a guard in our rooms. We did not have beds, in case our men should be overpowered by sleep as our opponents were. Our roof was our weak point, and many a night have we sat on the roofs watching by turns. We have had several small attempts to catch us napping and three great organised attacks. In each of these our opponents were beaten off with many casualties. Luckily the Infirmary was close at hand, and during each engagement a host of minor wounds had to be dressed.

The motto of the Oslerites before a battle was 'Get hurt'. Fortunately none of us were detained long in bed, the severest case being ten days. We gained great prestige by the fact that not a single man had entered the Oslerite rooms without the consent of the Oslerites, and that we had utterly wiped out both of the opposing forces and had swept their rooms.

Now I rather suspect that you will think all this physical fighting on your behalf rather puerile, and you will also fail to see how it could beneficially affect your candidature . . . Personally I can never hope to be associated with a more virile and self-sacrificing body of men and women than those who have borne the brunt of an unsuccessful battle in [sic] your behalf. They believed that you were their ideal Lord Rector and I was touched by the many ways they showed it. Classes, clothes, time, convenience were sacrificed; and even health, life and limb were endangered for 'the cause' . . .

The Scots diaspora takes the Rectorship to Canada

The rectorship has travelled to Canada and is established at Queen's University, Kingston, Ontario, a university and city where Scottish influence is strong. The university is a sister of Edinburgh University; the rectorship was specifically imported from Edinburgh in 1912.

The Rector is chosen by the students and serves for three years. He or she acts as an ombudsman for students and sits on the board of trustees and on certain committees such as the ones that decide who is to be appointed Principal and who are to receive honorary degrees. The Rector also joins the Chancellor and the Principal at ceremonial occasions.

For generations the post was held by prominent friends of the university. Examples are the former Prime Minister R. B. Bennett (1935–1937) and the businessman and chair of the Canadian Broadcasting Corporation Leonard Brockington (1947–1968). No students were elected in the earlier history of the rectorship. But in 1969, in an age of activism, the students forced the resignation of the incumbent, a Senator, and since then students have always been elected.

The person who was rector at the end of the period covered by this book, Ahmed Kayssi, has said:

I am not required to withdraw from my courses, and am in fact expected to maintain student status for the duration of my term in office. Past Rectors who have graduated before their term was finished chose to resign. How does one manage studying and doing this job? The ombudsman aspects of the job are flexible, so I usually schedule those meetings in the evening after classes are done.

Committee work is more tricky, and places a lot of burdens on my academic life. However, one forces oneself to be as organised as possible to make sure that tasks fit in. My remuneration has been fixed as free tuition and student activity fees for every year I'm in office.

Scottish Presbyterians in Upper Canada set up Queen's College for the education of future ministers and other young people. Queen Victoria granted its charter in 1841 as a college. The College had a Chancellor, Principal, Senate, and board of trustees. The Canadian Parliament raised the college to a university and introduced the rectorship in 1912. The town of Kingston also has the Royal Military Academy, the equivalent in Canada of Sandhurst in the United Kingdom.

The creator of Sherlock Holmes observes an election

The creator of Sherlock Holmes, Arthur Conan Doyle, was a medical student at Edinburgh from 1876 to 1881. A passage in one of his novels, *The Firm of Girdlestone*, describes an election of this period:

The whooping and yelling which proceeded from that usually decorous building [the university] might have been heard from Prince's Street to Newington. In front of the gates was a dense crowd of townspeople peering into the quadrangle, and deriving much entertainment from the movements of the lively young gentlemen within. Large numbers of the more peaceable undergraduates stood about under the arches . . .

The broad open quadrangle, and all the numerous balconies and terraces which surround it, were crowded with an excited mob of students. The whole three thousand odd electors who stand upon the college rolls appeared to be present, and the noise which they were making would have reflected credit upon treble their number. The dense crowd surged and seethed without pause or rest. Now and again some orator would be hoisted up on the shoulders of his fellows, when an oscillation of the crowd would remove his supporters and down he would come, only to be succeeded by another at some other part of the assembly. The name of either candidate would produce roars of applause and equally vigorous howls of execration. Those who were lucky enough to be in the balconies above hurled down missiles on the crowd beneath – peas, eggs, potatoes, and bags of flour or of sulphur, while those below, whenever they found room to swing an arm, returned the fusillade with interest ...

The crowd was most dense and noisy in front of the class-room in which the counting of the votes was going forward. At one the result was to be announced, and as the long hand of the great clock crept towards to hour, a hush of expectation fell upon the assembly. The brazen clang broke harshly out, and at the same moment the folding doors were flung open, and a knot of men rushed out into the crowd, which swirled and eddied round them. The centre of the throng was violently agitated, and the whole mass of people swayed outwards and inwards. For a minute or two the excited combatants seethed and struggled without a clue as to the cause of the commotion. Then the corner of a large placard was elevated above the heads of the rioters, on which was visible the word "Liberal" in great letters, but before I could be raised further it was torn down, and the struggle became fiercer than ever. Up came the placard again – the other corner this time – with the word "Majority" upon it, and then immediately vanished as before. Enough had been seen, however, to show which way the victory had gone, and shouts of triumph arose from everywhere, with waving of hats and clatter of sticks. Meanwhile, in the centre other two parties fought round the placard, and the commotion began to cover a wider area, as either side was reinforced by fresh supporters. One gigantic Liberal seized the board, and held it aloft for a moment, so that it could be seen in its entirety by the whole multitude:

LIBERAL MAJORITY - 241

But his triumph was short-lived. A stick descended on his head, his heels were tripped up, and he and his placard rolled on the ground together. The victors succeeded, however, in forcing their way to the extreme end of the quadrangle.

A character in the novel gives his opinion on the day's proceedings:

"What Goths! What barbarians! . . . And this is my dream of refined quiet and studious repose!"

"They are not always like that, sir," said his son, apologetically. "They were certainly a little jolly today."

"A little jolly! . . . You rogue, Tom. I believe if I had not been there you would have been their ringleader."

He glanced from one to the other, and it was so evident from the expression on their faces that he had just hit the mark, that he burst into a great guffaw of laughter, in which, after a moment's hesitation, his two young companions heartily joined.

BIBLIOGRAPHY

General Sources

Much material has been gathered from newspapers: *The Scotsman, Glasgow Herald* (later *The Herald), Times, Edinburgh Evening News, Edinburgh Evening Dispatch,* and some others.

The Edinburgh University magazine, *Student,* has been a rich source.

The *Dictionary of National Biography, Who's Who, Who Was Who.*

Who's Who in Scotland.

'The Contentious Breed', a series on BBC Radio 4 about the rectors, April and May 1994.

Anderson, Robert D., Lynch, Michael, and Phillipson, Nicholas, *The University of Edinburgh, an illustrated history* (Edinburgh, 2003).

Cahill, Kevin, *Who Owns Britain? The hidden facts behind landownership in the UK and Ireland* (Edinburgh, 2001).

Conan Doyle, Sir Arthur, *The Firm of Girdlestone* (London, 1890).

Crofton, Sir John, *On being an early Vice-Principal of the University of Edinburgh 1969–70.* An unpublished memoir written in June 1997 (a copy is in the university library).

Crystal, David (editor), *Cambridge Biographical Encyclopedia* (Cambridge, 1998).

Currie, Dr A. M., communications to the author, March and April 2004.

Donaldson, Gordon, *Four Centuries: Edinburgh University Life, 1583–1983* (Edinburgh, 1983).

Goring, Rosemary (editor), *Chambers Scottish Biographical Dictionary* (Edinburgh, 1992).

Grant, Sir Alexander, *The Story of the University of Edinburgh during its First Three Hundred Years* (London, 1884).

Hall, J. T. D., editor, *The Tounis College, an anthology of Edinburgh Student Journals, 1823–1923* (Edinburgh, 1985).

Horn, D. B., *A Short History of the University of Edinburgh* (Edinburgh, 1967).

Horn, D. B., *The Universities (Scotland) Act of 1858*; the *University of Edinburgh Journal, 19* (1958–1960).

Kayssi, Ahmed, conversation with and communications to the author, 2003 and 2004.

Kettle, Ann, *Governance and Management in the University of St Andrews: a worm's eye view.* Paper to European Academy of Management, 8 May 2004.

Parry, Melanie (editor), *Chambers Biographical Dictionary* ((Edinburgh, 1997).

Roy, Kenneth, editor, *Dictionary of Scottish Biography,* vol. I, 1971–1975 (Irvine, Ayrshire, 1999).

Swann, Michael, *Student problems in Edinburgh and beyond.* An address to the General Council of the University of Edinburgh (Edinburgh, 1968).

Turner, A. Logan, *History of the University of Edinburgh, 1883–1933* (Edinburgh, 1933).

Walker, Archibald Stodart, *Rectorial Addresses delivered before the University of Edinburgh, 1859–1899* (London, 1900).

Webster, Jack, *Why ask a boy to do a man's job? Scottish Daily Express,* 11 October 1968.

Allenby, Lord (1935)

Gardner, Brian, *Allenby* (London, 1965).

Hamilton, Ian, *Against Oblivion, Some lives of the Twentieth-Century Poets* (London, 2002)

James, Lawrence *Imperial Warrior, the Life and Times of Field-Marshal Viscount Allenby* (London, 1993).

Savage, Raymond, *Allenby of Armageddon* (London, 1925).

Sim, Dr Myre, letter to the author, 23 January 2003

Allsop, Kenneth (1968)

Crofton, Sir John, *On being an early Vice-Principal of the University of Edinburgh 1969–70*. An unpublished memoir written in June 1997 (a copy is in Edinburgh University Library).

Cuddihy, Robert, conversations with the author, December 2001.

Foulkes, George, letter to the author, 4 September 2003.

Travis, Alan, *Students were "frighteningly radical"*. *The Guardian,* 31 May 2000.

Balfour, Lord, of Burleigh (1896)

Balfour, Lady Francis, *A Memoir of Lord Balfour of Burleigh* (London, 1925).

Beatty, Sir David, later Lord Beatty (1917)

Chalmers, W. S., *The Life and Letters of David, Earl Beatty* (London, 1951).

Roskill, Stephen W., *Earl Beatty, the last Naval Hero* (London, 1980).

Van der Vat, Dan, letter to author, December 2003.

Brown, Gordon (1972)

Anonymous, *Lord Swann* (obituary). *Times,* 24 September 1990, page 14.

Crofton, Sir John, *On being an early Vice-Principal of the University of Edinburgh 1969–70* (unpublished memoir; a copy is in the university library). Letter to the author, 13 October 2004.

Naughtie, James, *The Rivals* (London, 2001)

Pym, Hugh, and Kochan, Nick, *Gordon Brown, The First Year in Power* (London, 1998).

University of Edinburgh, *Minutes* of the Court's meetings 1972–1975, *passim.*

Carlyle, Thomas (1865)

Fielding, K. J., and Henderson, Heather, *Carlyle and the Rectorial Election of 1865* (Edinburgh, 1979). Carlyle Pamphlets No 1, published for the Carlyle Newsletter.

Froude, James Anthony, *Life* of Thomas Carlyle (London, 1884).

Christison, Robert

Cushing, Harry, *The Life of William Osler* vol 2 (Oxford, 1925).

The Life of Sir Robert Christison, Bart. (Edinburgh, 1886.) This was edited by his sons but was written by him.

Churchill, Winston S. (1929)

Archive Arrangement Routledge Associates (compiler), *Index to the Diary of Beatrice Webb 1873–1943* (London, 1978).

Freshwater, Peter, *Winston Churchill and Two Rectorials,* University of Edinburgh Journal, 37 (2) (December 1995).

Jenkins, Roy (Lord Jenkins of Hillhead), *Churchill* (London 2001).

Seymour-Jones, Carole, *Beatrice Webb, Woman of Conflict* (London, 1993).

Webb, Beatrice, *Diary,* 21 July 1924, vol. 38, folio 4096.

Cunningham, Admiral Lord

Lewis, Dr Ian, letter to the author, 28 January 2003.

Myerscough, Dr Philip, letter to the author, January 2003.

Van der Vat, Dan, letter to the author, December 2003.

Derby, Lord (1874)

Prevelakis, Ekeutherios, *British Policy towards the change of dynasty in Greece* (Athens, 1953).

Vincent, John (ed), *The Diaries of Edward Henry Stanley, 15th Earl of Derby, (1826–93) between September 1869 and March* 1878 (London, 1994).

Dufferin, Lord (1899)

Lyall, Sir Alfred, *The Life of the Marquess of Dufferin and Ava* (London, 1905)

"Muir, James Hamilton" (Bone, James; Charteris, Archibald Hamilton; and Bone, Muirhead,), *Glasgow in 1901* (Glasgow and Edinburgh, 1901).

Finlay, Sir Robert Bannatyne (1902)

Anonymous: Edinburgh University rectorial Address; International arbitration; Rowdy proceedings. *The Scotsman,* 22 January 1904, page 8.

Fleming, G. H., *Victorian 'Sex Goddess', Lady Colin Campbell* (Oxford, 1990).

Fleming, Sir Alexander (1951)

Anonymous: Obituary. *Times,* 12 March 1955.

Amory, Mark (ed), *The Letters of Evelyn Waugh* (London, 1980).

Maurois, Andre, *The Life of Sir Alexander Fleming,* trans. Gerard Hopkins (London 1959).

McCluskey, Raymond, letters to the author, 2003.

Nuttgens, Bridget, letters to the author, 2003.

Gilmour, Sir John (1926)

Pottinger, George, *The Secretaries of State for Scotland 1926–76. Fifty Years of the Scottish Office* (Edinburgh, 1979).

Mackie, Albert, *Crazy students? We were worse.* The *Scottish Daily Express,* 2 November, 1954.

Gladstone, W. E. (1859)

Jenkins, Roy *Gladstone* (London, 1996).

Neaves, Charles, *Songs and Verses Social and Scientific* (third edition) (Edinburgh and London, 1869).

Goschen, George Joachim (1890)

Jenkins, Roy, *Gladstone* (London, 1996).

Jenkins, Roy, *The Chancellors* (London, 1998).

O'Brien, R. Barry, *The Life of Lord Russell of Killowen* (London, 1901).

Spinner, Thomas J., jnr, *George Joachim Goschen; the transformation of a Victorian Liberal* (Cambridge, 1973).

Grierson, Sir Herbert (1936)

Crofton, Sir John, *On being an early Vice-Principal of the University of Edinburgh 1969–1970* (an unpublished memoir written in June 1997; a copy is in the university library).

Davie, George Elder, *The Democratic Intellect. Scotland and her universities in the nineteenth century* (Edinburgh, 1961).

Davie, George Elder, *The Crisis of the Democratic Intellect* (Edinburgh, 1986).

Grimond, Jo (1960)

Grimond, Jo, *Memoirs* (London, 1971).

McDowall, Bill, letter to and conversations with the author, November 2003.

McManus, Michael, *Jo Grimond: towards the sound of gunfire* (Edinburgh, 2001).

Munro, J. Forbes, letter to author, 2003.

Smith, Trevor, untitled book review, *Country Life*, 7 February, 2002.

Haldane, Richard Burdon (1905)

Haldane, Lord, *An Autobiography* (1929).

Hamilton, Sir Ian (1932)

Anonymous: Obituary. *Times,* 13 October 1947, page 8.

Innes, Sir Thomas, of Learney, *The Tartans of the Clans and Families of Scotland* (Edinburgh and London, 1971).

Moncreiffe, Sir Ian, of That Ilk, and Hicks, David, *The Highland Clans* (London, 1967).

Van der Vat, Dan, letter to the author, December 2003.

Hartington, Lord (1877)

Blyth, Henry, *Skittles, The Last Victorian Courtesan, the Life and Time of Catherine Walters* (London, 1970).

Doyle, Sir Arthur Conan, *The Firm of Girdlestone* (London, 1890).

Edwards, Owen Dudley, *The Quest for Sherlock Holmes* (Edinburgh, 1882).

Fraser, Norman, *Student Life at Edinburgh University* (Paisley, 1884).

Jackson, Patrick, *The Last of the Whigs, a Political Biography of Lord Hartington, later Eighth Duke of Devonshire* (London and Toronto, 1999).

Mitchell, Dennis J., *Cross and Tory Democracy, a Political Biography of Richard Assheton Cross* (New York, 1991).

Strachey, Lytton, *Eminent Victorians* (London 1929).

Kitchener, Lord (1914)

Pollock, John, *Kitchener* (London, 2001).

Royle, Trevor, *The Kitchener Enigma* (London, 1985).

Lloyd George, David (1920)

Anonymous: Mr Lloyd George in Edinburgh; Students' boisterous reception. *The Scotsman,* 2 March 1923.

Anonymous: Mr Lloyd George. *Times,* 2 March 1923.

Anonymous: Political success; The necessary qualities; Mr Lloyd George's advice. *Edinburgh Evening News,* 1 March 1923.

West, Francis, *Gilbert Murray, a Life* (London, 1984).

Wilson, Duncan, *Gilbert Murray OM* (Oxford, 1987).

Lothian, Lord (1887)

Ashby, Sir Eric, and Anderson, Mary, *The Rise of the Student Estate in Britain* (London, 1970).

Cahill, Kevin, *Who Owns Britain* (Edinburgh, 2001).

Johnston, Tom, *Our Noble Scottish Families* (Glasgow, 1909, reprinted Glendaruel, Argyll, 2001).

Macleod, Malcolm (1994)

Alexander, Douglas, letter to the author, 15 April 2004.

Macleod, Dr Malcolm, emails to the author, 2004.

MacPherson, Archie (1985)

Gibson, John, *How Archie came from the bowery to be Rector.* The *Edinburgh Evening News,* 19 March 1985.

Nelson, Sarah, *The voice of football champions education, The Scotsman,* 3 July 1985.

Magnusson, Magnus (1975)

Currie, Dr Alex, former Secretary to the university, communication to the author, April 2004.

Minto, Lord (1911)

Johnston, Tom, *Our Noble Scots Families* (Glasgow, 1909, reprinted Glendaruel, Argyll, 2001).

Moncrieff, Lord (1868)

Johnstone, T. J., *Ruskin for Rector: the Edinburgh Rectorial Election of 1868* (Edinburgh, 1982) Carlyle pamphlet No 2, published for the Carlyle Newsletter

Omond, G. W. T., *The Lord Advocates of Scotland,* Second Series 1834–1880 (London, 1914)

Tyack, Geoffrey, *Ruskin and the English House.* In *Ruskin and Architecture,* edited by Daniels, Rebecca, and Brandwood, Geoff (London 2003).

Walker, Archibald Stodart, *Rectorial Addresses delivered before the University of Edinburgh 1859–1899* (London, 1900).

Muggeridge, Malcolm (1966)

Ingrams, Richard, *Muggeridge, the Biography* (London, 1995).

Muggeridge, Malcolm, *Another King, the Muggeridge Sermon* (Edinburgh, 1968).

Wolfe, Gregory, *Malcolm Muggeridge: A Biography* (London, 1995).

Munro, Donnie (1991)

MacDonald, the Rev Iain, email and letter to the author, April 2004.

Munro, Donnie, email to the author, April 2004.

Northcote, Sir Stafford (1886)

Lang, Andrew, *Life, Letters, and Diaries of Sir Stafford Northcote, first Earl of Iddesleigh* (Edinburgh and London, 1891).

McGonagall, William, *Collected Poems* (Edinburgh, 1992).

Pollock, Sir Donald (1939 and 1942)

Pollock, Sir Donald, *Message from the Lord Rector,* Edinburgh University Student's Handbook 1943–1944 (Edinburgh, 1943).

Robertson, J. P. B (1893)

Walker, Archibald, Stodart, *Rectorial Addresses delivered before the University of Edinburgh 1859–1899* (London, 1900).

Robertson Justice, James (1957 and 1963)

Marshall, Julian, *Julius Nyerere,* obituary. *Guardian,* 15 October 1999.

Morton, Eric V. B., *Odd Memories of Student Days,* Edinburgh University *Journal,* December 2002, page 248; and letter to the author, 10 February 2003.

Reynolds, Clyde, letter to the author, 28 January 2003.

Simpson, David, letter to the author, 25 January 2003.

Rosebery, Lord (1880)

Coates, Thomas F. G., *Lord Rosebery, his Life and Speeches* (London, 1900).

Crewe, Lord, *Lord Rosebery* (London, 1931).

Edwards, Owen Dudley, *The Quest for Sherlock Holmes* (Edinburgh, 1982).

Sim, Alastair (1948)

Bannister, Winifred, *James Bridie and his Theatre* (London, 1955).

Cowie, Dr Iain, letter to the author, 16 January 2003.

Sim, Naomi, *Dance and Skylark. Fifty years with Alastair Sim* (London, 1987).

Steel, David (1982)

Bartram, Peter, *David Steel, His Life and Politics* (London, 1981).

Steel, David, *Against Goliath, David Steel's Story* (London, 1989).

Stirling Maxwell, Sir William (1871)

Edwards, Owen Dudley, *The Quest for Sherlock Holmes* (Edinburgh, 1982).

Ferguson, Robert, *Guide to Pollok House*. National Trust for Scotland (Edinburgh, 2001).

Holmes, Rachel, *Scanty Particulars: The Life of Dr James Barry* (London, 2002).

Roberts, Shirley, *Sophia Jex-Blake, a Woman Pioneer in Nineteenth Century Medical Reform* (London, 1993).

Todd, Margaret (Graham Travers), *The Life of Sophia Jex-Blake* (London, 1918).

Wills, Jonathan (1971)

University of Edinburgh *Minutes* of the Court's meetings 1971–1972, *passim*.

Cuddihy, Bob, conversations with the author, December 2002.

Wills, Dr Jonathan, email to author, 25 June 2004; and conversations with the author, January and March 2004.

Wyndham, George (1908)

Bliss, Michael, William Osler, a Life in Medicine (Oxford, 1999).

Cushing, Harry, *The Life of Sir William Osler,* vol. 2 (Oxford, 1925).

Freshwater, Peter B, *Winston Churchill and Two Rectorials, University of Edinburgh Journal* 37 (2), December 1995.

Jenkins, Roy, *Churchill* (London, 2001).

Mackail, J. W., and Wyndham, Guy, *Life and Letters of George Wyndham* (London, 1925).

INDEX

Entries in **bold** indicate the main entries for Rectors, and in *italics* the page numbers for the bibliography.